Casting Off

How a city girl found happiness
on the high seas

Emma Bamford

ADLARD COLES NAUTICAL

B L O O M S B U R Y

LONDON · NEW DELHI · NEW YORK · SYDNEY

Published by Adlard Coles Nautical
an imprint of Bloomsbury Publishing Plc
50 Bedford Square, London WC1B 3DP
www.adlardcoles.com

Bloomsbury is a trademark of Bloomsbury Publishing Plc

First published by Adlard Coles Nautical in 2014

ISBN 978-1-4729-0661-8
ePDF 978-1-4729-0663-2
ePub 978-1-4729-0662-5

A CIP catalogue record for this book is available from the British Library.

This book is produced using paper that is made from wood grown in managed, sustainable forests. It is natural, renewable and recyclable. The logging and manufacturing processes conform to the environmental regulations of the country of origin.

Designed by CE Marketing
Printed and bound in Great Britain by CPI Group (UK) Ltd, Croydon CR0 4YY

Note: while all reasonable care has been taken in the publication of this book, the publisher takes no responsibility for the use of the methods or products described in the book.

Some names have been changed in this book to protect the privacy of the individuals described.

10 9 8 7 6 5 4 3 2 1

Contents

Panacea

Prologue

It was the day before the *Independent* was being re-launched with a new design and mid-negotiation over selling the paper to a former Russian spy that I handed in my notice. Not the most considerate of timing to quit my job on the newspaper, but it had to be done. I crouched by my boss's desk and spoke in a low tone, so that no one could overhear me. Reporters are a nosy bunch. Keeping a secret in Fleet Street is like trying to prevent a five-year-old from creeping downstairs to open their Christmas presents early. Delicate manoeuvring is needed and despite your best efforts it is likely to result in some tantrums and a big mess.

'I need to talk to you about something,' I murmured into the ear of Ollie, the news editor.

'Sure, what is it?' he replied, neither his eyes leaving his screen nor his fingers stopping their tapping on the keys. I say tapping but he's rather heavy of hand, so it was more like stamping.

'I'm going to quit tomorrow.' That got his attention; he hadn't seen it coming. He stopped and turned to me. 'Why?'

'I can't hack it any more,' he might have understood. *'I've got a better offer from the* Guardian/Mail/Telegraph,' he possibly expected. Hell, even *'I've had enough of this excitement and I've decided to retrain as an accountant,'* he could have considered reasonable. But there's no doubt that

the answer I gave him would never have crossed his mind in a million years of a month of Sundays and then some.

'Because I've answered an ad on the internet from a man who wants a woman to come and live on a boat with him and his cat. In Borneo. So I'm off.'

Since I was 16 I'd wanted be a journalist on a national newspaper. I know this because when my parents moved house and dumped a load of my old things on me, I found my UCAS application form in a box of old school files and in my personal statement I had written 'I want to be a journalist'. Pretty clear. At university I forgot this for a bit but somehow ended up falling into journalism anyway. Fate, some might say. Others might sagely label it sobering up.

I had been at the *Independent* for two years, working as a news editor, shaping the news content of the next day's edition and galvanising the reporters into action. I was contracted to work 40 hours a week; I put in 55 to 60. I wasn't highly paid but I was highly stressed. In a world where people can – and prefer – to get their news for free, updated 24/7, the British newspaper industry felt like it was struggling to take its last breaths, being suffocated by a combined mess of falling readership numbers and declining ad revenue. Budgets were non-existent and reporters were overstretched, writing for all sections of the newspaper at the same time. There was no money for freelances or for commissioning work from outsiders yet not enough in-house staff to carry the workload. Demand from on high for world-class exclusives was incessant and it often felt like the senior executives wouldn't listen to reason. On more than one occasion I'd had to lock myself in the ladies to cry.

Of course it could be a thrilling place to work, when a big

story broke or we had a breakthrough in a case we'd been campaigning for. The adrenaline rush that carried me through a day like that was immense and sometimes if I met friends for a drink after work I'd be practically incapable of coherent speech for the first 20 minutes or so, until I'd had a chance to come down off my jittery high.

But newspapers can also be a nasty environment, mainly for one reason – egotism. Fleet Street must have some of the biggest, baddest egos around. I've worked with an editor who literally screamed at people in front of colleagues and had a bully's instinct for preying on those least likely to fight back. A political columnist said that he was glad news reporters were being made redundant because he'd get more space in the paper. Another columnist demanded the quotes-of-the-day section be removed from its habitual spot so he could write a bit more. Gossip about newsroom punch-ups was not rare. I even heard tales of an editor stepping over a news editor who lay on the floor suffering a heart attack, just so he could get a conference started on time.

Good riddance to all those egos, I thought when I quit. (In the interest of fairness, I should add here that they weren't all total gits all of the time. One journalist offered to ask the managing editor if I could have the six months' worth of days off in lieu *he* had accrued so I could go off on my travels and still have a job to come back to half a year later. Another helped me research ideas for books to write about my trip and a deputy editor, who had twice got me to do his daughter's homework for her, tried to impress me by hoiking both feet on to the desk, splaying his hands on the floor and pumping out elevated press-ups in the middle of the newsroom. Past the bloom of youth he might have been, but he still managed two.)

What I hadn't expressed in that UCAS personal statement back in 1995 was that my 17-year-old self fully expected that, by the ancient age of 31, as well as being a successful journalist I would be married, live in my own detached house with a garden and have at least a couple of kids under my belt. It wasn't an aim, it didn't need to be worked and strived for, unlike getting into the right university and working at a career. It would just happen, naturally. My thirties were sooo far away and there was plenty of time for all of that. It was so far in the future that I'd possibly – the horror! – be wearing high heels instead of Doc Martens by then and carrying a handbag.

By 31 the Docs were long gone, the art of walking in high heels was perfected (well, improved) and there was a lot of stuff shoved into the recesses of that handbag. Yet there was no house, no husband and no children. There was a mortgaged-to-the-hilt-and-then-some ex-council flat, a few ex-boyfriends and some dates, the last one of whom tried to charm me by pointing out my knobbly knees.

Like many a single girl who went before me, there were moments, both privately and publicly (the public ones being mainly brought on by an excess of gin), in which I bemoaned my lack of a good husband and angelic children. OK, if I'm being honest, sometimes it really got to me. All my friends seemed to be getting hitched and popping out kids left, right and centre. Some even had the temerity to be on their second marriage by the age of 30 when I was struggling to get a fourth date. I desperately wanted to be married, like everyone else I knew. My (lack of a) love life was a standing joke at work. 'Get back on your shelf, Bammers,' was one of the set remarks whenever I filled in my colleagues on the latest round of dumping and being dumped. I still considered myself a hopeful romantic, though, and thankfully I didn't fall into that self-destructive trap of wondering what was wrong with me. Mainly I put it down to a run of bad luck.

A lot of the time I wasn't sure if my remorse was because I was single or because everyone else wasn't. It always mildly shocked me when I went to visit friends from university, friends whose hair I had held back from their faces when they were throwing up after one too many pints, and I now found myself at their homes, sitting in their gardens and playing with their children while their husbands fixed me a drink. It was all so grown-up. I felt left behind and left out.

'I've got some news for you,' said my old friend Katie when we were drinking tea at Jane's. Jane, naturally, lived in a house (although not a detached one) and had both a husband and a daughter. 'One of your friends is pregnant.'

'Not another one,' I said, rolling my eyes. 'Who?'

She laughed. 'Me.'

I'm not a total bitch and obviously I congratulated her and her husband Dave on their news but my joy was a little bit tinged with sadness through this 'great, there's another one moving on' mentality that I'd developed.

But Katie wasn't having any of this 'woe is me' attitude, once she'd gotten out of me what was wrong and why my smile looked forced. 'Are you crazy?' she said. 'Look at you. You can do anything you want to, go anywhere you want, be anyone you want. Me and Jane, we're stuck here now. This is it for us for years and years.' She looked at Jane, who nodded. 'Do it now while you still can.'

Well. It was a bit of a light-bulb moment and I felt a rush of exhilaration. Honestly, I'd never thought of it that way before.

What an idiot I'd been. Katie was completely right. I wasn't enjoying my job any longer, I had some savings in the bank, a flat I could rent out and no ties. Also, having dated half of the single men in my part of south-west London already, perhaps I might be able to make a more meaningful relationship work with someone from further afield. There was absolutely nothing to stop me going somewhere I wanted to go, doing something I wanted to do and being someone I wanted to be. The only problem was that I hadn't the foggiest where, what or who that was.

That evening when I got back to my flat I couldn't get the idea out of my mind. The one thought that kept popping into my head was to go sailing. As I had been falling out of love with journalism, blinkering myself so that I could only see the negative aspects of my job, I was falling in love with sailing. What had started out as a hobby for the odd week in the summer holidays had been inching towards an obsession. I'd signed up for courses; I'd read Ellen MacArthur's memoirs on the tube on the way to work, and Peter Nichols' tale of the first non-stop solo circumnavigation race back in the 1960s, won by Robin Knox-Johnston.

Ironically it was journalism that pushed me away from journalism and towards the sea. At the *Independent* I was approached by the marketing team behind the Clipper Round the World Yacht Race, a race with only amateur crew on board the ten yachts. Would I like a place on board in exchange for writing a blog about it on the Indy's website, Clipper asked. A thousand times yes! The catch? I had to do three weeks' training in the Solent and the North Sea, just as any paying crew member would. I used all my annual leave preparing for the race. More than 100,000 people gathered around the Hull docks to wave us off on a Saturday morning in September. I was assigned to the Hull and Humber boat and we were treated almost like heroes as we paraded through the throngs to our 68-foot boat for the race start. Strangers cheered and wished us good luck; some dashed forward to shake our hands. It was a surreal experience, especially since we were little more than novices, not experienced, professional racers. The route to La Rochelle in France was fast and furious – we covered the 800 miles in just three days with 20 knots (nautical miles per hour) of wind at our back. When I rejoined the boat, months later, in Canada to cross the Atlantic to Ireland, we went even quicker, making it to Kinsale in just nine days. I loved every minute of it – except, perhaps, for those minutes spent throwing up.

That experience helped to nourish the seed of an idea that was now germinating in my brain. If I was looking for something new to do with my life, something that would give me that buzz and make me feel alive again, why not go sailing? I already knew I loved it more than most other things in my life. I even knew – sort of – how to do it. Plus, sailing was fun, you could do it in sunny, exotic locations like the Caribbean and sailors were often pretty hot. It seemed like a win-win situation. Being on a boat seemed to be able to offer everything that a life stuck behind a desk could not: excitement, freedom, fresh air, movement, being outdoors, using my body as well as challenging my mind as I learned new skills like sail trim and navigation. The old excitement I used to feel when I got an exclusive story I now found in almost everything I learned on a boat – there was immense satisfaction in changing an engine impeller or parking in a difficult berth.

The planning commenced. I signed up for membership of an online site where boats advertised for crew. I fired off emails to lots of skippers, most of whom I never heard back from. It wasn't dissimilar to internet dating. I ended up in conversations with three men (for some reason, women very rarely seem to own boats). The first was Philippe, a 40-something Frenchman who'd got out of the New York finance world in the wake of 9/11 and had gone to live on a catamaran in the Caribbean (hello, exotic sunniness). In his Facebook profile photo he looked like Captain Jack Sparrow and he told me he'd just come out of a relationship. Alarm bells rang. I didn't fancy being some kind of emotional prop – that might kill the mood of the adventure. Vernon, in his sixties, was a British retiree with a yacht in Madeira, a Jaguar in the UK and a wife who didn't like sailing. He was trying to crew up his 32-foot Hunter for a six-week cruise around the Azores islands in the middle of the Atlantic Ocean. He'd built the boat for £50,000 and spent double that on kit for it. I drove out to Surrey to meet him for lunch one Tuesday. He seemed very organised, even precisely fixing the dates of the cruise and giving me information on which airline was cheapest to fly with, yet I didn't feel the necessary spark of excitement when I thought about going sailing with Vernon.

I did get that tingle of promise when I received emails from Steve, the skipper of a 46-foot yacht currently in Borneo, which he shared with his cat. His plan was to join a regatta for two weeks in Borneo – hello, more fun racing! – then cruise slowly eastwards to New Zealand, taking in the Philippines, Palau, Papua New Guinea, Vanuatu and the Solomon Islands. Steve was a British guy in his forties and his emails made me laugh. He said he liked a drink and a party, used to teach sailing for a living and was looking for crew. In his emails he was casual and friendly, and we became Facebook friends, which meant I had access to lots of photos of his wonderful-looking life on his boat in the tropics. He mentioned he and an ex-girlfriend had sailed with other crew before and he wrote that the sailing scene in Malaysia was pretty sociable, so it'd be easy to meet other boats.

Jane declared him 'fit' from his photos and practically married us off then and there. I wasn't as enthusiastic but tried to keep an open mind. I was already sure that we'd be friends. *And who knows – maybe I will like him*, I reasoned with myself. *After all, he's a sailor, a traveller. He's living this dream life that I want to try.* He offered me a two-week, no-strings-attached trial. I was sold.

Over the three months that I worked out my notice period at the *Independent*, I researched and planned for my trip. I didn't know how long I would go away for but I wanted to put some kind of a number on it so I looked at my bank statement, did a bit of arithmetic and was pretty much forced by the result to decide on one year. Phase two of the planning commenced. I bought my flight and travel insurance, booked in for my injections and sold my bike and car. I packed up my books, clothes, plates and duvet, kicked out my flatmate and handed over the keys to an agent so someone else could sleep in my bed and cook in my kitchen while I camped at a friend's place for my last few weeks. Surprisingly, it was just like planning a holiday. The hardest part had been making the commitment to myself to do it. Even leaving my flat didn't bother me – the draw of exploring far-flung desert islands and sailing through crystal-clear waters easily outweighed the advantages of a comfortable and familiar home.

In the southern Indian Ocean a 16-year-old American girl who was attempting to break the world record for the youngest person to solo non-stop circumnavigate broke something else instead – her mast. It didn't put me off.

At work the paper was still riding high on a circulation rise during the build-up to and aftermath of the 2010 general election. BP was being censured for the massive *Deepwater Horizon* oil slick in the Gulf of Mexico that had been dominating the front page for what seemed like weeks and at the same time former 'first lady' Sarah Brown was being told off for tweeting about her forthcoming memoirs before their official publication. The Isle of Wight festival was on and the new government's economic forecast was set to be worse than the ex-Chancellor Alistair Darling's projection of three per cent growth for the next year. The editor, Roger Alton, was replaced by his predecessor, Simon Kelner, and a new era of stress and hassle dawned. The deputy news editor was told in morning conference that there was 'too much passive news editing' going on and the news editor kept disappearing into secret meetings. The paper was sold, after nearly two years of rumours and counter-strikes, to the Russian Lebedev family.

It was an exciting time at the newspaper. But I no longer cared. My mind was on other, more fun things. I felt no fear, no trepidation about heading off alone into the great, wide world, to live in a 46-foot space with a man I'd never met. A year or so before I'd never have thought that this would be something I would ever do. My family was *very* surprised. But it just felt right to me. It was *exciting*. I had a fun-filled send-off party, drunkenly told all my friends and family that I loved them and toddled off to Stansted to begin my adventure.

Kingdom

1

Now, Voyager

None of the tips about beating jet lag worked on my cramped long-haul budget flight to Kuala Lumpur. I considered not eating the meals, to trick my body into lacking energy so that I just fell asleep. I tried putting my watch ahead eight hours as soon as I boarded the plane in London and immediately adjusting to the new time zone. I attempted to keep track of what hour it was in the country we were currently flying over and going with that. Then I remembered that I'd paid extra for those tiny foil-packed meals and was determined to get my money's worth. There was no entertainment system so no graphic of the aeroplane arcing its way across the world to give me a clue about where we were. And by trying to jump forward eight hours using an analogue watch, I was a bit confused about whether it was 4am or 4pm, so by the time we landed at Kuala Lumpur Low Cost Carrier Terminal I was a spaced-out, sweaty wreck.

I knew the temperature in Malaysia would be 30°C + and the humidity high, yet I was dressed in jeans, mid-calf Gore-Tex sailing boots and a T-shirt, with both a cardigan and a waterproof jacket tied around my waist. Why? Certainly not for the style. Simple – excess baggage. When I booked my ticket I opted for the 20kg option, reasonably assuming that when I went away on a two-week holiday I only ever packed about 12kg and never used most of it, instead living in the same four or five items. But then, like a good little journalist, I started thoroughly researching things one might need to pack on one's back when going travelling. Once I'd thrown in stuff I might need for an off-the-beaten-track, who-knows-where-I-might-end-up sailing adventure – life jacket, boots, waterproofs, thick, padded mid-layers and woolly hat in case I found myself somewhere colder than the equator, months' worth of contact-lens solution, a mosquito net, medication, make-up, high-heeled sandals for nights out, a sleeping bag, and sterile needles in the event I needed to go to some godforsaken hospital in the jungle – I was struggling with the pre-booked 20kg limit. Then I had to add some apparently essential items that my host was having trouble finding in Asia – a home-brew beer kit and a cat flap – and I busted the maximum 30kg limit. It cost me £93 in excess baggage for the first flight and about £13 for the internal one and was a lesson sorely learned. Especially as it happened I would never use most of it – including, thankfully, the sterile needles – and would instead mainly recycle the same four or five items of clothing. (Neither, it would turn out, were the beer kit and cat flap actually essential – the beer would not be drunk and the cat would never pass through the flap.)

At baggage collection at Kuching airport in Sarawak, Borneo, I waited an age for my two pieces of luggage, until it was just me and a pair of Malaysian girls left. I began to worry that bringing a 40-pint IPA home-brew kit into a

Muslim country was a crime and that the cat flap Steve had had delivered to my office and that I hadn't bothered checking was really choc-a-block with drugs.

I was contemplating my impending incarceration when my bag finally appeared. All OK.

The only instructions I had about where to go from here were in the form of a text message from Steve telling me to get to somewhere called Santubong, so I paid my 70 ringgit (£14) up front at a kiosk and got into a slightly shabby looking red and yellow taxi for the one-hour ride. We drove past palatial homes: white and square, with balconies and tall iron gates closing them off from the street. Not quite the jungle shacks I'd imagined for Borneo. Next came rough-looking collections of concrete shops like I'd seen on holiday in Mexico and Egypt, and then an out-of-town Pizza Hut and KFC complex and a suburban area that reminded me of Oxford's inner ring road. All the cars on the road were boxy in shape, with matt paintwork. Oxford's inner ring road in the early 1980s.

Steve had told me by text message to go to the police station as it was the nearest landmark to where he was anchored. The driver looked at me doubtfully as he pulled down a dirt alleyway. There were no houses in sight, only the police station set in a garden dotted with rusting cars. No people, either. I rang Steve while my bags were being unloaded.

'See a white gate at the end of the hill?' he asked.

'Yep.'

'Go through there, along the road and I'll jump up and meet you.'

The taxi driver still looked dubious but drove off and left me there anyway.

I propped my wheelie case against the bars of the police

station fence, imagining vicious police dogs running out at any minute, while I climbed, tortoise-like, under my rucksack, staggering a bit beneath the weight. I strapped my hand-luggage backpack on to the top of the wheelie case handle and, with another bag in my free hand, I set out.

'Private property. Keep out,' declared a sign on the gate. I hesitated. But the gate was open and this was where Steve had said to go. On the other side was a wide, tree-lined avenue. That was as much as I could make out in the dark.

I decided to dig out my head torch. I knew it was somewhere in my rucksack. I went back to the police station fence, propped up the unbalanced wheelie case again, put down the small bag in my hand, struggled out from under the heavy rucksack, dumped it on to the dusty floor and fumbled with the combination lock using what little light there was coming from the windows of the police station to see the numbers. Lock off, loosen straps, unzip, unpack, root around, find torch, attach to head, switch on, repack, zip, tighten straps, lock on, stand up, hoist on to back, bend over under extra weight to retrieve small bag from floor, take handle of wheelie case and start again.

So now I was through the gate and trudging, in the dark, up a path, imagining more guard dogs, rapists and robbers in the bushes, with a 25kg weight on my back, dragging a wheelie case not designed for off-roading and with two items of clothing tied round my waist, a head torch that did little besides illuminating the bats swooping between the trees above me and an ever-increasing sense of fear. Sweaty does not even cover it. *What on earth am I doing here?* I repeatedly asked myself but I didn't turn round. There was nowhere else to go anyway.

I kept walking for about another 100 metres or so until I reached a farmyard or garden of sorts. Here there were lights and, a little way ahead, two men who saw me. I stopped, remembering the Keep Out sign, and propped my wheelie case against my thigh to free up my right hand so I could call Steve on my mobile.

'I'm not sure I'm in the right place,' I said, keeping one eye on the men. Were they security guards about to shout at me for trespassing? One of them got on to a moped and started coming towards me. *Shit.* I took the phone away from my ear before I could hear Steve's reply. The guard pulled up a few metres away and said something in English that I didn't quite catch.

Then from nowhere a white man, even sweatier than I was and wearing only a pair of shorts, appeared and grinned from me to the guard and back again. It was Steve and apparently I was in the right place.

In the first half a second of seeing him in the flesh for the first time, two words flashed into my mind so clearly it was as if someone had shouted them. *Small! Bald!* I almost flinched. Next came *Ugly!* So much for Jane's theory that me and this shiny, half-naked sailor man were going to live happily ever after. *Never in a million years*, I thought, awkwardly accepting his welcoming hug. When he pulled back I could see bewilderment in his face as he looked at me. No doubt he was summing me up as *Sweaty! Dirty! Wearing a freakishly large amount of clothes!*

When I was a kid, I loved the Sweet Valley High books. One or two pages into each story, author Francine Pascal would describe what the protagonists looked like. In every book – and there were a lot of them – the description was exactly the same, down to the barrettes Elizabeth wore in her hair and the fact that Jessica, during a rebellious phase, had painted her bedroom chocolate brown. No doubt the author reasoned that including a detailed description of appearance and characteristics would help her readers picture the twins in their minds. I'm going to borrow a leaf from Ms Pascal's book here.

Steve was English, in his forties and about 5 feet 5 inches tall. What little dark hair that remained on his head was clipped right back to his skull. His tan emphasised the blueness of his eyes, which were fringed with black lashes that had been bleached blond at the tips by the sun. He had an angular, Roman nose and thin lips almost the same shade as his skin. Unusually for a cruiser he was clean-shaven. His body was small and wiry and curiously hairless. A tattooed lizard crawled up his right shoulder blade. He mainly wore only short shorts without underpants underneath. I came to know this because sometimes a ball would pop out if he sat with his legs splayed. His fingernails usually had a black rim around them from tinkering with the engine.

He'd had a traditional English middle-class upbringing: good school, university, job at an established company. Like many an early 90s bachelor before him, he'd driven a sports car and had a succession of women. He'd sailed for years and had long harboured a dream of living on a boat in a beautiful tropical setting. Eventually he'd saved up enough money to do it and he'd taken his girlfriend at the time along with him. But after a couple of years they'd split, she left and he stayed on the boat.

I have no idea what colour he painted his bedroom during his rebellious teenage years.

Steve took my rucksack and I followed him through the trees. Suddenly we were no longer in a farmyard but walking along a wooden pontoon, loading my bags into the dinghy and then climbing aboard his yacht, *Kingdom*, which was anchored a little way off. I don't know if it was nerves or jet lag but everything seemed to be moving in fast forward.

I followed him down the narrow companionway steps into the innards of the boat. It was boiling hot even though all the fans were on. And cramped. My bags seemed to be taking up all the room. I turned round and round, not knowing what to do with myself. The confidence I'd felt in London had totally vanished.

'Drink?' Steve asked.

'Yes please. What do you have?'

'Everything.' Which actually meant not much, unless I wanted alcohol. I took an orange juice and then, because I was so hot, another one, and somehow started to feel guilty. Steve was nervously pacing around the boat moving things. Neither of us really knew what to do or say. Maybe a beer or at least vodka in my orange would have been a good idea, I thought. Bit of social lubrication and all that.

I perched in silence on a blue sofa and looked around, feeling more and more uncomfortable. The interior was made of dark wood, like in many older boats, and that made the space feel even smaller. To my left were the steps up to the deck; in the centre of the saloon was a large table and the mast, which had a flat screen TV bolted to it. There was another blue seat opposite me. Cupboards lined two walls and washing was hanging from a line that had been strung up across the room, including a pair of extremely large faded jeans. They looked way too big to be Steve's, unless he'd lost an extraordinary amount of weight. Or possibly he just liked the baggy 1990s NKOTB look.

To my left, past one side of the stairs, was the galley, and to my right the forepeak cabin, which was a triangular sleeping platform with cupboards along each wall, and a bathroom. I could see a shower curtain through the open door.

A tabby cat wandered into the saloon. 'That's Layla,' Steve said. She stared at me with her yellow eyes and settled herself down on the top step. Cats bring out a kind of broody instinct in me. Dogs I can't deal with, but cats I like. I always say hello to any I come across in the street. Friends' pets usually seek out my lap to sit on because they know I'll lavish them with attention. One day, a few decades down the line, I imagine the neighbourhood kids will refer to me as 'the mad cat lady'.

I decided it would be a good idea to make friends. 'Hello, Layla,' I crooned at her as I approached, right hand lifted ready to stroke her soft, stripy fur. No miaow in reply. 'Don't touch her bum or she'll bite you,' Steve advised. I stopped, my fingers inches above her back. I eyed Layla; Layla eyed me. She didn't look friendly. At all. I retreated and sat back down on the sofa, sans cat on my lap.

I fidgeted, waited and sweated in my jeans, watching Steve pick things up and put them down again. He seemed vacant, unable to concentrate on anything or finish his sentences. *Why am I here?* I asked myself for the nth time. *This man is odd, borderline rude. Even his cat is standoffish. At the regatta I'll have to meet other people and jump ship.* Not a good start to my adventure. I took off my boots and socks, coat and cardigan, as much to have something to do as to cool down. Finally Steve broke off from his pottering to offer me a shower.

Although I was desperate to have a wash, it felt odd to

shower while a stranger was nearby. While the door to the head (bathroom) did close after a lot of rearranging of the shower curtain, the one for the cabin didn't. I prayed my small travelling towel would not fall down while I rooted around in my bag for some clothes, painfully aware that I was in plain sight. Despite the cold shower, the embarrassment and difficulty of trying to find underwear with one hand while the other clutched at the towel was making me hot again. The humidity in the bathroom while I dressed didn't help.

Steve showered after me and undressed with his back to me in the cabin, dropping his shorts on to the floor and stepping naked into the bathroom. I noticed he kept the door open, rather than struggling to shut it. A few minutes later, he walked right past me in just a towel to his cabin at the back of the boat. Easy. *I'll have to be less of a prude,* I thought.

When he came out he offered me a drink, 'A proper one this time,' and I accepted a beer. He finally sat down and we both relaxed. Steve said he wanted to set sail immediately for Talang Talang, a turtle sanctuary island 50 or so miles away, so that I could wake up to my first morning in a really beautiful place. I got a crash course in sorting out the anchor chain to stop it from tangling as it came up and then we were off. It was midnight and the hulk of the Gunung Santubong mountain was black against the night sky as we motored out of the river into a flat, calm sea.

After a while, and another beer, the breeze came up enough for us to sail, so we did. We talked, laughed and drank our way through the night, the awkwardness between us diminishing as the hours – and the alcohol – passed. Quickly it felt like we were great mates, with a shared sense of humour. We retold each other the stories of our lives that we'd already covered on email. I learned that Steve was a very sensitive man who had had a clear plan about wanting to live on a yacht and travel. I got the impression that when, in England, he met the girlfriend he'd later lived on the boat with, he'd found out early on whether she would be interested in a life aboard so that he could have a partner with him afloat. And he wanted that again, very badly, I realised, as I listened to his tales of disastrous internet dates since. His choosing to sit close to me might also have given me a bit of a clue.

Now is the time to make it clear you're not interested in him, I told myself. *Tell him you like someone else. Give him the old 'it's not you, it's me' line. Anything. Just so everyone knows where they stand.* It would have been the smart thing to do. But, ever the ostrich, I merely shifted my body a few centimetres further away, tried to give out 'not interested' signals and said absolutely nothing.

At some point, probably not long before dawn, I fell asleep in the cockpit and Steve fetched a blanket to cover me. When I woke, about 7am, we were approaching a tropical island: a steep-sided peak covered in dense rainforest, a few palm trees further down leaning crazily sideways, two wooden houses on stilts and a raised golden sand beach and spit covered with what must have been turtle tracks. I smiled to myself – this was more like it.

2

We will have a fishy, on our little dishy

This was it – my adventure, my new beginning, my chance to change my life and take it in any direction I wanted to. It was really happening. Sitting by myself on the deck, I felt one of those odd moments of pure happiness that had been all too lacking in my life recently, a swelling inside my chest that felt as if it could easily expand beyond the confines of my ribs. I didn't know this country, this boat or man but I did know that it felt natural just being there.

So far there was sun, there was a gorgeous yacht, a golden sunrise, tropical settings – and now there was yellow sea. That's right, yellow. Strictly speaking, if this new life of mine was going to live up to expectations, it should have been a beautiful blue sea. But it was yellow. Not in as disgusting a way that snow can be yellow, I'll grant you, but yellow all the same.

Steve and I had left the island with the turtle tracks early in the afternoon on a three-day passage to the town of Miri, where we would pick up our other crew for the approaching regatta. With no wind, we had motored the whole way, offshore and mainly out of sight of land, without stopping, past oil rigs and into these vast patches of thick yellow water. At one spot the change in colour was so obvious it formed a straight line on the surface.

'I've never seen yellow sea before,' I said. 'Brown, maybe, off the east coast of England, but not yellow.'

'It's the palm oil companies,' Steve said. 'When they cut down the rainforest for their plantations, the soil gets washed into the rivers and then the seas.'

'So when we get past the rivers the water will turn blue again?' I asked.

'Yes, it should do.'

'Great.' Back on perfect-adventure-setting track.

During the three-day passage we fell into a rough routine. We were both awake during the day, mainly motoring along because there was little wind. Steve would be downstairs doing 'boat jobs' while I was on deck, keeping an eye on the autopilot and looking out for ships or big floating logs the size of entire trees that we really didn't want to hit. Every now and then Steve would stick his head up and declare it 'a sailing breeze' and the sails would come out and the noisy engine go off and we'd sail in blissful silence for a while until the winds died and the engine had to come on again.

He taught me how to use the radar, how to trim the mainsail to get the best out of the light winds, to tell if one of the rare ships we saw was on a collision course. He was a very experienced sailor and I was a little bit in awe of him and flattered that he felt confident enough in me to let me keep watch over his boat alone. At night, he'd get some rest while I stayed awake on watch until 3am or 4am. Then I'd try to sleep but I was usually woken up by the heat and bright sunlight a couple of hours later so I'd invariably doze off in the afternoon as well. Sleeping at odd times meant missing meals. If we were both awake one of us would cook something, which was a bit of a struggle as I'd forgotten to tell Steve I was a vegetarian before I arrived and he had an aversion to most forms of carbohydrate, except beer.

'What do you mean, you don't eat rice?' I asked, incredulous. 'You live in Asia.'

'I just don't like the stodge. I need protein.'

As well as rice, his list of foods he didn't like to eat much of included pasta and bread – basically the main parts of a vegetarian diet, apart from, obviously, vegetables. He loved meat. Apparently we'd have to work out some recipes both of us could stomach, once we could get to the shops. The boat's stocks were meat-heavy and so for the first two days, excepting the tiny plane meals, I ate only one tortilla filled with pinto beans and cheese, a packet of three dry crackers and a salad made of raw cabbage, long-life feta and half an apple. *Good chance to lose a few pounds, being as how I'll be mainly living in a bikini*, was my first thought. It was swiftly replaced by painful, gnawing hunger.

Those three days were my introduction to the boat and how everything worked. I'd spent a reasonable amount of time on yachts by then and I knew to expect a run-through from the skipper on the use of various equipment like radar, autopilot, the man-overboard system, which rope controls what, where the switches are for the navigation lights, and so on. On *Kingdom* there was a fair bit more to the induction, especially where the saucepans were concerned:

'The washing-up has to be done in a specific way,' Steve said. 'First wash with salt water, then rinse with a minimum of fresh. And remember which foot pump controls which tap.' I nodded. The list continued.

'Always fasten doors open on their catches.'

'No metal implements to be used in the saucepans.'

'No hot saucepans to be placed on the work surface.'

'Pans and lids are to be placed separately back into their original plastic wrapping after use and stacked in precise order inside each other before being returned to the cupboard.'

'On deck, handles stay in the winches but must point forwards at all times.'

'All ropes must be folded into "elephant's ears".'

'Everything on deck – cushions, dan buoy, spare fuel tank, even the barbecue, has recently been reupholstered in special weatherproof fabric. There is a second set of covers to go on top of the cockpit cushions. These are not waterproof and must be removed in the event of rain.'

The rules seemed a bit anal to me but Steve always had a reason or a story behind them. If I ignored them all, we'd be sitting on soggy cushions, drinking salty tea stirred with rusty spoons while doors crashed loudly every time a wave hit. Keeping the winch handles pointed forward saved shins from bruising, covering everything prevented UV damage and rusting and not coiling ropes made them less likely to tangle. The multiple pan rules were because Steve had lugged an entire non-stick set back from the UK in a suitcase one year and he wanted to keep them as long as he could. It made sense but crouching on the floor, unpacking and repacking pans and lids out of and back into plastic bags became my least favourite chore, followed closely by dashing out in the rain in the middle of the night to remove 16 fleecy cushion covers that were tied and velcroed on to metal frames.

Although I was coming from a British summer, my body was in no way prepared for the heat and the strength of the sun, which was so fierce it burned through my factor-30 sunscreen in 20 minutes, even on partially cloudy days.

The first morning, I asked Steve to put suncream on to my back. I sat down at an angle on the seat next to him and handed him my Piz Buin. He started to rub it in, sliding his hands all over my back, touching every inch. My first thought was *That's a thorough application*, but when it continued for a lot longer than it should have done and progressed to shoulder kneading, I said thanks and twisted away. *Stop being such a prude*, I reasoned with myself. *He's just a very tactile person. It's not like he's groping you. He didn't flirt while he was doing it, didn't mention it afterwards, just asked you to put some cream on his back in return.* I wanted to keep the mood on the boat light and I didn't want to come across as standoffish so, despite my discomfort, I said nothing.

For the three days we'd been on our way to Miri we'd had a fishing line strung off the back of the boat but had no bites. At possibly the worst time for it – less than three miles away from port, while we were doing 7 knots with our largest and trickiest-to-handle spinnaker sail up – the reel started screaming. Steve sprang into action and donned his cod piece. It reminded me of something a Tudor might have worn: a belt fastened around his waist, and down the front, over his groin, was a plastic plate with a sort of spout sticking up and out from it, like a hollow strap-on penis. Steve took the fishing rod out of its holder on the back rail and slid it into the spout, gripping it with one hand while he reeled in the line with the other. He had to plant his feet wide on the deck to keep his balance. It was ridiculously phallic.

I stood ready with the enormous gaff hook while Steve, hand still on groin spout, struggled against both the fish, which was fighting for its life, and the drag of the boat.

'When I lift him out of the water, you put the hook through his gill,' he said. 'It'll probably come out of his mouth.' Nice behaviour for a vegetarian.

After an epic struggle, I saw the fish's silvery back break the surface of the water. It looked huge and angry. Steve kept pulling it in, bit by bit, until it was close enough for me to reach. I leaned out from the back corner of the boat, swallowing back my squeamishness. It took a couple of goes before I managed to hook the gill. Fortunately the spike didn't come out of its mouth. While I held it wriggling on the hook, Steve fetched a knife. I turned away when he killed it.

I'm not sure who was more excited about the catch – the skipper or the cat. Layla appeared, yowling, and Steve danced a jubilant jig in his codpiece, showing off. He was the hunter, the provider of food, the man. He weighed the fish – 5.2lb – and said he thought it might be a Spanish mackerel.

We had only one and a half miles to go before we hit land and we were still sailing under spinnaker so the fish was hung from the back rail, a noose around its tail, while we took down the sails, hung out the fenders and moored up.

Once we were settled, Steve put some potatoes on the barbecue and started to cut up the fish. According to an illustration in his book of fish species, we'd caught a bluefin tuna. He cut off the head and tail, then sliced through the backbone to make steaks for the barbecue. What we weren't eating that night went in the fridge. Layla licked pools of blood from the teak deck and nibbled on hand-fed titbits of sushi. She was in cat heaven.

Back in London, I had had a fantasy of what life on a sailing boat would be like and, specifically, what meals on a yacht would consist of. I imagined breakfasting on tropical fruits, lunching on fragrant rice piled high on banana leaves and dining on fresh fish we had caught ourselves that afternoon, just before sunset, and blackened on a beach fire built from driftwood. I'm a bit of a daydreamer like that. Also, from a practical point of view, it made sense to me to eat a lot of fish if you lived on the ocean. So I was fully prepared to relinquish my five years of vegetarianism for pescetarianism and give this tuna a go. And I was pretty impressed with Steve for catching it, reeling it in and knowing how to kill, gut and prepare it. I didn't think anyone I knew back in England would have had those kind of real-life skills. Still, I felt a bit anxious about eating it.

Steve was proud to cook me my first fish in half a decade – and a fish that he'd caught himself, with his bare hands (and a codpiece). He laid the folding cockpit table with knives and forks and chilled white wine. He carefully lifted four foil-covered packages from the barbecue and set them down on the plates. He sat opposite me and made sure I had butter for my potato, that I had salt and pepper for my fish. His mood was infectious and, while my mouth wasn't quite watering, I was looking forward to my dinner. I wanted to like it. I peeled back the foil, loaded my fork, put it into my mouth and chewed. Steve, who hadn't started eating, watched me expectantly, blue eyes fairly twinkling with anticipation.

'So, what's it like?'

I didn't want to be rude but there was no getting away from the fact. 'Tastes like canned tuna.'

It wasn't, it turned out, a bluefin tuna, a delicacy the world over, particularly in Japan. It was, more likely, a skipjack or, possibly, a mack, which, someone would later tell me, goes into cat food.

I ate the potato, left the fish and stayed a vegetarian.

3

Getting into the groove

So who are the other crew who are arriving for the race, then?' I asked Steve the next morning as I bobbed about in the small inflatable dinghy, scrubbing the yacht's sides to get her camera-ready. 'All women? Is that by coincidence or by design?'

He laughed. 'Design, daaarling. No, I don't really like having other men on my boat, telling them what to do. Egos can get in the way. I find it easier with women.'

'OK,' I said, thinking back to his advert that I'd answered. Had it specified female crew? I couldn't remember.

'Tomorrow we've got Claire and her cousin arriving, who Claire says is a "hottie".'

'What's her name?'

'Not sure.'

'And where do you know Claire from?'

'She crewed in a race I did a while ago. She had a bit of a thing for me. But she's not really my type.' *Maybe the cousin will be your type*, I thought, *and that will take some of the pressure off me.* I was thrilled to have a bigger crew. I'd never sailed with fewer than three people before joining *Kingdom* – and across the Atlantic we had a boat of 20 – and I am firmly of the opinion the more, the merrier.

Lizzie 'the hottie' lived up to expectations – long, wavy blonde hair, smooth skin with not a freckle or a scar, long limbs, full lips, the clearest eyes I'd ever seen. She was everything I wanted to be but was not. Quieter than her cousin, once she warmed up she was full of jokes and had a dirty sense of humour. She was jet-lagged, having flown from Scotland to Singapore to meet her older expat cousin Claire. Claire had high, Scandinavian cheekbones but the blonde hair was where the family resemblance stopped. Tall and strong, she looked like she could hold her own with the male crew on the racing boats she sailed in regattas in Thailand and Singapore. 'Medium build' was Steve's unkind way of describing her. A successful lawyer, she was a natural organiser and knew a lot about yacht racing. For Lizzie, who had just finished her studies to be a vet, it was her first time on a boat.

It was the night before the race week began and there was no organised event so we took a taxi into Miri town centre. As I stepped off the boat, Steve handed me the head of the tuna we'd caught in a plastic bag.

'Is that for the bin?' I asked.

'No, we'll find someone to give it to.'

I was incredulous. 'Find someone to give it to? Who's going to want a fish head?'

'It's a delicacy out here. They love it. They'll make a curry out of it or something.'

I walked with Claire and Lizzie to the car park to find the taxi we'd ordered. Claire was carrying the rubbish to throw into the big bins and I had the fish head bag. None of the

Malays we passed were eagerly eyeing it up, licking their lips or seeming about to snatch it off me and toss it into their curry pot and I felt too embarrassed to offer it to anyone. When Claire went to throw the rubbish in the large bin, I passed her the head. Gone. Embarrassment over.

We got into the taxi, girls in the back; Steve, who had caught up, in the front.

'Where you wan go?' asked the driver.

'Do you know a good restaurant in Miri?' Claire asked. 'Good local food? Sells beer?'

He nodded and started the engine.

'Where's the fish head?' Steve asked me, twisting round in his seat.

I blushed, although possibly no one could tell through my sunburn. 'Erm, in the bin.'

'What? Why? We could have given it to the driver.' He turned back to the driver. 'You like fish head, yes?'

The driver took his eyes off the road to look at Steve briefly then returned his attention to his driving. He didn't speak.

'For curry? Soup?' Steve persisted. 'Mmm, very tasty.'

Still nothing from the driver. Either he was as revolted as I was at the idea of a fish's head floating about in a spicy stew or, more likely, his English wasn't that good. Whatever the reason, nothing more was said about the head.

He had, however, understood enough to drop us at the Ming Café. I know it is the title of an esteemed Chinese dynasty – and some pretty expensive crockery – but the word still made me chuckle. The waiters and waitresses wore black T-shirts with the café's slogan printed in bad English on the back: 'I pissed in Ming Café.' And what was the top item on the menu? Fish head curry.

Food etiquette was not the only aspect of culture – and life – shock I would experience. The regatta, which started the next day, with its frenzied whirlwind of activity – what with the regular briefings, the events, the dinners, the moving from town to town, the meeting of new people all the time and trying to remember their names, their boats' names, which categories they were in and who their crew were – would turn out to be a good stepping stone between my old life in London and my new identity as a traveller and cruiser. Its ordered structure was familiar, even if the Borneo setting and the people I now lived with were not. And I had little time to wonder what I was doing here. We were so busy, I just had to get on with things.

Steve had suggested we do a 'shake down' – practise sailing together as a team – the next morning, before the first race. He was very patient teaching Lizzie how the boat worked and even more patient when she and Claire were both very sick in the fairly choppy seas. We managed one hour of shaking down and throwing up before limping back to the shelter of the marina.

It was already dark when we got to the pre-race dinner that night and the hall was stunning. Built of wood in a style based on the traditional Borneo longhouses, where an entire community lives in one large shed, it had a high vaulted ceiling and was full of round tables which, in turn, were full of mainly white people in loud Hawaiian shirts. A white-haired man in the loudest Hawaiian shirt in the room whistled and beckoned us over. 'I've saved you some seats,' he shouted across the hall.

'That's Ron from *Blue Steel*,' Steve said. 'I bet he's saved places for us because he knows I've got a crew full of women.'

So women are currency here, I thought, sarcastically. I knew Steve well enough by now to know that he had a tendency to be a show-off – and what better way to draw attention to yourself than by making an entrance with three younger women? The *Blue Steel* crew didn't seem at all slimy and were just friendly, older chaps excited to be on holiday, drinking, partying and racing. They were Canadian Ron, the captain, who lived on his boat full time and made his living from picking up backpackers and taking them on sailing trips around Thailand and Malaysia. He was tanned and always holding a beer can across his skinny body. Big John was a Teutonic giant, quick with a joke and always ready with a story to tell. Also from Canada, he was a builder by trade but should have been a cowboy. Posh Simon was younger, in his thirties, and knew Claire from the racing scene in Singapore, where he lived with his wife and daughters. And Trevor was an Englishman who'd taken advantage of the tax breaks the local government offers foreigners to retire to Malaysia and spend their pensions there.

'Erm, where are all the hot men?' Lizzie asked me as we took our seats. She evidently had the same theory as me about sailors being a handsome bunch – and apparently didn't consider Steve to be good-looking, either. We scanned the crowd. Old sailor, old waiter, Malaysian government official (old), ancient mariner. It seemed that all of the other competitors were married couples in at least their sixties. *Blue Steel*, being all men with an average age of about 45, were the closest thing there was to boat totty. We sighed and got stuck into the complimentary Carlsberg.

Then Adonis appeared in the room. Tall, blond, tanned, toned, square of jaw and green of eye. And way, way, below the age of retirement. Steve nudged Claire. Claire nudged me. I nudged Lizzie. We all four, Steve included, stared, agog. We couldn't take our eyes off his face. His were the kind of all-American, high-school-prom-king good looks that make Abercrombie and Fitch model recruiters weep. And in his wake tiptoed a veritable princess: tiny body, blonde mane, white smile as dazzling as her dress.

Josh. His name was Josh. And she was Kristin. Steve stood behind them in the drinks queue and dug for information, acting like an honorary member of our new girl gang. Josh was the son of a rancher who had sold off a lot of land to developers and made quite a bit of money. Kristin was freshly arrived from the US and was an actual beauty queen. They seemed madly in love, very nice people and, for Americans, were surprisingly good at taking the piss.

The next few days passed in a blur of races: short ones, long ones, windy ones, becalmed ones. We tried as hard as we could, Lizzie and Claire still suffering from seasickness, and we varied between coming third and falling back to ninth place. It was fun and exhilarating and I loved every minute.

While we were all together, Steve treated me no differently from Claire and Lizzie. The suncream applications became more clinical, and for that I was glad. But whenever we were alone, he would seize the chance to flirt. As I washed up after lunch during one off-shore race, making sure to stick to the washing-up rules and put the pans back in their plastic wrappers, Steve said to me from out of nowhere: 'You're much prettier than in your Facebook pictures,' as he walked past. I didn't quite know what to say to that but he'd wandered off again before I'd had a chance to try to think of a suitable reply. It was another indication that he liked me in that way more than I liked him. But *I can handle this*, I told myself. *He'll get the message eventually and stop trying.* (*OK, Miss Naïveté*, I'd tell myself now.)

When we reached Kota Kinabalu, exhausted and demoralised after being hit by the bad wind fairy on the 65-mile passage race from Labuan, Lizzie and Claire went ashore to look into booking a trip to see orangutans, leaving Steve and me on the boat by ourselves. He was in the aft cabin, trying to sleep as he'd managed only 90 minutes over the past 36 hours, he'd been so busy trying to squeeze every last drop of speed out of his boat and enthusiasm out of his crew. I lay down on my sofa bunk, desperate to get some rest. I heard him get up and come through to the saloon and opened my eyes just in time to see his face approaching mine as he tried to kiss me. So much for getting the message that I wasn't interested. Beer fumes from his breath flooded my nostrils. I turned my head over towards the wall. 'No,' I said. He stopped and walked back to his cabin.

'Are you coming for a cuddle?' he called.

'No.'

'Sure?'

'Yes.' My pulse was racing and I felt quite vulnerable. It was weird – he was my skipper and my friend and I trusted him in those roles. But this was a different situation and I felt unsettled. I was alone with this man, on his boat, which was also his home, anchored off, and I didn't know how to use the dinghy to get to shore if I needed to. I sat up in the bed and listened. He was still in his cabin and it didn't sound like he was coming back through. My head felt cloudy and confused and I was very, very tired but I couldn't sleep after that; I just lay there, wired, until it was time to get up to go to an afternoon press conference that all crews were supposed to attend.

I still felt unsettled so when I climbed into the dinghy I decided to say something to clear the air.

'I feel a bit funny,' I started.

'About what?'

'About what happened earlier.'

He laughed. 'You'll get over it.' And that was that as far as he was concerned. For the rest of the evening I kept away from him, trying to shake the uncomfortable feeling I had in my stomach. It was not dissimilar to when someone tells you a big, shocking secret and you can't tell anyone but have to process it by yourself. Lack of sleep was no doubt making me more emotional but for some reason I couldn't bring myself to tell Claire or Lizzie. Embarrassment that I'd got myself into this position, probably.

The last day of racing was much, much better. In our free Borneo International Yachting Challenge T-shirts we'd been given we looked a bit more like a crew for the two races in the bay just outside Kota Kinabalu. There were no waves to speak of and – yes, thank God! – there was some wind. It was almost perfect. I had a good feeling about it until Steve said he wanted to take me off bowman's duties and put me on the helm instead.

'What? Why? Am I not doing a good enough job?'

'No, you've been fine. It's just that I'd like a chance to work the bow and you like helming, you say.'

My feelings were hurt at the perceived demotion – *Has he done it because I snubbed his advances yesterday*, I wondered

– but I took the helm, worrying slightly because I'd never steered in a short, fast race before. He told me to watch the tell tales on the sails – ribbons that indicate how the air is flowing over the sail – but I was ashamed to tell him that I didn't know how to respond to them. My hands were sticky with sweat as we approached the starting line of the first of two races.

It was fantastically exhilarating. I concentrated on the feel of the boat and its speed while I got the hang of reacting to how the tell tales were fluttering and adjusting my steering angle. Steve called it 'getting into the groove' – gathering enough speed to build apparent wind and heel the boat over.

As we approached the finish line of the first race we were between two boats with less than a metre either side, the crew of the leeward yacht yelling at us to come up and give them room.

'We can't come up,' I shouted back. 'There's a boat on our windward side.' We could have let the sails luff, lost speed and dropped back out of the way but I wasn't going to tell them that. I held my nerve – and my breath – and we slid forward between the two yachts and our bow crossed the line just ahead of theirs. We came fourth.

After that beautiful finish we cocked up our approach of the first mark of the final race, so we had to tack, tack, tack to get round it. All the jubilation after the day's first race quickly dissipated as our speed dropped to frustratingly low levels. Then another boat, *Pandemonium*, came up to the mark. I was waiting for Steve to tell me to turn and he thought I was going to judge it by myself. We were too slow to tack away, too late to dip down and so – crunch! – our beams 'kissed'. 'Sorry!' we shouted out to *Pandemonium*. 'No damage done,' they called back and very kindly didn't protest us at the end of the race. We caught up under kite and overtook them and three others in quick succession by stealing their wind, and crossed the line fifth.

We derigged and popped the Veuve Clicquot Claire had carried over from Singapore and celebrated with a lunch of cheese sandwiches. Steve was in his element as he posed for photos in the cockpit surrounded by his crew of women, Layla in his arms. I was just as elated – I'd helmed us to victory (well, fourth place) and I'd held my nerve to steer us between those boats. There were no worries about demotion now – I was pleased and proud that Steve had trusted me to steer.

After the champagne was gone we had some cava, then some more cava and then, when there was no more left, some very strong gin and tonics. There was music and dancing and general merriment. Lizzie was doubly excited – she'd caught the racing bug and had conquered her seasickness.

I was sitting on the port side of the yacht, my legs dangling over the side, when Steve came to sit next to me, his shoulder touching mine. We talked over the race, the day's highlights, wondered about how we would be placed overall, whether we had a chance of a top position after handicaps were taken into consideration. It was all fairly innocuous stuff. As I stood up to get my things together to go ashore for the final party, he gave me a sly look.

'I'm not going to be able to stand up for a few minutes,' he said.

It took a second for the penny to drop. *Oh my God. He's telling me he's got an erection. What do I say to that?*

'Oh. Errm,' I eloquently stuttered before dashing away.

I am quite prudish – see earlier anecdote about struggling in the shower – and overtly sexual behaviour puts me off. I knew that Steve was much more open about his sexuality. I'd laughed at tales of bedroom antics he'd related and I was getting (a bit) more comfortable with his 'hands on' approach to things. I had thought that I was relaxing a bit more into my new life, becoming a bit cooler, less uptight, more assertive. My reaction to this comment of his, though, and my inability to say 'Shut up. Stop being gross. It is never going to happen, ever,' showed me I was just as much the placid, timid sheep here in Borneo that I had been in London. And that was so disappointing. I'm not sure why I expected that changing my surroundings so completely would correlate to a radical overhaul in personality in just three weeks. But I had expected that – and I cursed myself for my weaknesses when I saw that it wasn't the case.

We were anchored off Sutera Harbour Golf and Country Club, which was hosting the finale dinner and which had given competitors complimentary use of its facilities for three days. Lizzie, Claire and I took full advantage of what are still, to this day, the nicest marina toilets I have ever had the pleasure of using. There were fluffy towels and mahogany lockers. There were limestone cubicles and hairdryers, sachets of shampoo and conditioner and toothbrushes for the taking. Considering most showering facilities for sailors resemble the clinical bathrooms found in Soviet government-run health saunas, but with less hot water, we were in heaven.

Our Malaysian hosts had pulled out all the stops for the final party. Our dinner was held in a marquee stretched out over the tennis courts with hundreds of strings of white lights dangling from the silky white ceiling. It looked like the setting for an American movie wedding. Steve had packed a cool bag with bottles of wine and beers and I felt incredibly embarrassed that he had brought it along – until I saw that the country club was charging 26 ringgit (£5) for a glass of wine and then I didn't feel so bad.

June, a New Zealand sailor from one of the catamarans, stood up to make a brief speech, thanking the Malays for their generous hospitality in their language. She'd had some help translating her words into Bahasa Malaya and stumbled over them a little but the officials were loving it. So, apparently, was Steve, whose eyes welled with tears that he dabbed away with the tablecloth.

'Steve, are you all right?' I asked.

'She's so sweet,' he sniffed. 'It was such a beautiful speech.' And the tears came again.

After we helped *Blue Steel* celebrate their overall first place win, while trying not to be too gutted that we'd not made the podium, we weaved our way to the dinghy. Steve was too drunk to read the combination on the lock and, because it was upside down and he didn't have his reading glasses on, confused the sevens with twos.

'Ladies first,' he said, after we'd taken the lock from his hands and sorted it out for him, and he stood aside, giggling. I'd started to notice that he almost had two personalities, which I had nicknamed (not that originally, granted) Macho Boat Steve and Camp Shore Steve. When he was on the yacht, especially during the racing, he was a more masculine version of himself, in control and running the ship, so to speak. He even dressed better and seemed more attractive. If he had had only this one personality I might have been interested. But when we went on to land he camped up: his lisp, his facial expressions, his gait, his double entendres. He cried at speeches, for chrissake, with tears and everything.

He managed to drive us back to the yacht but when the three of us climbed aboard he stayed sitting in the dinghy, tied to *Kingdom*, bobbing about in the bay. 'I just want a quiet moment to myself,' he said. I had my suspicions that he was still a bit tearful over June's gesture. It took Lizzie a good 20 minutes to coax him out of the dinghy, crooning at him like one would to a small child. He fell asleep at the nav station, lying foetal on the stool, his head under the table.

What better way to recover from a hangover than by relaxing next to the pool of a five-star country club with a fresh coconut to sip from? It was the first time I'd drunk fresh coconut water. I knew the health freaks back home went nuts for the stuff, shelling out £3 a can in Whole Foods in Kensington High Street to rehydrate after their yoga workouts. I shouldn't mock – I loved my yoga workouts; I was just too tight to hand over £3 for a drink afterwards. It was sweet and a little bit salty, like those rehydration sachets your mother makes you drink after you've had a dose of the runs, and I knew it was probably doing me the world of good.

Lizzie and I went for a dip in the pool. The water was refreshingly cool and we bobbed about gently, not bothering to exert ourselves by doing any real swimming. I knew I'd signed up to be on the boat on my own with Steve and had flown all the way out here to do just that. We got on well as friends – both online before I came to Borneo and in person. But his behaviour was making me nervous as it was clear he wanted more and I did not. I didn't feel threatened by him exactly, more uncomfortable. It had been fine when there were other people on the boat and I had really enjoyed our being a crew of four – five if you counted the cat. I tried to talk to Lizzie about it.

'I really hope Big John comes on board,' I started. Steve had told me that Big John had asked if he could join us on *Kingdom* for a few weeks after the girls had gone. She looked at me, her blue eyes inscrutable. 'I mean I think it would be more fun, you know, with more people around.' Damn my inability to vocalise what I actually feel. What I should have said was, 'I don't want to be on my own with Steve. What would you do if you were me?' Instead I fluffed it and she replied with some platitude or other and I lost my chance to talk things over before she and Claire left.

She probably thought I was an utter loon to have flown halfway round the world to join a lonesome man on his boat, anyway. It was a standard reaction before I left when I told friends and family what I was doing. They were used to my going off sailing with people I didn't know for a week at a time but this was more than that – they knew it and so did I. 'You what? On a boat with a man? Alone?' was the stock response. Usually it was followed by 'Have you seen *Dead Calm*?' or 'Is it going to be like in that film with Oliver Reed, you know, that old one, where they have sex all the time?' Looking back I can see where they were coming from but at the time I was so caught up in my own excitement of what an adventure it was all going to be that I just laughed along with them.

Maybe I shouldn't have been so blasé – he tried to kiss me again that evening when we were standing in the cockpit. 'You just need more time,' he said when I moved away, seeming not in the least offended by my blunt refusal.

It is a well-known fact that women are wont to change their minds at the drop of a hat. And so it was that, not two days after trying to tell Lizzie that I was unwilling to share a 46-foot boat with the skipper, I ended up sharing a cabin with him. One minute I was innocently unpacking my rucksack into a spare locker he had in his cabin, the next I was not-so-innocently occupying the port side of the double bed. Reader, you're shocked? Well, imagine my surprise.

At school, for my A level in English Literature, we studied *Tess of the d'Urbervilles* and had deep discussions about how much of a part the comely farm girl has to play in her own seduction. Having reached the ripe old age of 31, I admit I was no Tess Durbeyfield ingénue, and I wouldn't go so far as to say that the wicked cur Stephen seduced me. But I'd like to think that the thoughts that passed through my mind might also have occurred to Hardy's heroine when the villain of the piece kept needling away at her: 'Oh, I can't be arsed with this. Maybe it'd just be easier to go along with it.' Also, as they say about Dr Pepper: 'Try it. You might like it.'

I was lying on the sofa, talking to Steve, who was busy in the galley cooking our dinner. I was a few gin and tonics into the evening and he was making me laugh. Now that we were on our own, he felt the need to show off less and was back to being Macho Boat Steve. Layla miaowed bad-temperedly.

'What?' he asked her. 'You don't get the joke? Well, we think we're funny, even if you don't.' He stirred the white sauce he was making for cauliflower cheese, put the spatula down on the work surface and leaned over to have another go at kissing me. This time I didn't stop him. Maybe it was the strength of his attraction to me that knocked me out of my flip-flops. Or perhaps it was the gin.

Actually, these are just excuses. In reality, I was angry with myself for being such an uptight *English* person. There were things about Steve I liked – his sense of humour, his kindness, this lifestyle he offered, his skills as a sailor. OK, so he wasn't my usual type – and my type is very specific: tall, posh, fair-haired, plays 'rugger', preppily dressed, younger than me. Steve was none of these things so I had automatically discounted him. Now I wondered if that was fair. Also, keeping him at arm's length was a way of protecting myself. If you don't start a relationship, you can't get hurt when it ends, is I suppose what a psychologist would say my motivation was. I knew, deep down, that this fear of getting my heart broken yet again was why I had never got that husband, family home and kids in the UK. So if I was changing everything else about my life, why not this pattern of behaviour, too? Perversely, it was a way of being less passive and taking control for once.

Layla seemed to be a bit startled by what was going on but came to accept it when she realised that she wasn't going to have to share her Whiskas biscuits. The new arrangements would work well in Big John's favour, too, as he'd have the forward cabin all to himself.

I wasn't entirely comfortable with what was happening between us but I felt unable to stop it. I did think that perhaps I was loosening up a bit and should just go with the flow and see what happened. After all, that was part of the reason I'd come away, to change my life.

4

Culture club

Kota Kinabalu was my first taste of a large Asian city. The big draw for tourists is Gunung Kinabalu, the great hulk of a mountain that glowers behind the city. People book months in advance for the chance to scramble up its sides. I suppose they must do it for the challenge as it certainly wouldn't be for the views from the top: we could see the mountain from where we were anchored but only once or twice did we glimpse its peak; most of the time it was shrouded in mist. The rest of the city is all shopping malls divided by a system of highways that would put Spaghetti Junction to shame.

Being in a city has its advantages for the cruiser, though: access to a wide variety of food. After Lizzie and Claire left, Steve and I spent three hours in a branch of the Malay supermarket chain Giant stocking up on various essentials that would be impossible to find once we were off the beaten track: pesto sauce, tortilla wraps, tonic water, muesli. Our trolley overflowed.

We got to the till and started to unload the 800 ringgit

(£160 worth, which is an obscene amount to spend on food in Malaysia) of goods on to the conveyor belt. Steve, being a keen environmentalist, always told the shop that he didn't want plastic bags as we'd brought our own reusable fabric ones. Often the staff didn't understand and put our items into plastic bags; we would unload them from the plastic and repack them in our own bags, leaving a stack of plastic by the till. Even the eggs came out of their boxes and were re-nestled, one by one, into special containers we carried with us. Clearly they thought we were mad but they gamely went along with us and our funny foreigner ways. In Malay supermarkets the practice is to seal each plastic bag of shopping with a bit of branded sticky tape, I presume to reduce the temptation to slip the odd extra item inside on the way out. Our no plastic bags scheme – 'Selamat kanbumi!' Steve would say to the employees, which he told me translates as 'Save the planet' – mucked up their anti-shoplifting system and the only way they could get round it was to stick a piece of the branded tape on to each and every item we bought. So it went into plastic, out of plastic, into fabric, was plucked out of fabric by a member of staff, sticky tape was applied and then it went back into fabric again. No wonder it took us three hours to do our shopping.

This branch of Giant had a non-halal section, where Steve found some bacon and sausages to restock his freezer. When we placed some smoked Danish on the conveyor belt the young till operator's eyes nearly leapt out of his head. He stopped the belt and stared from it to us and back to the bacon again. He rang his bell for a supervisor but none came. He broke out in a sweat. We realised what was happening – that he couldn't bring himself to touch the haram meat to scan it, even though it was in a sealed pouch. I tried to be helpful and ran the packet through the scanner myself, stuck on a piece of tape and put it in our cool bag. I repeated the action with all the other non-halal items. But he was still freaking out. He put two layers of plastic bags over his hands, like gloves, I assume because he was worried the bacon had sullied other items it had come into contact with, and more on the glass surface of his scanning machine. I have truly never seen a man so frightened before. His eyes were rolling around in their sockets. I felt so guilty for putting him through that. I tried to tell him, 'I'm with you, buddy – I'm veggie,' but he either didn't speak any English or he had forgotten it in his sheer terror.

Much more interesting than supermarket shopping were our trips to the fresh food 'wet' markets. Some foods we recognised – bananas, cauliflower – but others were a complete and utter mystery. It was food shopping by lucky dip; one trip we bought some purple tuberous things that I guessed might be yams, a hairy coconut with a leek growing out of the top of it and a big green dusty thing that may or may not have been a mango.

Food shopping would become a bit of a bone of contention between Steve and me: I was happy to just go to the local market and eat whatever we could find, doing without, say, almonds or wholemeal flour if I had to. But I had only been away from the UK for a few weeks and trying exotic foods was all part of the adventure. I could remember what good, unsweetened bread tasted like (my tip to you – never buy a prepacked sandwich in Malaysia. Salty fish paste does not go well with white sliced that is so sugary you can feel cavities developing as you chew); Steve had been abroad for a decade and he wanted to eat like he would have done at home: stewed lamb shanks, bacon and eggs, cauliflower cheese – even if that meant days of asking around for a specialist store that stocks Cheddar, and then an hour and a half bus trip either way to procure 2kg of the stuff. The way he looked at it was that it was worth the effort and he had the time and money to spend. Me, I would have been content dining out thrice daily on greasy roti telor bread, mee goring (fried noodles) and nasi goring (fried rice) and spending less than £2 to cover all three meals.

As arranged, Big John turned up at the dockside with an impressively small amount of luggage – unlike me, he knew how to pack – and the three of us went to meet Josh and Kristin for dinner at an Italian restaurant on the waterfront. Josh told us he had been sailing for three and a half years, through the Mediterranean, the Red Sea, Indian Ocean and South China Sea to Malaysia, where he had joined a rally and the race. He was keen to do the same route Steve had told me he planned to cover. I asked him where the one place he really wanted to go was. He replied Palau, an island east of the Philippines in the Pacific Ocean.

'And why do you want to go there?' I asked him.

'Imagine paradise,' he said, fixing me with those green eyes. 'Everything you dreamed paradise could be. Well it's there and it's called Palau.'

Palau was on the route Steve had mapped out to me in his emails. Josh's enthusiasm was catching and I felt my pulse quicken with excitement. Paradise? Far-flung, exotic places? Sailing there on your own – well, Steve's – boat? That was more like what I had imagined my trip to be, not this: eating pizza in a city. Granted, the city was Kota Kinabalu in Borneo, which technically qualified as a far-flung, exotic place, and the restaurant was by the sea. It's just that it was by an open sewer, too, and the whiff was ruining the whole dining-al-fresco-in-paradise vibe quite a bit.

Josh dropped into the conversation the fact that he knew Paul and Rachel Chandler, the middle-aged British couple taken hostage by Somali pirates nine months earlier. I felt a jolt. It was an odd convergence of my old life back in London and my new one at sea: only a couple of weeks before I left London, when the news came out (prematurely, it later emerged) that the Chandlers were about to be freed, I was asked to write a feature for the paper about why people give up everything to go sailing.

Now, hearing Josh's claim that he knew the couple, I felt the familiar journalistic tingle. When you think you might be on to a good story, your pulse quickens, you get a shot of adrenaline in your gut and your mind clears instantly, allowing your concentration to sharpen so that you can focus on getting every single detail correct. I hadn't felt that intense 'story alert' moment for a long time. Without meaning, or even wanting, to, I started to interview Josh. I guess old habits really do die hard, even when you are consciously trying to leave them behind.

'How do you know the Chandlers?' I asked him. Steve shot me a look, almost as if he had noticed the switch my brain had made from chatty mode to reporter.

'I spent six months with them and taught them to dive,' he said.

I asked him what they were like. The usual response: nice, normal people, he said. But then he added: 'They'd take chances. They'd, like, break away from the safe convoy when we were coming across the Gulf of Aden and they'd go off and anchor somewhere by themselves.'

He explained that to get through the danger zone, the section of sea closest to the Somali coast, ten boats went together in convoy, sailing at night with their lights out to reduce their chances of being seen. The Chandlers got through safely that time; it was later, when they were still in Seychelles waters, that they were captured, he said. For a split second I thought, *That's a story I could write and sell*, but then, just as quickly as the idea came, it went again. *It's not you any more*, I told myself. *Let it go. You're a sailor now.*

I turned to Kristin and asked her how long she'd been sailing for. Never, before she joined Josh for the Borneo race, she said. That was odd. From how she talked about Josh's mother a lot and the way they seemed so close, I had formed the impression that she was the original girl-next-door and that an engagement was on the cards. But Josh had been sailing for months and months. So were they a new couple? I wanted to ask but didn't dare. As the conversation continued, Josh mentioned that before Kristin flew out he had had two other female crew members. *Doubly odd*, I thought, but forgot about it as the conversation moved on.

As we left the restaurant in search of a taxi, she took my arm. 'It's so nice to meet another young couple,' she said.

My immediate reaction was to snatch my arm out of her grasp and shout: 'Whoa! Hold it there, lady. You've got the wrong end of the stick. Steve and I are soooo not a couple. This is just an ill-thought-out fling I'm starting to regret. And he's not even young.' But that would have been mean in so many ways so I didn't and just smiled politely. I didn't expect to see her or Josh again, anyway, as the following morning the two-man, one-woman and one-cat crew of *Kingdom* were setting off to explore the wilds of Borneo.

They have satellite TV, it turns out, in the wilds of Borneo. A few miles north-east of Kota Kinabalu we anchored off a stilt village at Teluk Ambong where the wooden houses, bleached pale grey by the sun, had taken over the beach. They were so close to the water that at high tide the fishermen could drive their boats right up to their homes, tie up and step off into their living rooms.

As we were well out of the city, I put on my 'shore clothes' – cropped trousers and a long-sleeved cotton shirt, before getting into the dinghy. After spending most of my time in a bikini, I felt ridiculously covered up but this was an out-of-the-way kampong (village) in a Muslim country and I didn't want to draw attention to myself.

It was just a short walk from the beach, between the wooden stilts of the houses, avoiding wandering goats and ducks, before we were in the quiet 'street' – a wide strip of sand that separated two facing rows of houses. There was no one else around. Jim strode along the only constructed pavement, a pathway made of strips of wood, into the kampong shop to buy some smokes and Cokes. I had a look round its shelves – out-of-date sweets, dusty crackers, biscuits and soap.

Jim said something I didn't understand to the shopkeeper, who smiled and nodded his acknowledgment as we left.

'What did you say to him?' I asked Jim, following him down the narrow path.

'Terima kasih. It means thank you.'

'Terima what?'

'Terima kasih. Like "tear up my car seat".'

'Oh, that's good,' I said, really liking the mnemonic. 'Tearup ma kaseet!'

'You got it,' he said. 'Just drop the t at the end.'

'Tearup ma kasee!'

We probably could have gone ashore naked and not generated more excitement than we did in our modest clothing. While we were in the shop the news of our arrival had spread fast around the kampong and now there were gaggles of children waiting to see us. A chorus of 'Helo!' (that's 'hello' in Malaysian) came from a large group of boys, aged five to maybe 12, who had gathered in the street right outside the shop. They all had short black hair and very white smiles and grinned at us and then whispered something funny to their friends, who screamed with boisterous laughter. They wore football shirts – Manchester United, Liverpool – and ate bags of crisps, dropping the empty packets on to the sand when they had finished.

'What your nem?' they asked us, over and over, pushing and shoving at each other to shake our hands first, touching their right palm to their chest between each shake, to bless us. 'Where you plom?' *Plom?* I wondered. *Is that a Bahasa word? Ah – Where are you from?* 'Foto! Foto!' they yelled at Jim, pointing to the camera hanging from his neck. He obliged and they adopted the stance of boys the world over: feet wide, smiles wider and flicking Vs at the lens.

The girls were just as curious but their shyness was greater than their courage and they watched us from a safe distance, hiding behind a car and peering over the roof. A few were brave enough to wave back to me but none would come near.

Jim went off to say hello to the village imam and Steve and

I took a stroll along the 'street'. This was the first non-Western settlement I'd ever seen that wasn't a city. The houses were all about ten feet off the ground, with wooden steps leading up from the soft white sand. There was no glass in the windows, just slats or netting, and many had curtains made from old bedsheets. Often the front door was open and we could glimpse into people's bare living rooms, smiling back at the grandparents, parents, teenage children and babies who sat on the bare wooden floor, staring out at us. The roofs of the houses were corrugated iron and chickens scratched around the stilts at ground level as goats rambled past, herding their kids in a line. To my naïve eyes these families seemed dirt poor, with their ramshackle huts for homes and their children dressed in charity-shop-rejected clothes, yet there were Astro satellite TV dishes attached to the sides of half of the houses and 4x4 trucks parked here and there. Apart from the discarded crisp and cracker packets the children had dropped, the village was neat and tidy.

Steve rummaged in his backpack.

'What are you looking for?' I asked.

'The headsets,' he said. 'I'm going to give them away.'

He had brought along two sets of foam-covered earphones that we'd been given for free when we'd bought internet dongles in Kota Kinabalu. On the yacht, before we came ashore, I'd thought he was crazy – what useless piece of charity was this? After school I had been so focused on getting straight to university and then into a journalism career that I had never had a gap year: never taught children in Africa or witnessed the favelas of South America. I only knew 'favela' meant slum because I'd learned the word in my GCSE geography class. In my limited experience charity was doing things like baking cakes and selling them to your friends' mums or dropping a few pennies into a can being shaken in the street. My sketchy idea of charity in a developing country involved handing out American $1 bills to desperate one-legged adults or buying bags of rice or apples for starving children. Real Comic Relief tear-jerking montage stuff. Giving out flimsy electronic equipment in a village in Borneo did not quite fit in with that. I imagined us having to force them on some bewildered kids who would later toss them aside, not even knowing what they were, so that they could return to scavenging for grubs among the jungle trees. But as Steve pulled them from my bag, a young man ran straight over and asked us how much we wanted for them.

'How much?' I whispered to Steve, thinking I must have misheard. 'He wants to *buy* them?'

'No, no – free gift for you,' Steve said to the youth, handing over the headsets. The young man climbed happily with his prizes up the stairs into a house. So much for my rose-tinted view of Borneo village life – probably he was going to plug them straight in to his PS2 so he could turn the sound up as loud as he liked without risking his mother shouting at him to 'turn that racket down'.

I thought again about the 'shacks' that I had seen and adjusted my perspective. Apparently this was suburbia, Borneo-style. The houses were built of wood on stilts because that was the way they had always been built here. The children were clean and healthy, the TV dishes and cars showed that people had jobs. It was no slum. Clearly I had a lot of learning to do.

5

If Carlsberg made coconuts ...

Two picture-perfect islands were waiting for us to explore them: Pulau Mantanani Besar and Pulau Mantanani Kecil. Sitting off the north-west coast of the peak at Borneo's tip they were the inhabited larger (*besar* means big) island and his little (*kecil*) brother, whose only feature is a dive platform and a couple of huts. We tackled the smaller of the two first. At high tide the beach was only a metre deep and covered with driftwood.

'Watch out for snakes,' Steve called back over his shoulder as he led the way.

'Shit! Really?' I said, hesitating. Jim strode ahead and I copied his high-stepping gait to the heart of the island, where we found a man-made clearing with a few tall trees dotted about. The whole island was only about 40 metres wide and we'd seen all there was to see within a few minutes. The real entertainment was to be had in the sea. Jim was in his element snorkelling in the incredibly clear water around the reef. I love swimming – in a pool – but am more than a bit daunted by the sea. I generally prefer to be on it, rather than under it. If I'm in deep or cloudy water my imagination runs away with me and I picture things coming up from the deep to touch me. It's not only sea monsters and sharks I worry about, any little aquatic creature will do it. But I wanted to try snorkelling and Steve showed me how to roll out of the dinghy and held my hand as we followed tiny shoals of fish into very shallow water. I willed my heartbeat to slow and concentrated on steadying my breathing but the tips of my fins started catching on coral, adding to the feeling of claustrophobia. In my panic I imagined I was only millimetres away from scraping my bare stomach along the coral and when I tried to lift my body further away my feet sank deeper and I kicked the coral harder. It was just too much and I had to get out.

'Maybe it was a bit too shallow for you,' Steve tried to reassure me as I tried to haul myself, in an ungainly manner similar to a whale beaching itself, back into the dinghy. I promised him I'd try again another time and instead enjoyed the views by putting my mask back on and sticking my face under the water, turning myself into my own glass-bottomed boat. With my body safely out of the water, it was fascinating to watch tiny black fish with luminous blue stripes and their little yellow cousins darting in between the golden corals.

In the afternoon I was sitting in the cockpit of the yacht when a couple of fishermen approached us in a small blue wooden skiff. In the bottom of their boat was a collection of coconuts and one man hauled out three on to our deck. I said 'Helo!' and got a reply in Bahasa. They clung to the side of the yacht, holding the two boats close together, and grinned at me. Steve and Jim had heard the outboard engine and came on deck to see what was going on.

'We should give them some money for the coconuts,' I said to Steve, quietly. 'No,' he said. 'They were a gift.'

'That's what people do out here,' he added, smiling at the Malay men.

I thought he was being tight and forced him to ask the men if they wanted money. 'Ringgit?'

They shook their heads but continued to cling to the boat and point to Mantanani Besar. We decided between the three of us that they probably wanted to take us on a tour of the island so we changed into our shore clothes. I asked Steve if we should pay them for this.

'They just want to show us around,' he said. 'They aren't interested in money.'

He went downstairs and came back up carrying an inflatable globe. 'Sekolah?' he asked the two fishermen. They smiled and pointed to land.

'What's that for?' I asked him.

'I want to give it to a school and they said there's one on the island.' *Another odd piece of charity*, was my first thought. But then I remembered the kampong and the headphones. *Hey, what do I know? I keep being wrong about this.*

The fishermen led the way to a beach and we tied our dinghy next to their boat and followed them along a rough path through the jungle to the sekolah, a series of one-storey pre-fab rooms that were deserted. An Indonesian teacher there spoke some English and Steve enthusiastically handed over the globe and he accepted it graciously, if slightly bewildered. To get back to the beach we took a different path that led us to a village, with more wooden stilt houses arranged more randomly than in the first kampong I'd seen. Big handsome cockerels strutted around like they owned the place and three tiny girls watched us with wide eyes from the front step of their home. Jim took their picture and no one ran over screaming 'paedophile'. It was a peaceful place with not many people about. Those that were smiled and waved at us and carried on with their laundry-wringing or cigarette-smoking. At the jetty Jim got chatting to a Filipino immigrant who had a newborn son and Steve took pictures of the animals on the beach. I watched the cows chewing lazily on coconut husks while ducks and skinny cats zigzagged across the white sand. To my British eye they looked ridiculously out of place, as if a whirlwind had picked them up from a farmyard and transplanted them on to a beautiful tropical beach.

When we got back to the dinghy our original 'guides' were waiting for us and asked us for petrol. Steve said he'd give them two litres but when he checked the tank it was nearly empty. Then they asked for money. 'Ringgit. Ringgit.' I gave them 10 (£2); they asked for 20. Jim said it was all the money we had. Ten ringgit should have bought them five litres of fuel; maybe four and a half at over-inflated island prices. I began to worry things were going to turn nasty.

'We never should have offered them money for the coconuts,' Steve hissed at me under his breath.

Thankfully the men took off in their boat and we motored back towards *Kingdom* but a few minutes later, presumably after refuelling, they caught us up. What had seemed like friendliness two hours earlier was now bordering on being menacing. They made us follow them in a more circuitous route back to the yacht and broke away as we approached the boat, only to return a while later to try to sell us some fish that looked a few days old. We fobbed them off with a couple of beers. The lack of a shared language and assumptions on both sides had caused the confusion and we still weren't entirely clear about what they had wanted or if we had offended them by offering money in the first place or by not giving enough in the end.

The incident took away our enthusiasm for the fresh coconuts. Rolling about, unopened, on the floor of the cockpit they remained – at 3.33 ringgit a pop – probably the most expensive coconuts in the world.

6

What's the worst that could happen?

The thing with drinks like Dr Pepper is that the sweetness can quickly turn to a bad taste in your mouth. Jim left us in airless Kudat to meet a friend in the Philippines earlier than expected and Steve and I were alone. Tempers were frayed in the heat and, without the cushioning effect of Jim's presence, *alone* seemed suddenly like a big deal. Steve seemed very happy that it was finally just the two of us. He became even more tactile, more coupley. With every approach he made I could feel myself backing away, mentally and physically.

It's a funny thing, gut instinct. The moment I saw him for the first time, that night I arrived in Borneo, I knew he wasn't the one for me. All those times he'd tried something on during the race I'd known it, too. But something had compelled me to overlook that gut instinct: sailing, living on a yacht, exploring the world. Steve and I shared this dream. We got on as friends, he made me laugh. *Maybe the rest might come*, I'd try to convince myself as I lay awake in his bed while he snored in the cockpit where he had fallen asleep, drunk, after another heavy night with Jim. *If I can suppress that little shudder, maybe the rest* will *come in time.*

I had always rejected men in the past if I deemed them not 100 per cent perfect. And that philosophy hadn't netted me the things I'd wanted. And rejecting this man just because sometimes I was embarrassed by him or thought him camp wasn't going to help me achieve this new dream, either. *You need to grow up*, I told myself firmly, yet again. *You're not exactly perfect yourself. Just loosen up, be less of a worrier and see what happens.*

As we weighed anchor and left Kudat, the tension – both between us and within me – dropped with the mercury. We sailed to Pulau Bangii, the nearest island, and wandered around the kampong, with its village green surrounded by thatched huts. Back on the yacht I had my first naked on-deck shower and we hung from the swim ladder off the back, letting our bodies float behind us in the 2-knot current stream. At night I did yoga on the back deck, my nose in chataranga inches from the (stinky) cat litter tray, using the starlight and lightning flashes going off all around me to see by as I changed asanas.

Conversation turned to future plans. Steve wanted to know where I wanted to travel to. I was still desperate to visit Papua New Guinea, Vanuatu and the Solomon Islands, which were the same places he was planning to go with the boat. He asked me how much time I had to do it in.

'Oh, I don't know – six months?' My only previous experience of long-distance sailing was crossing the Atlantic Ocean with the Clipper race and we had done that in nine days, so six months seemed a reasonable amount of time.

Steve was thinking more along the lines of two years. *Two years!* I explained that I had a finite amount of time and money, that I wanted to try to make it to my brother Tom's wedding in December and that at some point I would need to find work. He knew a woman in a marina in Thailand, he said, who could help me get a job as crew on a superyacht.

'And, if you want, I'll stop cruising for a few months while you work and I'll just concentrate on doing jobs around the boat,' he offered.

I didn't know what to say to that. It seemed a very over-the-top gesture to make – I had left the UK just three weeks before and had been sharing a bed with this man for only a week or so (and was already having doubts about that) and here he was offering to make long-term plans with me. I felt guilty that he saw this as a committed partnership while I just viewed it as a fling. Now Jim was gone, Steve wanted to pick up where he thought we had left off.

It was windy where we were anchored and the wind roughed up waves that hit us on the beam (side) of the yacht, so that we were rolling over and bouncing up again like a weeble, the glasses and crockery clinking in their cupboards. A look at the chart showed us a shallow, protected anchorage nearby, called Mitford Harbour. It was surrounded by coral and we had to creep our way in, Steve 8 metres up the mast sitting on the first spreaders, keeping a good lookout for large coral heads, or bommies, and me on the autohelm and throttle, creeping us forward and adjusting our heading on Steve's directions to sneak us slowly and carefully along through the deepest water.

Inside the harbour it was magical. There were no other boats and no signs of human life. There was an awful lot of animal life instead. Every few minutes a shoal of tiny silver fish performed a spot of synchronised swimming, leaping out of the water to avoid a predator. From a distance I couldn't tell they were individual fish; their timing was so immaculate that they looked like one large spurt of water from a fountain. We took the dinghy ashore in the afternoon and immediately spotted monkey footprints in the sand, about the size of a toddler's but rounder and with clear imprints of opposable big toes. The only human footprints were those Steve and I left.

The white beach was dotted with tiny pearls of sand, thousands of them, stacked up next to holes about the size of a pea. I bent over to look at one more closely and caught some movement in my peripheral vision. Turning my head, I saw a little translucent crab. This was his hole he had dug out, working the discarded sand into ball shapes with his pincers. Once my eyes adjusted I could make out hundreds of these ghost-like crabs all over the beach. Despite their near-invisibility I didn't have to worry about stepping on one for as soon as my flip-flopped foot came anywhere near they darted off across the sand at incredible speeds and shot down into the safety of their holes.

Steve had reached the few scattered mangrove trees across to the right so I walked over to join him.

'Any luck with monkey sightings?' I asked.

'No. You?'

'No. Only the tracks in the sand.'

'Shh!' he said, holding up one hand. 'What was that?'

'What?'

'Can't you hear it? A kind of squealing.'

We held our breath, listening intently. And there it was, like a quieter version of a pig's squeal, followed by a splashing noise.

'Monkeys?' I whispered.

'I don't think so. Come on.'

We climbed over the exposed mangrove roots, following the sounds and scanning the surface of the water. I spotted something, a head, but it wasn't a monkey. Then I saw another sleek black head and another.

'They're otters,' Steve said.

There was a family of eight of them and they were having a whale of a time playing in the water, swimming, diving and calling back and forth to each other with their squeaky squeals. We watched, enchanted, for a few minutes, taking photos, until one of them saw us and stood up on its hind legs, front paws dangling. Suddenly it herded up its companions and they dived under the water and were gone.

In the absence of man-made sound, the jungle was creating music around us. The sounds were distinctly tropical and nothing like what I had heard back home: cicadas singing, geckos calling and unseen monkeys chattering. I heard a woodpecker drilling away at a tree and the repeated cries of what I termed the Laughing Policeman Bird. Its call was a cross between the unnerving guffaws of the model constable in the penny arcade and the sarcastic laugh of Nelson from *The Simpsons*. 'Haa!-ha! Haa-ha! Haa!-ha!' it cried, over and over, rising in pitch. Even the plant life on the edge of the rainforest was noisy – the coconut palms rustled scratchily in the breeze and the driftwood cracked as it dried.

Feeling more in tune with Mother Earth and taking advantage of the slower current in the protected harbour, I decided to have another go at swimming. I jumped in from the yacht and started breaststroke, up and down the 46-foot length of the boat, concentrating on my breathing and on keeping count of the number of lengths and total distance covered to crowd thoughts of biting, nibbling, fishy things out of my brain. I was doing OK, just about managing to push down the fear, when I reached the stern of the boat and saw something in the water about a foot or two in front of my face. It was brown, long and thin and its head was raised above the surface, moving from side to side. I screamed and splashed my way towards the ladder to get on to the boat and to safety. Steve heard the commotion and came to see what all the fuss was about but froze when he saw the look of terror on my face.

'Emma! What is it?'

I couldn't speak. Time had slowed down and my progress was agonisingly slow.

'Tell me. Then I can help you.'

'S-s-snake!' I managed to stutter. A few more strokes and I was at the ladder, adrenaline helping me haul myself out by my arms faster than I'd ever managed to before. My legs were shaking as Steve handed me my towel.

'A snake?' he asked. 'In the water? Wow – that's really rare.'

'It was there, I'm telling you. I wasn't just imagining it. I even looked at it twice to make sure it really existed. That's it. I'm not going back in the water.'

He was comforting but disbelieving and, once I'd started to calm down, his incredulity was infectious. I began to doubt myself. Was it really a snake? I could have sworn I'd seen it raise its head out of the water, like a cobra about to strike, and turn towards me. Now, on the safety of the boat, I wasn't so sure. When Steve returned to his work, I wandered about the deck of the boat, looking into the water for an infestation of snakes. I couldn't see any. But what I could see, just off the bow, was the seed pod of a mangrove tree being carried slowly along in the current. I frowned and leaned over the rail to get a closer look. Hot embarrassment crept up my neck and into my cheeks. The pod was brown coloured, long and thin and stood vertically in the water, its tip slightly curved over. As the gentle waves pushed it along, it bobbed up and down, rotating slightly from side to side. As they say, you can take the girl out of the city... but you can't put her in one of the wildest places on earth and not expect her imagination to go into overdrive.

That afternoon we were trying to repair the leech line, the rope that runs through the back of the mainsail, when Steve said: 'This is doing my head in.' I thought he was referring to the sewing.

Then he added quietly: 'I'm going to ask you to move back into the forepeak.' Just as abruptly as I had ended up in his cabin, I was now being kicked out of it. An enormous rush of relief flooded through me.

I had stayed in that aft cabin for two weeks but I had had very, very mixed feelings about what I was playing at. I knew Steve liked me a lot – always touching me and telling me he adored me and would do anything for me. He made it obvious that he wanted a girlfriend. I should have sat him down, right at the beginning, and spelled it out to him but, hating confrontation as I do, I was too much of a wimp. It wasn't fair to him and it was a very silly thing for me to have done but done it I had. I had made my own bed and for a while I literally had to lie in it.

It was a surprise, his asking me to move out – perhaps he was more perceptive of my feelings than I had given him credit for – but now, I thought, there would be no guilt that I was leading him on and we could have fun and enjoy making each other laugh without any added pressure.

'We can still sail as friends,' Steve said and made up the bed in the forepeak for me, tucking me in that night. I felt like a weight had been lifted.

The other issue that had been preying on my mind was the money situation. Back in the UK, when I had been chatting with Steve over email, we'd had a brief discussion about finances. He told me he normally charged people £25 a day, plus a share of food, alcohol, fuel, gas, laundry and marina fees when they were on board short-term. Over a longer period of time it worked out cheaper, he said. 'When I was cruising with my girlfriend it worked out at about £15 a day each.' We'd passed the free two-week trial period and I'd asked him a few times for his bank details so I could set up a standing order but he'd fobbed me off with, 'Oh, it's not all about the money, is it?' I wanted to get it sorted out so I pestered him again for his details and he gave them to me. I knew Jim had paid the £25-a-day price with us and Steve hadn't charged him extra for any alcohol – and he'd drunk a lot over a week – and I had been here a month so I set up a payment to him of £15 a day and told him that I'd sorted it out. Another problem solved. Things were looking up.

Fair winds blew in and we took advantage of them to move to the Turtle Islands, where we'd read there was a sanctuary and a hatchery. We took the dinghy to Pulau Gulimaan, where, the *Lonely Planet* had informed us, hawksbill turtles went ashore to lay their eggs. But this was not their breeding season, the book said. *The* Lonely Planet *is wrong*, I thought after we landed on the island: there were turtle tracks everywhere, distinctive wide marks where the female's belly had been dragged up the steep beach, lined on either side by small, deep indentations left by her claws. We thought the tracks might have been old but when we reached the other side of the island we found a hatchery with 13 egg collections labelled as having been laid the previous night. It looked like a sandy allotment. A pair of white shorts were drying in the sun outside a hut but there were no workers around. We cleaned up plastic bottles from the beach and I found some turtle egg shells. With hard but flexible skins and spherical in shape, they looked and felt like deflated ping-pong balls.

At dusk we returned to the island, hoping to spot a turtle come ashore by moonlight to dig her nest and lay her eggs. There was a stony-faced warden at the hut who told us we had to leave because we needed permission from the other island, Selingaan, to visit here.

'Let's go,' I told Steve but he wouldn't budge.

'Leave this to me,' he said. 'The Malaysians are so polite, we can get anything here if we're nice and smile.'

And he was right (again. Had I not learned anything yet?). Despite firmly ordering us off his land, the warden seemed happy to chat and took us to see a green turtle, about four years old and 30cm long, that he and his colleagues had fished out of the sea that afternoon. It was unable to dive and they were worried that the sun exposure would kill it so they'd brought it ashore and placed it in a small saltwater pool built out of concrete next to the hut. In the adjacent pool was a team of hawksbill hatchlings (take that, *Lonely Planet!*), each about three inches long. They were swimming around in a haphazard fashion, bumping into each other and the sides of their pen, wiggling their flippers out of synch.

The warden let us help him put them in a basket so he could release them on the beach. They were so light and quite soft and one hooked its back flippers around my little finger as it sat in my palm. Another fell on to its back in the basket and couldn't right itself, no matter how hard it waved its flippers in the air, so I turned it over. On the beach, the warden tipped them on to the sand about two feet from the water's edge and while some of them were off to the sea like a shot, others needed a bit more time to think about it and to build up either their courage or their sense of direction. It was a struggle for them to swim out; every time a wave lapped on to the sand it carried a group of floundering hatchlings back with it.

Steve stayed up half the night listening for turtles. He described it to me as a very human sound, like a diver gasping for air. The next morning, still full of excitement, we motored in the dinghy to Pulau Selingaan to ask for permission to come ashore at night to take part in one of the turtle vigils they held there. We were flatly refused and, deflated, set off back to *Kingdom*.

While we had been away another yacht had anchored close by us. Steve diverted to head towards it and as we approached a very tanned, forty-something man wearing a floppy hat, a lot of sun block and a long-sleeved shirt came on deck to greet us. Australian? I wondered.

'G'day! How's it going?' he said.

It being a small world, you can bump into someone you know even when you're on anchor hundreds of miles away from the nearest city in a country none of you can call home. Steve recognised the Aussie, Greg, from a regatta in Thailand. Greg and his wife Debs, both in their forties, were cruising Borneo aboard *Southern Cross*. We chatted briefly, us sitting in the dinghy, them crouching on their deck, and they recommended that if it was turtles we wanted to see we should visit Pulau Langkayan, a small island with an upmarket resort on it where the staff will radio you on your boat if a turtle comes ashore at night so you can go and take a look. But Langkayan was back beyond where we'd come from and we were running low on fresh water reserves so we thanked them for the tip and sailed off towards the town of Sandakan instead.

Blue Steel was at anchor off Sandakan yacht club – well, I say yacht club, but it was more a drinking venue for non-boat-owning rich Chinese locals – and we bumped into Ron as we walked into the town centre for dinner. He had a case of lager balanced on his shoulder that he'd picked up from a local Chinese restaurant. Again, I say restaurant, but it was more another drinking venue – this time for gambling, down-and-out Chinese locals. They didn't speak any English other than 'Eighty ringgit', the price of one slab of Carlsberg. We swung by to stock up.

Ron was in Sandakan to pick up Flora, a traveller he'd had aboard a few weeks earlier for the World Music Festival near Kuching, and her friend Becky, who had never been abroad before, and had in fact barely left Swindon, but had somehow managed to scrape together the cash and the courage to fly to the Borneo jungle to live on a boat with a strange man. It sounded familiar. Ron was taking them up the Kinabatangan river to see the rainforest wildlife and asked if we felt like tagging along. Go on a bona fide river jungle expedition with the chance of seeing pygmy elephants, orangutans and proboscis monkeys in their natural habitat? You didn't have to ask me twice.

7

The jungle books

We went in convoy up the river, *Blue Steel* leading the way, as Ron had been there a few times before. The GPS was useless – it showed us motoring across dry land – and the water was a murky yellow-brown, meaning we couldn't see any obstacles like rocks or sand banks. We followed Ron, sticking to the outside bends of the river's curves, using the logic that that was where the water flowed fastest, so the river was likely to be deepest there, and gritted our teeth, praying we wouldn't get stuck in the mud.

I'm not very good at judging distances but I'd estimate that the Kinabatangan was a couple of hundred metres wide. When we first entered the mouth, from the sea, it was lined with mangrove trees that gave way to nippah palms, dense, stubby little trees with no visible trunks. The water was full of clusters of lily leaves that had broken away in the force of the current and were being swept downstream and, more worryingly, branches and giant logs the size of battering rams. As well as keeping an eye on the depth reader and monitoring the curve of the river, we had to keep watch for these monsters and dodge them – while not running aground. They were doing a few knots downstream and we were motoring at a similar pace upstream and our combined speeds could have taken a nasty chunk out of the hull.

After a few miles the nippahs changed to grassy banks and we passed scattered houses set back from the water's edge. Naked children were being bathed by their mothers in the brown water. I wondered if they didn't end up dirtier after their baths than they were before. One woman was hand scrubbing her laundry, her bare feet sinking into the mud. They stopped what they were doing in order to stare at us as we crept by.

A right-hand turn after the houses and then we were into the jungle proper: trees of every height and shade of green imaginable, all crowded together and jostling for space, the shorter ones ducking their heads under the canopies of their taller cousins, the giants luxuriating in the space their height afforded them and stretching out their branches to catch as much sunlight as possible. I'd seen rainforest before, in Australia, but then I was driving or walking among it and everything was happening above my head. Here, with the water separating us from jungle, we had perspective. I could see the wood *and* the trees and it was unbelievably beautiful in a chaotic, here's Mother-Nature-at-her-rawest kind of way.

I couldn't wait to spot some jungle animals. When I wasn't checking the instruments or the water's surface for objects I was scouring the trees, desperate to catch a glimpse of a monkey or an elephant. But all I saw was birds. Large white egrets surfed down the river, perched serenely on floating logs. Every time we approached one it would unfold its long neck, extend its wings and flap, flap, flap until it was up and away. There were eagles soaring above us, from time to time diving to the water to snatch fish in their talons, and kingfishers who were no more than orange and blue blurs as they zoomed by.

Another of the boats in Sandakan had given Steve the latitude and longitude co-ordinates for where they had seen wild pygmy elephants. 'They said it was wonderful,' he had reported back. 'They were on anchor and a whole family of elephants crossed the river right in front of their boat, babies and everything, swimming at night.'

Thus started Mission Elephant. *Blue Steel* went off and did their own thing. *Kingdom* stayed put and day after day, armed with a hand-held GPS, camera, sunhats and a cool box loaded with drinks, we drifted along with the current in the dinghy for hours, searching out the shy creatures. But they were too elusive for us and we spotted neither grey hide nor whiskery hair of them, even though we blasted eight miles up the river in the dinghy, further than we dared go in the yacht. During daylight hours the Kinabatangan was busy with tourist boats shooting back and forth, the guides on board trying to locate the elephants for their clients. A couple of times we jumped into the dinghy and followed them but it led to nothing.

Disappointment at the lack of elephant sightings aside, there was plenty in the jungle to marvel at. This was a habitat that had grown up over hundreds of thousands of years and it was teeming with life. At night the frogs' croaks were as loud as dogs' barks. In the day the Laughing Policeman Bird was always chuckling away at something and the Orgasmic Bird's fevered cries rose to ecstatic heights. And, a couple of times a day, there was the call of the hornbill.

The endangered hornbill is like a large toucan gone wrong.

Imagine a black parrot but in place of its short, triangular beak it has a long bill, more like a pelican. It has a protuberance shaped like an upward-curving banana on the top of its head, just above its eyes, that can be white, red or yellow. In appearance, it is exactly what a prehistoric jungle bird should be. It looks like it is from the age of dinosaurs and it sounds like it, too; a hornbill's cry is loud and jolting, almost like the supersonic boom given off by a jet when it breaks the sound barrier. The first time I heard it I thought there were pterodactyls flying about above my head.

Back in London, I used to cram so much into every day: 11 or 12 hours in the office, two hours of commuting, a trip to the gym or a run, cooking, cleaning, catching up with friends. Now a whole day could easily pass by with me doing little more than going on a couple of outings to look for animals. Each day was luxuriously long – like that feeling you get a few days into a vacation when you finally start to relax, but a more extreme version. The heat and humidity of the jungle sapped a lot of energy but that was OK – there was little to do anyway and nothing urgent. Things between Steve and me had settled and I loved sleeping by myself in the forepeak, stretched out to try to expose as much of my skin as I could to the puff of the fan.

I learned to drive the dinghy and we did drifts every day, switching off the engine, settling down in the bottom of the boat to be swept along by the current, our backs leaning against the inflated rubber hull, just staring out at the jungle as it inched past. After a few non-events, I learned to recognise the kinds of trees monkeys like to live in and we discovered the best time to go monkey-watching was just before dusk. The sound of crashing branches was the first sign we were in the right place. We'd hear noises and then look around the canopy until we saw leaves moving. Then I would adjust my eyes, like you do for those 3D-image posters that were all the rage when I was about 13. Remember those? You let your eyes go out of focus and some of the meaningless dots and swirls would recede or move forward until you could see the three-dimensional image of Jesus, or if you couldn't see it you'd wait until your friend said something like, 'I can see his beard!' – and then you'd lie and pretend you could, too.

The same thing applied to the monkeys except going boss-eyed didn't help. What I had to do here was look for grey or brown patches among the leaves and watch them until they moved. Once I'd got one monkey in my sights I could then see all of the others, like I'd passed some secret test. It seemed as if only then would they come out for our entertainment, leaping from branch to branch or sometimes huge distances from tree to tree, like circus performers. Tiny babies clung to their mothers' bodies while older children played, daring each other to jump from a greater height or starting a wrestling match. The long and short-tailed macaques, with their sad-looking faces and grey fur, were the most hyperactive breeds. But I loved watching the proboscis monkeys, a species only found on Borneo. They may have been slower but they were so entertaining. They have a distinctly unathletic build, with enormous Tellytubby bellies and skinny little arms and legs covered in two-tone red and grey hair. When they walk along a branch they waddle like a nine-months-pregnant woman, even the males, who are easily identifiable because their tiny red penises are always hanging out and often standing to attention. Their upturned noses and round faces make them look either benignly surprised or angrily glowering, depending on whether their chins are tilted up or down. They are possibly one of the oddest yet most human-looking creatures around. I was spellbound.

They were fond of sitting in the Y-section of a tree where two branches joined and on one evening we saw them not long into our drift. We were looking at one family, about 20 or 30 metres above us, and keeping as quiet as we could. But we were spotted anyway. The big male saw us and actually did a double-take. Then he hauled himself to his feet, his hands on different branches, and stuck his head as far forward as it would go to get a better look at us. If his eyes had popped forwards out of their sockets and a cartoon-style car hooter noise gone off, it wouldn't have seemed out of place. He stayed like that for ages, occasionally looking away and then turning back to us and craning his neck forwards again, holding on to his branches the whole time. *Blue Steel* Ron had said that jungle sights were 'better than a movie'. I'm sure Mr Tubby, up there in his tree, watching these funny-coloured, non-furry animals sitting in the bottom of a grey rubbery triangle, would have agreed with him.

On that trip I fell in love with the rainforest. Despite the hideous heat and humidity, the flies and mosquitoes and the fear of crocodiles that kept us out of the cooling waters, it was the most amazing place I'd been to. The most beautiful scenes in England, even at the height of spring or in the full colour of autumn, just cannot compete. If I look out of my parents' window on to the rolling valleys of Derbyshire, there is undeniably beauty there but it's of a quieter, more tamed variety. Refined, in a mute-toned, prim, British way. The Borneo rainforest might be bold and brassy in comparison, with its primary colours and rowdiness, but that wild sluttiness only added to its appeal for me.

During the hottest part of the afternoons the animals took a siesta and Steve and I retreated to the shade of the yacht. One day I was lying in a hammock on the foredeck that Steve had strung up between the roller furler and the mast, trying to keep as still as possible to get some respite from the constant, abundant sweating in the stifling rainforest humidity. It was a big hammock and Steve climbed in the other end, disturbing me while I was trying to read. Reading is one of my big loves but working in the newspaper industry had killed off the enjoyment for me – when you have to read tens of thousands of words a day, the last thing you want to do in your free time is pick up a book. Your brain is 'literally' tired. But by now I had been away from London long enough, my mind had had time to heal itself from its exhaustion. Like getting over a sickness, it was starving for stories and I made sure I fed it everything I could get my hands on – even some sickly sweet romance novels another boat had lent me. Steve wasn't a reader and didn't really understand the enjoyment of it. Reading was something he did when there was nothing else to entertain him. His stock of non-boating books were the Harry Potter and the His Dark Materials series. Oh, and one on the enjoyment of tantric sex.

He put his feet on my lap. Even though we were sleeping in separate cabins, he was still touchy feely with me, often hugging or stroking me. I felt bad enough for rejecting him that I tolerated it when we were alone on the boat, but as soon as there was anyone else around I made sure I moved out of reach.

'All right?' I asked, trying to be polite, even though I was mildly annoyed at being disturbed and his feet on my lap were making me hotter.

'Not really,' he replied. 'I want a girlfriend and it seems you've decided it's not going to be you. But I'm finding it really hard to understand why. When we're on land we're one thing in front of other people – not touching, conforming to 'normal' behaviour, but when we're on the boat, we're something else. If we were away at sea we might find we ended up having a relationship anyway.'

I had put down my book to listen to him. Now I fiddled with the edges of the pages as I thought about what to say. He was the one who had asked me to move out of his cabin, implying he wasn't interested in being a couple, either, so why was he now saying the opposite? I was certain that, despite my earlier behaviour, even if we were off in the middle of nowhere I wouldn't change my mind. Moving my legs as far away from his feet as was possible in a hammock containing two people, I told him I'd make an effort to behave 'normally' all the time, if that was confusing him.

'So no more cuddles?' he asked.

'No,' I replied, thinking, *They are always instigated by you anyway, never me, so that isn't going to be hard for me to stick to.*

'OK,' he agreed, looking away at the jungle and adding that he 'might have to go and listen to the Archers', which was code for meaning he needed to cry. *Oh crap*, I thought. *What mess have I got myself into?*

'Look, Steve, I'm sorry,' I said. 'I feel like I'm hurting your feelings and I don't want to.'

He nodded, his hand covering his face, his mouth creasing into a grimace, and I stayed, squirming in the other end of the hammock, until he had finished. After he had calmed down, he said he would email other women who had replied to his 'crew wanted' adverts. He had put them on the backburner while I was on board, he said.

Through other conversations we had had, I had come to understand how difficult he had found it – and still was finding it – to meet someone. He had chosen this life on a boat and he wanted to be with a woman who would enjoy it. The trouble was that most yachties are already firmly established couples who sell their homes and businesses to live out their jointly held dream. Steve said he wasn't interested in Thai or Malaysian women so that meant he had to advertise to Westerners. He'd tried internet dating and even placed a small ad in a magazine. The distance between the UK and Malaysia meant there was no casual meeting up for a coffee to see if they got along and calling it a day after an hour or so if there was no chemistry. Instead, a long-distance relationship had to be cultivated over the phone and email.

'And because of the time difference,' he explained, 'the only time they can talk is after work, which means I have to get up at 4am if I want to talk or chat over Skype or Facebook.' A few women, he said, had flown out to visit. Of the three, he had liked one and had gone to the UK to visit her. She was a successful businesswoman and, even though he never described her, I built up an image of her in my head: like Deborah Meaden from *Dragon's Den* crossed with Karren Brady; busty, fond of sober but expensively cut skirt suits and always, for some reason, wearing a chunky necklace of oversized navy blue beads.

'So what happened?' I asked.

'She was too commercial, so I ended it.' Music can sometimes be disparagingly labelled as 'too commercial', but people? 'She liked to own things,' he clarified. Ah. And there aren't a lot of chances to go shopping in the Malaysian jungle. Hell, shopping out here consisted of old guys in a little wooden boat bringing you a pumpkin.

I felt sorry for him. I'd tried internet dating in London and had never quite been able to reconcile the idea of the person I'd built up in my head from his profile, photos and emails with the actual, real-life man standing in front of me. And that was easy dating, as I could walk away if I didn't like the guy. That's not exactly possible when you've whisked the lady off to a picturesque, remote spot in the hopes of letting the romance flow and you find out you're incompatible and the furthest you can get away from each other is 46 feet. Maybe 56 feet, if one of you climbs into the dingy.

Over the following days there was no awkwardness on Steve's part so I concluded that he was fine with everything. Now we were 'mates' he started to tell me about the women he was hearing from. He'd read me their emails and show me photos they had sent as they downloaded, very slowly with the dreadful connection we got and only then if we anchored in certain places. I began to realise that he had very high standards: one was rejected for her poor grammar (although I have been guilty of doing the same in the past); another because she was too chubby; a third purely because she was American. I am not chubby nor American and, as an editor, my grammar is not too bad. *That must have been how I slipped through his filters*, I thought. I was glad he felt able to talk to me about it and the underlying atmosphere that had permeated the boat since Claire and Lizzie had left dissipated. In my new spirit of openness, I had tried it, found I didn't like it and now it was time to move on and focus on having fun – and ignore that little twinge of guilt that was niggling in my belly.

8

The (pygmy) elephant in the room

Elephants everywhere!' read a text from Greg and Debs up the Kinabatangan on *Southern Cross*. Steve and I had left the river to go to Sandakan town to restock but we didn't need any more motivation than that to return to the rainforest.

'*Kingdom, Kingdom*, this is *Southern Cross*, over,' came Debs's voice over the VHF when we were halfway up the river.

I grabbed the handheld radio and pressed the button to transmit. '*Southern Cross*, this is *Kingdom*. Hi, Debs. We're fine, thanks. How are you? Are the elephants still there?'

'G'day, Emma, how's it going? Want to switch to channel 68, over?' I'd forgotten that we weren't supposed to be clogging up the emergency channel 16 with idle chit-chat. It was easy in the lazy heat of Malaysia to forget all the strict boat protocol stuff that sailors religiously stick to in the cold waters around the UK. But at least I didn't use 'over and out' to sign off.

I left Steve steering the boat up the river, dodging the enormous drifting logs again, while I nipped below to plug my camera in to charge while the yacht's engine was running. As I reached for the inverter, my mobile phone vibrated with a text message. Messages from home were rare – I suspected it was very much 'out of sight, out of mind' – and a strong enough signal to receive them even rarer. It was from Lou, an old flatmate and a friend back in London, the inbox said. And it was a baby scan.

Hot tears sprang into my eyes and an unmoveable lump suddenly appeared to lodge in my throat. I stared at the grainy grey image. 'Looking forward to meeting you, Aunty xx', she'd written. I hadn't even known they were trying for a baby. Huge sobs burst from deep inside me and I jammed a hand over my mouth to stifle the noise. Hunched over in emotional agony, I ran into the bathroom, locked the door and cried and cried and cried.

Plenty of my friends had had children and I don't know why this one was more of a shock than any other but it hit me really hard. Maybe I would have handled the news better in London and it was receiving such a stark reminder here, in a tropical jungle, of all places, of what others had that I didn't that affected me so strongly. My life here in Borneo was child-free and there'd been none of those reminders about what I 'should' be. The people I hung out with were generally older and even if they had children they were grown up. Feeling left behind hadn't crossed my mind the whole time I had been here – and even for months before I left the UK, as I'd been so absorbed with preparing for my adventure. In a way it was like relapsing on the booze after going cold turkey for a while – just one hit affected me so much more strongly than before. It took me a good 20 minutes to calm down and compose myself before I could go back on deck.

I felt like such a ridiculous, hysterical *woman* explaining when Steve asked me what was wrong. I kind of mumbled out my answer while he put a comforting arm around me. He didn't laugh at me, he didn't try to push his case again; he was kind and understanding and it felt nice to be able to count on him as a friend.

When we reached them, Greg and Debs said they had seen elephants a day or so earlier. We immediately got started on round two of the Great Elephant Hunt but still had no luck. Greg and Debs came with us, showing us the places where they'd had sightings before. There was a muddy footprint here, some trampled grass there, but no actual elephant life. Steve and I were starting to think we were cursed. We hadn't come across a crocodile, either, even though several yachties had reported seeing a large one, which seemed to get bigger with every telling of the tale, until it reached a massive 5 metres from snout to tail tip.

As a change of scene from the main river, Greg took us in their dinghy up a small tributary where, he said, macaques liked to hang out. It was barely wider than the boat and we had to push branches away from our faces to work our way in. Dejected by our unsuccessful day's safari – there weren't even any monkeys there – we took advantage of the shade to have a rest and a drink. We were chatting about how unfair it was when Greg asked: 'Why is there an elephant over there?'

I thought he was joking but he was looking off into the bush and I followed his gaze. And there he was: a male with short tusks, standing, on his own, staring at us. He had approached so quietly that we hadn't heard him coming.

I assumed that elephants would make a lot of noise, snapping every twig they stepped on, but no. It was like an apparition.

The elephant stood on the spot, swaying his trunk from side to side. He took one small step forwards, tentatively, but then moved backwards again. He did this a few times while we stared.

'I think he wants to get in the water to go for a swim,' Debs said. 'But he's too scared to do it while we're here.' Greg and Steve grabbed an oar each to punt the dinghy backwards to give the elephant a bit more space. The elephant's behaviour was flighty, like a bird that has seen a tasty crumb it wants to get hold of but it isn't sure if it's safe to go forward to snatch it up. Except he was 2 metres tall and weighed more than the four of us and the boat we were in combined.

After a few minutes of toing and froing he made up his mind that we were too much of a menace and turned away and lumbered off into the trees. We were so close to the river bank that I was able to scramble up after him. I walked in the direction he was going slowly, partly because I was barefoot and also because I was wary of the rest of his herd suddenly coming charging towards me. I think Steve was a little bit startled by my behaviour – she's too much of a wimp to swim in the sea but brave enough to go off-roading barefoot through jungle – but he recovered himself after a minute or so and followed me.

The elephant was gone but I found something much more surprising. The beautiful rainforest, the wild jungle that I loved, which was home to so many thousands of animals, from the tiniest tree frog to herds of wild elephants, was a façade. Literally a front, hiding a palm oil plantation. The jungle extended only about a hundred metres back from the river's edge; after that it was neat, cultivated row upon row of palms, all exactly the same height, extending as far as I could see. When the farming corporations had cut down the primeval forest they had left a thin strip in place so that it looked like business as usual from the river. I suppose that in doing that they had at least preserved something of a habitat, albeit a small one, for the animals. (And, the cynics might add, for the tourists.)

Steve was totally opposed to the logging and palm oil industries. Every chance he got he would take a pop at them. My opinion is that poorer people don't always have the choices we do in life. Not everyone is fortunate enough to be able to save some money and go off to see the world for a year or buy a boat for £100,000 (half a million Malaysian ringgit) and live without working for the foreseeable future. Europe built its wealth and civilisation on agriculture and development and using what resources it had, and that is what Malaysia is doing now, except instead of timber and coal it is palm oil. Maybe there is a happy middle ground between development and conservation but I don't know much about it and I don't want to judge people when I'm ignorant of the facts myself. That was the argument I put forward if it came up in conversation between us. But standing there, rooted to the spot by the shock of seeing what had been done to the rainforest, I felt unbelievable sadness. I only hoped that the cultivation wasn't mirrored on the other side of the river. The hills we could see opposite as we had motored along the Kinabatangan seemed to still be covered with original trees – palm-oil plantations form a very distinctive pattern, like pompoms, from a distance – so maybe it wasn't as bad as it seemed.

That was probably optimism talking. Every day we had to

check the anchor chain to make sure there was nothing lodged up against it that could drag the anchor and set *Kingdom* adrift. One evening there was a log 20 feet long caught on the chain. It was so heavy that Steve had to use the dinghy under engine to tow it off the chain and let it flow down river. And that happened more than once. *These are big bits of valuable hardwood*, I thought. *Surely the loggers wouldn't just toss them away?* But if the trees were being cut down not for timber but to clear the area for planting, that would explain the jetsam. Probably it was a combination of both.

You wait ages for an elephant and then an entire herd comes along at once. Like with the monkeys, as soon as we'd seen one, we saw them all. Steve and I were across the river from *Kingdom*, in the dinghy, when I saw ripples in the water a short distance away. The ripples got bigger and bigger and something dark broke the water's surface.

'Steve,' I whispered, pointing. 'I think there's a crocodile.' As we watched, a black head emerged – and then a trunk. It looked like the same young male elephant and he had been sitting completely submerged in the river. Maybe they really were hiding from us? Whether or not it was the same animal, and he had finally got that swim, he was alone. I had read that young males were often cast out from the herds by the dominant male once they became seen as a threat. He lifted himself out of the water and on to the bank, climbing easily up the slippery step, his hide slick with mud. And he ambled off again.

After that a whole herd came right to the water's edge, exactly opposite *Kingdom* and *Southern Cross*, and stayed there for two days. We didn't even have to get in the dinghy, we could sit on the yachts and watch them eating, eating and eating. Called pygmy elephants, they are considerably smaller than their Asian cousins but they are not tiny, like their name might suggest. There were calves that were probably about my height, and full-sized adults with and without tusks. When they weren't eating they were bathing. I don't know when they slept because after dark Debs and I went closer in her dinghy and they were still wide awake, and eating. Their eyes shone white in the light of our torch but they didn't mind us and didn't stop munching on their midnight snacks. Their trumpeting calls and bellows echoed through the jungle, competing with the hornbills for the loudest cry. The tourist boats didn't faze them much, either. They seemed to be on a bit of a mission to eat up all of the available grass in that area before moving on. Now I had seen how narrow the forest was I understood why reported sightings of them were so frequent and why they didn't just go deeper into the vegetation to avoid humans. They had little choice but to plod up and down this small promenade, hunting out what food they could, putting up with the paparazzi and being chased along the banks by over-eager tourists who jumped out of their boats.

The excitement of elephant hunting over, things turned a bit more introspective on the boat. In the middle of the night I would wake up to go to the toilet to find Steve on his computer in the cockpit, emailing his women, trying to strike up a relationship across thousands of miles. Flies would swarm around him and the laptop, attracted by the light of the screen.

I asked him if he was having any luck.

'Four attempts have been failures now,' he said.

'Am I a "failure"?' I made quotation marks in the air with my fingers.

He said nothing, just gave me a look over the top of his reading glasses, like a stern schoolteacher telling me off for being dim.

The next afternoon, trying to be helpful, I suggested he could rewrite his advert to make it more obvious that he was looking to meet a long-term partner.

'Your original ad was a bit ambiguous,' I pointed out.

'What? What was ambiguous about it? Why didn't you realise I was looking for a girlfriend?' he demanded.

'You said you wanted someone to come "for fun or something more". That doesn't necessarily mean a relationship.'

He handed me a printout of the reply I had sent to his advert. I took the paper and read it, wondering how he had a printed out copy of a message sent five months earlier, what was going on and why I felt a bit like I was being ambushed. In the email I had introduced myself and written mainly about sailing, stating what I had done and what my level of experience was. It wasn't formal like a job application; it was friendly and chatty, but there was no flirting or innuendo. At least none that I'd intended.

I tried to point that out to him but he didn't believe me.

So much for the tense atmosphere dissipating. Now it was as thick as fog. Next up was a question about how if I wanted a boyfriend 'so badly', I wasn't able to 'let myself go' and be with him.

'What?' I said. 'What do you mean I want a boyfriend badly? When have I ever said that? Not everything is about looking for a boyfriend. I didn't come away to look for a boyfriend. That's you. That's what you're doing. You want a girlfriend so badly it influences everything you do. But I'm not like that. If it happens, it happens.' I had joined *Kingdom* looking for excitement, for travel, for something completely different from life back home. All joking about hot sailors aside, that was why I had replied to Steve's advert.

His eyes widened in disbelief and then his expression changed to a sneer. 'Oh, and while we're on the subject,' he went on, 'isn't it convenient that you arranged to pay the lower rate to me? Funny how you shagged me early on.'

My cheeks started to burn and my head swirled. I could recall that, in an exchange of emails ages ago when we'd talked about his girlfriend and money, I'd joked, 'So if I shag you I get a 60 per cent discount?' Obviously I had intended it as a gag and I was sure from his reply at the time that he had taken it as one.

But there was no joking now – he was straight-facedly accusing me of sleeping with him to save myself £10 a day. I felt ashamed of myself, both for writing the shag joke (I remembered going to delete it before I sent the email but then changing my mind because I was trying to be witty and I really wanted the chance to go sailing in Borneo) and for setting up the standing order for £15 a day without double-checking with him. I had offered since, twice, to increase the rate if he wanted me to but he had just dismissed the subject.

Waves of hatred were coming off him. Maybe his 3am emailing sessions weren't going well and he was tired and frustrated. I didn't know. And right then I didn't want to find out. I went to do the washing-up to distract myself and to try to empty the thoughts from my mind, but it was no good. I felt victimised, embarrassed, guilty and angry with myself for being an idiot in everything I had done and said and, even more, for what I had not said. I started to cry. Steve heard me – not difficult when you're sat only a metre away, and came to put his arm around me. 'What's wrong?' he asked.

'Well, you just accused me of prostituting myself, that's what wrong,' I replied.

'I'm sorry. I didn't mean it to sound like that.'

I offered to go online and change the payments to £25 a day and transfer him the difference for the days I'd already been on board.

'Thank you,' he said. 'I'd appreciate that.'

Living with one person is tough enough. Living with one person in a small space where you do everything together 24/7 is harder. And living with one person who you used to sleep with in a small floating space where you are together 24/7 and you can't get off is the hardest of all. The pettiest little annoyances become big issues pretty quickly, and when you do argue, tension lingers in the air for a long time afterwards.

Knowing this, Steve announced that he wanted to 'play a new game'. 'We tell each other something about the other one that annoys us. Then we can clear the air.'

'Erm. Right. Why?'

'Come on, just try it. You can go first.'

Hmm, I thought. *What have I done wrong now?* I was going through a stage where it seemed I couldn't do anything right – handle the sails, wear the 'correct' clothes, clean the toilet, play with the cat. Every time he would stop me and show me how to do something differently, i.e. his way. So, the game. *What should I say?*

'OK.' I took a breath. 'Don't tell me what to eat or comment on what I eat.' This was one thing that had been really annoying me. It started with Steve saying he disliked stodgy rice and progressed to his transferring his fear of all carbs and putting on weight on to me. He was Dr Atkins's biggest fan.

'So no more talk about obesity?' he tried to joke. But I was on a roll now.

'No, and no pointing it out when I do or don't have seconds at dinner or want a biscuit. And no more grabbing hold of my belly and wobbling it up and down. It's so frustrating, at 32 years old, with a good education, my own home and a pretty responsible job, to be told what to eat as if I were a small child. Carbs are not the enemy.' My voice was rising as I warmed to my theme. 'I happen to think my diet is pretty good, with lots of fruit and vegetables, thank you very much. I only weigh fifty-eight kilos, for God's sake!'

He was right – this new game was fun. I felt a lot better for getting things off my chest. *I should do this more often, rather than hold things in because I worry about upsetting people*, I thought. Now it was my turn to take it. I steeled myself, ready for the onslaught.

'Please can you not leave the foot pumps sticking out of the floor when you've finished at the sink,' he said, and wandered off. That was it. I felt pretty small. But I helped myself to a biscuit without having to sneak it and that felt good.

To make amends for the earlier arguments about the advert and money, I offered to polish all of the stanchions, the posts that hold up the safety lines around the deck of the boat. There were 24 of them, all stainless steel and growing rust. I thought it'd be a bit like doing the housework: a bit of scrubbing, a bit of buffing and Bob's your uncle (actually, he is but he prefers to go by Robert). How silly I was – the man who keeps his saucepans wrapped individually in plastic is not going to be placated with a quick squirt of Mr Muscle.

He showed me the technique. First I had to stick blue masking tape around the base of each stanchion, to prevent polish from staining the teak deck. 'But this tape is expensive, so don't use too much of it,' he said. Next I had to apply a special product and use a toothbrush to scrub away at the rusty sections, rubbing until the pale pink paste turned grey. I'd wipe it away, check for any residual rust, and keep repeating the procedure until it was all gone. Then I'd get a clean rag and rub, buff and polish until my fingers blistered and I could see myself reflected in thesteel. The base of each stanchion had two thin steel legs coming out of it and the plates were fastened to the deck with screws and, of course, the rust liked to develop in these awkward-to-reach places. It took me nearly an hour to do each stanchion, crouched or kneeling for three days under the beating sun.

But all that good, Protestant hard work didn't make me feel any better. In a way it made things worse because I began to be angry that I was actually paying Steve £25 a day to work on his boat. I know that I offered to do the job and he was busy doing other things – wiring a rotating glitter ball into the cockpit (like that was an essential task), changing oil and water in the engine and batteries, mixing up that home brewing kit I'd lugged from the UK but forgetting to add the sugar so that the yeast didn't ferment and the whole brown, sludgy lot ended up being thrown into the river – but I started to get a real bee in my bonnet about it. *He needs to decide whether he wants a paying customer or an employee*, I muttered to myself as I rubbed away.

When I took a break to read a book it sparked off another argument. He said I wasn't helping out enough, that I should 'take care' of downstairs while he did everything on deck. By downstairs duties he meant doing all of the cooking, washing-up and cleaning. I was furious – I hadn't travelled all this way to be someone's housewife or maidservant. I had come away to sail, travel and explore but, sitting on anchor up a river, we were doing none of those things.

I started to think about leaving *Kingdom* and sent a text to *Blue Steel*'s Ron asking if he was looking for crew. I also checked the crew website for other boats and sent out three emails. In one I asked the skipper outright whether he was looking for platonic crew or a girlfriend. I didn't want to make the same mistake twice.

I don't know if Steve sensed that I was looking to make good my escape because the morning after I'd sent the emails he apologised for some of the things he'd said, and explained he felt 'resentment' towards me. *No shit, Sherlock – even Dr Watson would have noticed that.* I asked why he resented me and he said it was because I hadn't been paying him enough money – 'It costs me £60 a day to run this boat,' he said – and for not wanting to go out with him.

Ron texted to ask if I wanted to go with him. I confessed to Steve and he was shocked and upset, telling me *Blue Steel*'s planned route, from Kota Kinabalu to Kuching to Tioman and then around Singapore to Thailand, wouldn't be very good. I asked Debs, as an independent source, what she thought of that journey and she said the water was dirty and it would mainly be motoring, rather than sailing, and dodging fishing boats. I also had an email from a man called Will about a one-year trip from New Zealand to the east coast of America.

'Why on earth would anyone want to go that quickly?' Steve asked, incredulous.

'I do,' I said.

'But why? You came away to change your life and you want to stay the same. You don't think about what's important in life.' He meant that I had lived a fast-paced life in London and now I was refusing to slow down. That wasn't entirely fair of him – I had slowed down, it was just that my idea of slow was much quicker than his. The first few weeks of my time on *Kingdom* had been great and we'd travelled a long way but the last month we'd been pretty much in the same place. I loved the rainforest but I was itching to move on, to discover the new things out there. Steve still didn't know when he was going to set sail for the Philippines and I didn't want to spend another three months pottering back and forth between the same towns we'd already been to.

'Well,' he said, 'it seems like you've already made up your mind to go with Ron.' And I almost had. I started looking up flights to KK and Kuching. But then I was uploading photos from my camera to my computer of the Kinabatangan river, Banggi with the otters and a coral cay we'd stopped at, and I got all dewy eyed as I relived all the wonderful things we'd seen. I told Steve I'd like to stay. For some reason, although we had our problems, I felt a loyalty to him and I didn't want to let him down. Also Big John had told me he had seen cockroaches on *Blue Steel* and I really can't stand the scuttling, shiny-shelled, filthy beetly things. So, blaming my horror of arthropods rather than my inability to confront the real issue, I put my head in the sand and tried to convince myself that everything was OK.

9

Almost heaven, West Virginia

It is possible my attempt to leave gave Steve a bit of a kick up the backside because only a day or two later we were motoring out of the Kinabatangan and on our way to Sipadan, an island famed as one of the best scuba-diving sites in the world. *Southern Cross* was heading the same way as us and we set a course for Semporna, the town nearest to Sipadan. On our way we heard *Southern Cross* talking on the radio to a French yacht called *Sunrise*. The skipper, Nic, had been anchored and a local approached in his boat, not saying anything, just watching closely. Nic looked down and saw he had automatic guns lying by his feet. We heard him tell Greg over the VHF that he would leave the area. He sounded remarkably cool about it. That's the French for you.

Here, on the north-east coast of Borneo, almost as far south as the Indonesian border, with the Celebes/Sulu Sea bringing fresh water, we were worlds away from the yellow murkiness of the Kinabatangan. The water was up to 200 metres deep and the most beautiful, iridescent blue.

Unfortunately, Semporna was a dump of a town: dirty,

smelly and busy. We wanted to get in and out as quickly as possible so that we could go to Sipadan.

'You know you can't go to Sipadan,' a guy who owned a dive company, Scuba Junkies, told us. 'It's a restricted area. You need a permit to dive there and they only give out fifty each day. It is forbidden for you to anchor there.' Great. That was that plan gone.

Sipadan is a world-class diving site which attracts people who want to see everything, from tiny seahorses to big pelagic fish and sharks, all in one place. To protect its wildlife, habitats and status, the resorts on the island were closed down and the number of visitors limited. The conservation practice worked: they practically guarantee that you will see turtles there. Obviously I wasn't so big on the diving but I was keen to do my glass-bottom-boat bit. I still hadn't seen a turtle, other than the rescued one and the hatchlings on Pulau Gulimaan. The closest I'd come was a few ripples on the surface. But Steve definitely wanted to don his scuba gear. We could, we were told, anchor at Mabul, an island eight miles away from Sipadan that had a few small dive resorts on it.

So we went to Mabul. The contrast with Semporna was unbelievable. It was a tiny sand island with four or five resorts on it, low-rise buildings set back from the water and blending into the jungle. There was one very smart-looking Chinese resort with wooden bungalows on jetties that extended a hundred metres or so over the sea so that the guests were completely surrounded by turquoise waters. It was six-star honeymoon stuff: raked sand, cordoned-off swimming areas, eco-huts in local hardwood. A few yachts were already anchored. *Southern Cross* had overtaken us and we saw *Sunrise*, the French boat that had had the run-in with the armed fisherman.

Surely this was paradise – even more of a paradise than the other places I had visited. The novelty of beautiful islands wasn't even close to wearing off, especially with one as stunning as Mabul. The water was the clearest I had ever seen. As we motored along we passed over a huge clear area, about a quarter of a mile square, that had no reef or rocks on the bottom, just pure white sand and thousands upon thousands of spotted starfish, all lying a similar distance away from each other to form a pattern so perfect it was hard to believe someone hadn't placed them all out by hand. Beyond the starfish was a coral reef. We had to be careful to drop our anchor over a white patch of seabed so that we dug into sand, rather than destroying reef. But as we paid out the chain we drifted backwards until we were floating safely above small patches of coral. Within an hour we had visitors: the usual little silver shoals I called poo fish, because they liked to hover around the head's outlet pipe, and some rich, dark blue fish that had skins like velvet, with long U-shaped tail fins that swayed gently in the current. They looked like jewels against the white sand beneath. It was here I learned that fish talk. Those velvety blues chirruped so loudly I could hear them while I stood on deck.

And turtles, turtles, everywhere. They surfaced by the side of the yacht, taking a gasp of air and diving down again. They popped up in front of the dinghy when we were motoring ashore and we'd have to alter course quickly to avoid running them over. There were hawksbills and green turtles and Greg taught me how to tell the difference between them, to look for the point at the bottom of the shell, near the tail. If there was a point there, it was a hawksbill; if not, it was a turtle.

The Australians were pure water babies. Debs was a school teacher but she had been a kayak champion in her youth and still had an athlete's body, lean and long, and Greg had been a pearl diver in the north-west. He had an enormous ribcage and incredibly broad shoulders and could free-dive for minutes and minutes on end.

I don't know how Debs knew I was afraid of snorkelling but she took it upon herself to ease me into it gently. The last time I had tried, with Steve, I had freaked out and had to scramble back into the dinghy. Debs took me out on to the reef, miles away from the yachts, in her dinghy. It was just the two of us and I didn't know her very well so I felt like I had to be on my best behaviour. Also, here was another woman, who was less likely to put up with wimpy crying at the sight of a few little Nemos than a man would. Steve had instructed me to roll into the water from the side of a dinghy and made me wear my snorkel on the left-hand side, because 'that's what scuba divers do'. He would pull me along, trying to be encouraging, but in reality just adding to my panic because I wasn't in control of where I was going or at what speed. Debs was much less regimented about it.

'All right?' she asked, as she stopped the dinghy engine and lifted it up out of the water, to reduce drag because she was going to tow it along with us as we swam. She pulled her mask over her eyes, put the snorkel into her mouth and jumped. No rolling, no faffing, no nonsense; just easy and relaxed. I swallowed hard and looked down. I couldn't see any fish around the boat, just clear water and some coral. There was no way I could witter on about wanting to stay in the dinghy and do my glass-bottomed-boat act in front of this fearless Amazonian Australian. I closed my eyes, held my breath and jumped. And it was great. Debs stayed close to me but didn't crowd me. She'd look out for interesting things and point them out to me then surface and tell me all about them while we trod water.

'Is that a clownfish?' I asked, recognising them from the movie *Finding Nemo*.

'Yeah,' she said. 'They're such territorial little guys. If you get too close they'll have a go at you, swim right up and bump into your mask.' It was funny to imagine this little fish, all of 5cm long, trying to take on a human being.

She dived down and fetched up a cowrie shell for me to see. The mollusc was still alive and a thin, suede-like membrane covered the outside of the shiny shell. It was soft to the touch and when we brushed our fingers against it, it recoiled inside its shell. She told me about corals that looked like brains, like trees and like antlers, and even about ones that picked up their legs and walked. I had trouble remembering the names of all the fish she showed me so I made up my own: fusiliers were 'yellow and purple fish' because, well, they were yellow and purple. A weird creature with a wobbly skirt that changed colour to match whatever it was next to swam past: Debs explained it was a cuttlefish. I was astounded as it bore no resemblance to the flat bony shells my auntie used to give to her budgie for it to sharpen its beak against. I saw something that looked like a bright red rose and showed it to Debs. She said it was nudibranch eggs. I had no idea what a nudibranch was but if its eggs were that beautiful, I imagined the creature itself must be spectacular. (I was a little disappointed to see one in a book and find it looked like a multicoloured slug.) The longer I spent in the water, the more comfortable I felt as

I began to recognise that the fish were more afraid of me than I was of them – they would always move out of my way, even if I swam right into the middle of a large shoal.

By the time we saw a turtle swimming near us, I was confident enough to follow it, off the edge of the coral drop-off and into 40 metres of deep blue water. I kept my eyes on the animal rather than looking around for the bottom. I think the turtle was just as curious about me as I was about him. He fixed me with a beady eye and slowed his pace so that we swam along in synchronicity. I waited for him when he dived down to check out an interesting patch of grass and stuck my head above the surface at the same time he did when he had to take a breath of air. We had lost part of one of his back flippers so I nicknamed him Stumpy. Three hours passed in what seemed like minutes. We only got out because we started to feel cold, even in the 31°C water. On deck, drying in the sun, I was so elated I radiated happiness. I was so proud of myself for conquering a fear and, more, for actually enjoying it. I'm sure the magical beauty of Mabul had as much to do with it as Debs's kindness and patience. Who could resist taking a look at all this extraordinary life under our keels once they had had a glimpse of how astonishing it was?

Steve had managed to get a pass to Sipadan and joined a dive tour for the day and I was sitting in the cockpit, still euphoric, when he came back in the dinghy.

'I've got some great gossip!' he yelled, over the engine, as he tied the dinghy alongside.

'Gossip?' I asked, surprised. The only people we knew here were Greg and Debs, and I'd been with the latter all day.

He switched off the engine and climbed on board. 'It's about Sexy Josh and Kristin. You're not going to believe this.'

On his dive trip, most of the other customers had been couples but there was an English woman who he had 'befriended': a thirty-something blonde called Jenny. Steve had been chatting to (chatting up, probably) Jenny and told her that he lived on a yacht. She knew someone who lived on a boat, she told Steve. She'd met him in Langkawi when she was on holiday last year and he'd swept her off her feet – after he'd told her he was single. He'd taken her camping in the rainforest, they'd gone out for trips on his yacht. They'd had a holiday romance and, afterwards, they'd become friends on Facebook. Jenny was so smitten that she'd arranged to come back to Borneo this year to meet up with him; they'd had lunch in Kota Kinabalu. The guy was Sexy Josh, Steve told me with glee, and Kristin had, apparently, seen some Facebook messages and hit the roof. But Jenny didn't know that we knew the Americans.

'I've invited Jenny over for drinks tonight,' Steve said. 'I'm picking her up in an hour and I'll stop by *Southern Cross* and *Sunrise* on my way to Mabul and ask them over, too.'

So we were seven crammed into the cockpit. I liked Jenny: she was about 35, slim and pretty, and worked in advertising. Once she'd sunk a few G&Ts she started telling everyone how she wanted to get married and have children but that she hadn't been on a date for two years. *What about Josh?* I thought. It was very nice to have confirmation that I wasn't the only single girl left in London but it also made me feel like a bit of a cliché. She even lived two roads down from me in Clapham.

Before Steve drove Jenny back to her dorm room on the

island, the pair of them, plus Greg and Nic from *Sunrise*, arranged to go diving from the dinghies the next day. Nic had told us he was a dive photographer. He travelled around in his yacht, mostly by himself, shooting underwater life and publishing his best pictures in spectacularly beautiful books. He was the epitome of cool.

Steve and I swung by *Sunrise* the next morning to fix the time they were all going to meet. Nic, fresh from the shower after a dawn solo-dive, crouched down to talk to us, dressed in a sarong, his long, wet, dark hair hanging loosely around his shoulders. He had that slightly arrogant French look and his thickly lashed green eyes danced with amusement as he spoke in halting English.

I had the boat to myself (plus the cat) for the latter half of the morning while the others were diving and, when Steve and Jenny returned to *Kingdom* for lunch, I listened to him flirting with her while I made a meal for the three of us. *Here we go again*, I thought. She came back with him after the second diving session, too, for sun-downers, and invited us to her resort for dinner.

'I've got to go because it's my friend's birthday and I promised him I'd be there,' she said. 'But why don't you two come, too? It's a self-service buffet and I don't think they'd notice.'

At Jenny's resort the benches were packed with young people, a bit like the dining hall at university, except with better tans.

We loaded our plates and found a table at the back that had space and tried to act like we belonged there. Two young, shirtless Americans were sitting opposite us.

'Good diving today?' one of them asked.

'Yeah, great, thanks,' Steve replied. Maybe they thought we were all divers, just like them. Steve had had done his usual trick and brought a cool bag loaded with drinks. We emptied our borrowed plastic water beakers and filled them with wine.

'Hey, where did you guys get wine from around here?' the dark-haired American asked. 'All I can find is that Filipino rum. Say, are you guys from that sailboat out there?' We admitted that we were. 'I knew it,' he said, looking at Steve. 'You've got wine and you're wearing a shirt.'

'Wearing shirts?' I asked.

'Well, divers and sailors always have their uniforms. Sailors always wear shirts, see, and divers wear T-shirts.' I looked around at the other divers in the room. Of the men that were clothed, each one was dressed in a round-necked T-shirt. Steve was in his uniform of Hawaiian shirt and shorts. Greg and Debs arrived – Greg in a collared shirt – and then Nic, also in a Hawaiian shirt. Come to think of it, I had never seen Steve in anything other than a casual, short-sleeved shirt with a collar. The American was right.

Cruising sailors are not known for their sense of style. When you do see a man in a T-shirt, it is invariably printed with the logo of a brand of beer of a country he has visited or the name of a marina he has stayed at. These T-shirts are usually freebies. Colours have faded in the UV, whites have turned grey from being hand-laundered in buckets of rainwater and the rigging has torn holes in almost every garment. The women aren't much better: they either dress like men in shirts and shorts or wear shapeless, baggy dresses. They are usually bra-less and because of their average age this really isn't a good idea. For a relatively young cruiser, Steve had an even worse sense of style. When I had first arrived on *Kingdom*, I had seen a pair of his jeans hanging up, drying, and had been confused about why such a small man would need such a large pair of jeans. And heavily stonewashed ones at that. All of the cupboards on the yacht with hanging space were crammed with short-sleeved shirts in garish colours and giant patterns. His 'best' shirt was collarless with long, voluminous sleeves and lacing across the gaping neck. It looked like Errol Flynn's undershirt but he thought it made him look dashing. He had a go at me once, upset, about why I never complimented him on anything he wore. How can you tell someone that you never say they look nice because you think every piece of clothing they wear is hideously ugly?

Dinner over, we moved the party upstairs and sat on stools around the bar. Jenny went to her dorm to shower and Steve was talking to Greg and Debs so I started a conversation with Nic. The wine was finished and we switched to Tanduay, strong Filipino rum that is loaded with chemicals that makes you really, really, drunk very, very quickly. I was soon seeing two Nics. Before coming to Thailand and Malaysia he had been diving and working in Madagascar. He thought Steve was my boyfriend so I quickly set him straight on that front, explaining I was a paying customer and that I'd come out to Borneo to race.

'Race?' he said, clearly not enamoured with the thought. 'I do not like this racing. The last thing I raced after was my wife – and I lost.'

Steve was pulling faces at me behind Nic's back, miming smooching and in a nudge-nudge-wink-wink fashion encouraging me to introduce the Frenchman to the concept of the great British lunge. I wasn't interested in Nic in that way.

Jenny came back, dressed up and with a full face of make-up, and pulled her stool close on the other side of him. Clearly she was. *How's Steve going to take that?* I wondered.

The dark-haired American from dinner appeared in the bar and I went over to talk to him. His name was Luke and he was from West Virginia. I am a sucker for a southern accent, either British or American. And for a suntan. And for a pair of green eyes. He was only 25 and had already owned, built up and sold his own construction business. He had left behind a beautiful actress girlfriend to 'be free', he claimed. Rock climbing was his passion but he thought he'd give diving a try and had come to Mabul to do his dive master. I have absolutely no interest in rock climbing or dive-master studies but I could have listened to that accent and stared into those eyes for days. He was gorgeous and his old-fashioned charm was doing funny things to me. He suggested a walk on the beach and led me outside by the hand.

A walk turned into kissing on the sun lounger for what must have been hours. We saw Nic come out and help Jenny into his dinghy. Then Steve stormed out of the bar and set off along the beach.

'I've got to go,' I told Luke, grabbing my shoes and running after Steve. 'Steve! Steve!' He must have heard me but he kept marching on. 'Steve! Wait!'

He stopped abruptly and turned to me. 'Where the fuck have you been?' he spat.

I stopped dead. 'What? Here on the beach.'

'I've been ringing you. I didn't know where you were.'

'I left my phone on the boat.'

'I didn't know if you were coming back or staying out all night.' He was furious.

'What? Of course I'm coming back to the boat. I was just there, on the beach. I stayed near the door, so I could see when you came out.'

'Wait there,' he ordered.

'What? I'm here now. I'm coming.'

'No! Wait there! I'll get the dinghy and come and get you.' He stamped angrily away, leaving me, confused, waiting in the sand.

We'd moored the dinghy at another dive company's shop and it would take him ten minutes to walk there and another five to drive back to me. I went back to the sun lounger but Luke was gone. No doubt as soon as he'd realised he wasn't going to get his end away he'd legged it immediately. I sat on the sand to wait for Steve, wondering if he would be so angry that he would go back to *Kingdom* and leave me stranded on the island all night to teach me a lesson. He finally appeared and I waded out to the dinghy.

'You are so off the boat,' he said.

'Fine.'

We motored along for a few metres.

He began again. 'I didn't know where you were.'

'I was keeping an eye out for you,' I explained again. 'I wasn't just going to go back with some guy.'

I couldn't understand him. 'Why are you so angry with me?' I had to shout for my voice to be heard over the engine as we went faster through the deeper water.

He was silent. Then he said: 'When was the last time you were in love with someone and switched it off, just like that?'

Love? Where was this coming from?

'Never,' I said in a small voice.

'I'm jealous, OK? Do you get it? I was fucking jealous.

I can't deal with this. You are so off the boat. Tomorrow you are gone. Understand? Get the fuck off my boat.'

The weird thing was, although I thought he was massively overreacting, I wasn't shocked or surprised by being ordered to leave. It could be that the alcohol was keeping me calm but I didn't care that I was suddenly homeless on a tiny island in the middle of nowhere, with no idea of where to go to next. Two months ago, I'd have been panicking that I didn't know where to go, how to get around, how to speak the language. The visits to remote villages, the getting by on sign language, the snorkelling had taught me that. I was becoming braver. I'd been away long enough now to feel OK with things when I was outside of my comfort zone. Also, I was incredibly relieved that the decision to leave had finally been made, one way or another.

A small part of me wondered whether he would regret his angry words and apologise to me in the morning but he didn't. We avoided each other, Steve spending the whole day in the cockpit reading, of all things, and me inside. I directed most of my attention towards Layla, who decided to be nice to me now that I was leaving. Late in the morning, Jenny and Nic came in off the reef in his dinghy. She must have spent the night on *Sunrise*.

I had to make plans. Steve was avoiding the subject so I didn't know when I would have to leave or how – maybe he would dump me in Mabul that same afternoon and I'd have to bribe a dive company to take me to the mainland and stay in a god-awful hostel in Semporna while I sorted myself out. My friend Grace was going travelling around India and texted to ask if I wanted to meet her. I rang the Indian embassy in Kuala Lumpur and they said it would take a minimum of nine days to get a visa and I would have to wait, passport-less, in KL while it was processed. I still had 25kg of belongings with me and, as wonderful as it would be to see a familiar, friendly face, I couldn't bear the thought of lugging sailing boots, thermals and a lifejacket from hostel to hostel in India. I still wanted to sail.

Steve said he was going to collect his re-filled dive tanks from Mabul and while he was ashore I checked my emails. There was one from a guy called Tyrone who was looking for crew and whose advert I had replied to a couple of weeks earlier. They were in Sandakan. Could I call?

Steve came back. He had been waiting with Jenny for her transfer to the mainland to catch her flight home.

'I hope you don't mind but I talked to Jenny about our situation,' he said. I didn't mind at all. She'd advised him it was better for me to leave the boat now while we were still friends, he said. He agreed but said I could stay for a few days while I sorted myself out.

'I didn't make a play for Jenny last night,' he said, 'and she didn't make one for me because you were on the boat and it would have been too messy.' He was telling me that I wouldn't be his girlfriend and that he couldn't get another one while I was here. I thought he was going a bit too far with that – Jenny clearly fancied Nic, as she'd spent the night with him, not Steve. It had nothing to do with me. But if it hurt Steve's feelings less to believe that I was the only obstacle between him and true love, I wasn't going to say anything to shatter his belief.

'I've had an email from another boat looking for crew in Borneo,' I told him.

'Great!' He seemed pleased and relieved, not like the last

time, when I had broached joining *Blue Steel*.

Everything happened so fast from then. I rang Tyrone, expecting a booming black American man's voice on the other end of the phone, but getting a Northern Irishman. He explained they'd just arrived from Papua New Guinea and that a crew member was leaving in Sandakan to go home. They'd be going up to Kuching and on to Singapore, Langkawi and Malaysia. This was a fairly similar route to the one I'd turned my nose up at with *Blue Steel* but now urgency made it seem much more appealing. But how to bring up the subject of whether he was a skipper advertising for a wife?

'So, are you a couple and you're just looking for some extra help?' I asked, tentatively.

'What? No. We're just four crew – me, two guys and a girl. It's Katherine that's leaving.'

Excellent news.

I wanted to make sure I covered all the bases this time. 'I should probably tell you that I'm a vegetarian, in case that's a problem.'

Tyrone laughed. 'Well, we are about to lose our vegetarian and I think the boys were looking forward to cooking meat again but it's not a problem.' This was getting better and better – they were used to having a veggie on board. There was an awkward silence. *Please pick me!* I prayed silently.

'Well, you sound nice,' he said. 'Can you come on Monday?' Yes! I was in! We settled on Tuesday, to give me more time to figure out how I was going to get to Sandakan. It was three days away.

We had a farewell dinner and beers ashore again with Greg and Debs and Nic. Luke from West Virginia wanted me to stay with him but I didn't want to do anything to risk Steve rescinding his offer of taking me to Semporna on *Kingdom* so that I could get a bus to Sandakan.

Back in that stinking pit of a town I scouted out the bus stop and bought a ticket for the next day and posted 5kg of my stuff back home to my parents so I only had one bag to handle. I was learning how to be a better traveller.

Steve's emotions were running high. From anger that drunken night and acceptance he moved on to sadness and tears, frequently coming to hug me.

The morning I left, he handed me one of the boat's water bottles. 'This is so you can take a little piece of *Kingdom* with you,' he said and I was touched at his gesture. He was calm as he walked me to the bus stop and I was the one who got upset. I was feeling guilty for having hurt his feelings and a little bit afraid of going off by myself to who knows where with God knows who. Again. Steve didn't hang around to wave the bus off. Once I was in my seat and my bag was loaded into the hold, he turned his back and walked away. I watched until I couldn't see him any more. It was over.

Gillaroo

10

Never judge a book

You remember that stuff I said about hating creepy crawlies? Well, that was life on *Gillaroo*. There was an infestation of ants that crawled everywhere – over the galley surfaces, the ceilings, across the toilet paper, along the beds. And cockroaches. Big, fat, one-inch-long cockroaches that waited until the sun had gone down before scuttling out of their secret hiding places to climb the walls – usually of my cabin, centimetres from my pillow. Entomophobia aside, *Gillaroo* was far from being a luxury yacht. There were no hammocks or home comforts, no fans to help us cope in the tropical humidity and heat, and we not only washed in rainwater collected on deck, pouring a couple of litres into a plastic bucket and then tipping it over our heads, we drank it. You might well expect that I took one look at that catamaran and its back-to-basics living conditions with wildlife included and got the hell out of Dodge. But actually I loved it. I told you I was learning how to be a better traveller.

I was nervous as I waited in Sandakan yacht club to meet Tyrone. Because we didn't have that back history of emailing and Facebooking, I didn't even know what he looked like. So when he appeared, although I didn't know what I had expected, I knew enough about yachties to know what I *wasn't* expecting. And here it was. He was white, really white, like he lived in the rainy UK, and spent all his time indoors sheltering from the precipitation, not on a yacht that had been travelling non-stop through tropical climes for two years. There was a woman with him, wearing a matching sunhat tied neatly under her chin. She was extremely pale, too. *How was it even possible?* I asked myself.

'Hello,' I said, getting to my feet. 'Are you Tyrone?'

'Yes,' he said, shaking my hand. 'And this is Katherine. She's the one that's leaving. She's flying off tomorrow.'

The slightly surreal feeling I was experiencing continued when we climbed into the dinghy. There was no outboard. Without a word of explanation, they each picked up a wooden oar and began to paddle us out into the sea. It was a big, heavy dinghy and the progress was very slow.

'Which boat is *Gillaroo*?' I asked Tyrone.

'This one here,' he replied, pointing his oar at a large red and white catamaran at anchor. Eventually, after many, many more minutes of silent paddling, we were pulling alongside one of the hulls. They were low at the back so it was much easier getting aboard than trying to clamber up *Kingdom*'s ladder. Tyrone handed up my bag and I walked into the boat's cockpit. It was huge – the size of a standard living room in a house. There was a red fabric roof over our heads, keeping out the sun, (Aha! A clue to the pastiness!) and benches with red cushions on them ran down the port and starboard sides. On the starboard side was a table big enough to seat eight people and a stack of white, plastic outdoor chairs. And there was a stainless steel chair at the helm, which was on the port side. You could have held a party for 20 people in that cockpit, it was so roomy. *I think I'm going to like living on a catamaran*, I thought.

A young guy appeared from inside.

'This is Hugo,' Tyrone said.

'Hi,' said Hugo, stepping forward to shake my hand.

Here was a tanned person. So someone went on deck sometimes. He was 19, from New Zealand, and had the widest smile possible, his sharp top canine teeth emphasising the breadth of his grin. Hugo was a little bit shy – although I suspected he would come out of his shell when around kids his own age – and obviously well brought-up, as he was always keen to help with anything. *Gillaroo* was his second boat and I was impressed that someone so young had made it so far from home by himself. His only drawback was he was flat broke. 'Is it ixpinsive?' he asked of everything, as he had barely two pennies to rub together until he got back home.

If I thought the outside of the boat was large, the interior seemed even bigger. There was another wooden table, with a curved sofa around two sides of it, in the main cabin, which was split 60:40 into a saloon and galley. The port side was the saloon, with the table, a large shelf-cum-nav table along the outer edge, radios, screens, gadgets and technical bits and pieces. On the starboard side the galley was a U-shape, with a cooker at eye level and a separate hob. Tyrone showed me the port hull. Down a few steps was a corridor with a double aft cabin on the left, at the back of the boat. Straight ahead were cupboards for storing tools and spares; to the right, going forwards, was a bathroom and, on the other side of the heads, a single cabin that contained a bed easily big enough for two people. It was the same layout in the starboard hull but instead of tools the cupboards housed food and box after box of books. On top of the boxes of books were stacks of more books. There was a library on this boat. I couldn't believe my luck.

Katherine showed me the aft starboard cabin. 'This is yours,' she said.

'Wow, it's huge!' I said, turning full circle. The bed was raised, because the engine bay was underneath, and I had to climb on to a small bench to get on and off it. It was so big I could lie like a starfish and still have spare room either side of me. This was lucky as there were no fans or aircon on the boat so quite often I did have to lie like a starfish, to get the maximum amount of air circulating around me to cool down.

'The house battery bank is in here so sometimes Tyrone has to come in to change the switch,' she said, showing me a large red knob. 'So don't touch this unless he asks you to.'

'OK,' I said.

'I gave it all a good clean. And I've left you a few bits – body lotion, vitamins, things like that.'

'Thanks,' I said idly, exploring the cabin. There was a tall set of shelves and a small wardrobe with sheets and sleeping bags stored in them. I reached into a shelf and pulled out a child-size pair of Crocs. 'Are these yours?' I asked.

'No, they were gifts we picked up to give away to local children but got left over.'

'Oh.' I put the shoes back in their place, next to a set of playing cards. 'So if this is your cabin,' I asked Katherine, 'where are you sleeping tonight? Do you want me to stay in the saloon?'

'No, I'll bunk in with Tyrone,' she said. I was surprised

– they didn't seem like a couple at all. I put him in his late forties and her in her early twenties. And if they were a couple, why was she leaving? Then I thought about Steve and I and wondered if it might be a similar situation.

After I had unpacked – my things took up maybe a quarter of the storage space – the four of us had tea and cake at the table outside. It was all very civilised – a teapot, tea leaves, cake served on plates. Except there was very little conversation. Conscious of the silence, I gabbled on like an idiot, asking questions. Where was the other crew member, I wanted to know. Where were we going next? When? Then what? Where had they just come from? What was it like? Where had they been to stay in Borneo so far? Did we always have to paddle the dinghy along? What was that red wooden thing hanging off the transom (back of the boat)?

They looked a little startled at my barrage of questions but they answered them. The remaining crew member was Chris, an American who was off doing some inland exploration on his own. They weren't sure when he would be back – he didn't have a phone so they were waiting for an email from him – but whenever it was that he did put in an appearance, we'd be off towards Kuching. In the meantime the outboard was having to be mended after it fell off the dinghy and filled with water. There was also a rudder that had to go back into the catamaran. They had been to Tawau, to Mabul for just one day and the Kinabatangan. They hadn't stayed to snorkel in Mabul and they hadn't managed to see elephants up the river. They had come from Papua New Guinea, a place they all loved ('When we were in Manus' became one of the most common sayings), and it had taken them two weeks to cross to Borneo. I wanted to know all about PNG and bombarded them with loads more questions.

The red thing was a canoe that Tyrone had built himself. He used to make them commercially, he said, back in Ireland. Through the course of the conversation, it turned out he had built *Gillaroo* as well. *Hang on a minute*, I thought to myself, *building a nice little canoe is one thing but a 48-foot, ocean-going live-aboard catamaran? That is something else.* I started to look at this slightly geeky man in a whole new light.

Time for my Sweet Valley moment. Tyrone was the 6-foot 2-inch, 52-year-old Northern Irish son of a bank manager who had peacocks and a pet sheep when he was growing up. He had been a computer programmer back in the early days, a volunteer trek leader in Africa for a group that worked with troubled kids, a maths teacher and a canoe builder. He looked like a mish-mash of all of those careers – he had a strong, lean body any man half his age would have been proud of, and a handsome, square-jawed face topped with a full head of floppy brown hair. His good looks were held in check by his nerdy elements: his glasses, those tied-under-the-chin sunhats and his manner of opening his eyes really wide in surprise. He and his brother Sackville (yes, really) had come up with a scheme to build their own catamaran and sail around the world with a crew consisting of Tyrone, Sackville, Mrs Sackville and the little Sackvilles and Tyrone had moved to the Irish countryside, built a polytunnel yard and started to craft this enormous boat himself, over five years. They had bought the plans from a naval architect, Derek Kelsall, and changed them slightly, to give longer hulls than the original design. For five years Tyrone laboured away in his polythene workplace in the middle of nowhere, while Sackville, home in Florida, researched equipment and gizmos and ordered the sails. Somewhere along the line there had been a brotherly falling-out and the Family Sackville no longer wanted to cruise, so Tyrone cobbled together a crew of friends and volunteers old and new. He hired a local farmer to drag the boat a hundred yards into the Irish Sea, hoisted an orange, white and green ensign and set sail for Spain, with a plan to keep going west for two or three years until he ended up back where he had started.

By the time I joined, the ensign was a bit faded and frayed along the edges, the orange stripe noticeably thinner from numerous patchings-up. The interior was starting to look worn – two years in the tropics had given her a nasty fungal infection, with mould growing everywhere it could get a hold, and a bad case of rust which was mostly confined to the cutlery drawer. The painted *Gillaroo* sign had worn off the dinghy's bow, the spinnaker had ripped apart and been sewn back together multiple times and there were a few nicks in the cat's topsides. But these were mere battle scars – she had sailed the high seas and lived to tell the tale.

As Tyrone and *Gillaroo* went along their merry way, some problems with the boat started to emerge. The wrong size rig had been ordered – five per cent larger than was originally planned – so she wasn't sailing right. By New Zealand, he had to stop for five months to do some major work: the keels had to come off and be moved, the front of the boat redesigned and the trampolines moved. 'This was a mistake,' Tyrone uttered about every third sentence as he introduced me to the boat's systems and told me *Gillaroo*'s story. 'That wasn't a very good design.' I think by the time I met Tyrone, two-thirds of the way through his journey round the world, he could see only the flaws in *Gillaroo* and nothing of the astonishing feat he had accomplished. He had built a boat in his backyard, for God's sake, and safely sailed himself, and at least 10 other people so far, across thousands of miles of open water. They'd crossed the Atlantic and Pacific oceans, visiting some of the remotest places in the world, and the boat was still in one piece. I wished I could open his eyes to seeing his achievement for what it really was.

Katherine (who, I discovered, was older than me – perhaps there really is something in staying out of the sun's ageing rays) left the following morning, Tyrone and Hugo paddling her ashore, and over the next couple of days I concentrated on settling in. I was given a kind of training manual that set out what was expected of the crew. The sailing would be divided into watches of three hours each, and I'd be on watch from 6am to 9am and 6pm to 9pm when we were on passage, and in charge of navigation and sail plan at those times. In between I was free to do what I wanted unless more hands were needed on deck for any reason. Breakfast and lunch were fend for yourself but dinner was a family affair, to be served before sunset to preserve power. We were to take it in turns to have a cooking and washing-up day. A small amount of paper could go down the toilets, it was best to charge computers and phones in the morning when there was spare solar power, any expenditure on food, fuel and so on was to be recorded in a notebook and divided equally every so often. While sailing at night, the person on watch had to wake someone up if they needed to go forward of the cockpit. We reefed the sails (furling them in and tying them down to make them smaller) once the wind reached 20 knots and put the engines on if our sailing speed dropped below 4 knots. There was nothing about dashing out in the rain to remove fleecy cushion covers – they were waterproof and fine in all conditions – and absolutely no mention at all of any saucepan protocol.

In fact, the only really strict rule seemed to be about alcohol – absolutely no drinking on passage and, if you want to get right royally pissed when at anchor or in a marina, you were to find yourself a bed ashore for the night. It was very much a community spirit – all for one and one for all, only without the swords and giant feathers in our hats – and it felt great to be trusted. I was happy to contribute to boat tasks and work off my own initiative because there was a strong feeling of all mucking in together. And I could read – oh, everyone was a great reader, even Hugo, which I found unusual in a 19-year-old lad. These were my kind of people and I felt so much more at home.

Hugo was a guy who took everything in his short-legged stride. He was between school and uni and had decided to head off for his summer break. There's nothing too surprising about that – the overseas experience is practically a rite of passage in New Zealand. But Hugo didn't fly off to Bali to get pissed with his mates; he found someone at the yacht club who was looking for crew, borrowed a waterproof jacket from his dad and hopped on board. The captain was a cruel drunkard and Hugo mutinied when he reached Vanuatu. And yet he didn't call on the banks of mum or dad and fly back home. He posted up an advert on the yachties' notice board and ended up not long afterwards on board *Gillaroo*. Still in his teens, he found himself with the responsibility of ensuring the boat's safe passage during his watches at night, alone, while the rest of the crew and the skipper slept. I think he was a romantic soul because every evening he would go forward to the front of the boat to watch the sun wind its way down the sky to vanish beneath the horizon. His enthusiasm for anything was tempered only by his poverty.

I offered to go shopping to re-provision the boat so that we could leave as soon as Chris arrived back. I already knew where the supermarket was, and the dodgy Chinese beer-selling restaurant. And, after weeks of pooh-poohing the idea of schlepping around town to buy sausages here and fresh milk there, I converted. Tyrone and Hugo said they hadn't tasted cheese for months so I set myself a mission to buy some.

I had to take a bus to an out-of-town shopping area. I texted Debs to ask her if she knew which bus I could take. 'Any number between 4 and 8,' she replied, 'going to Kim Fong.' I walked to the bus station and there were three number 4s so I got on the one at the back, which was the only one that had any passengers on it. 'Kim Fong?' I asked the driver. It was a woman – not at all what I had expected – and she beckoned me on with her hand. I sat near the back and waited. In Malaysia there aren't bus timetables, as such – the buses leave once they have enough passengers. It was a long wait at that bus station. So long, in fact, that a woman got on, selling snacks of dried fruits and nuts. Eventually the engine started and we belched our way along but there was confusion about where I was supposed to get off because I'd given the driver and conductor the name of the highway, not the stop I wanted, and I nearly ended up being left in the middle of nowhere. But through counting on fingers, gesticulating and taking a leap of faith, I ended up in the right place.

When I was shopping in Sandakan with Steve I had passed a small Chinese store that sold imported Australian cheeses and frozen non-halal meats, and I set off from the bus stop in that direction. I was walking along a wide road with broken paving slabs and overgrowing weeds. Coming towards me was a Malay who started shouting things at me. 'Sorry?' I asked and he yelled something else utterly unintelligible. A young man who had been walking behind overtook me.

'Don' worry,' he said, 'that man crazy,' and he twirled his finger by his temple in the international sign of madness. He shouted something at the other man, who left us alone, and continued to walk alongside me.

'Oh, terima kasih,' I replied.

'You speak Bahasa?' he asked me, surprised, and said a long sentence that I didn't understand.

'Only a little,' I shook my head. 'About two words. Terima kasih and jumpa lagi.' These mean thank you and goodbye and, even though I was pleased to have learned them, I would hardly have said I knew the lingo.

'You speak Bahasa,' he said, a statement this time, and again said something I was unable to translate. 'You understand me?'

'No.'

'Where are you going?' he asked in English, which seems to be the standard question asked in Malaysia, rather than 'How are you?'

'To the shop.' He was very young – maybe 19 or 20 – and quite slight and harmless enough. We kept walking.

Again he said something in Bahasa, then checked whether I had understood him. *Why are you speaking to me in a language I don't understand?* I thought.

'I finish job,' he announced, 'and now I go my home. You wan come?'

'No, thank you. I have to go do my shopping.'

That Bahasa phrase again and a raising of the eyebrows. Then: 'Is OK. Is nobody there.'

Now I understood. He was propositioning me. He probably couldn't believe his luck, coming across an English woman walking down the street on her own, showing a little ankle and a bit of collarbone. I mean, everyone knows British girls are easy, don't they? Even at 11am in the morning when they are clearly doing the supermarket run. I imagined that that phrase in Bahasa was something dirty like: 'You whore infidel. Look at you walking around in your sexy baggy T-shirt and your provocatively shapeless pants. You are obviously gagging for it and I will fuck you,' and that's why he kept checking whether I understood him.

'OK. I go to do my shopping now,' I told him again, firmly. 'Terima kasih. Jumpa lagi.' I used my two Bahasa phrases and crossed the road. He shrugged in a 'nothing ventured, nothing gained' kind of a way and kept on walking home.

11

My new family – and other animals

I was woken at midnight by the sound of the newly fixed outboard starting. Chris must be back, I realised, and got up to greet my new crewmate. From what I'd heard of him from Tyrone and Hugo, Chris was the most outgoing and chatty of the three and liked a drink and a party. I was looking forward to getting to know him. Tyrone arrived back with the dinghy, ferrying a cross between a scarecrow and a beanpole who, when he stepped into the saloon, had to duck his head to fit through the doorway. We said quick hellos and shook hands then it was back to bed ready for an early start.

We left at 6am for Langkayan, the turtle island Debs and Greg had told me about, and I got to know Chris a bit better. In appearance he was a little like an Elizabethan playwright: long, shaggy hair, pointy nose, quick and intelligent eyes, a thin moustache and goatee beard. He wore trousers he'd cut off halfway up the calves and raggedy shirts he left unbuttoned to let the air circulate round his 25-year-old lanky, hairless body. He was proud of his straw hat he'd got in a New Zealand $3 shop, even though it had clearly been sat on many a time, and, when he wasn't reading books on world economics, wandered around the boat strumming his guitar or blowing on a mouth organ. He'd been travelling for about 18 months since he had been made redundant and had decided to learn how to sail. He'd taught himself and to a pretty high standard, too – he'd learned astro navigation from a book and could pinpoint our location with the sun or moon, a sextant and a watch. He tried to teach me and was very patient, twisting his beard hair between thumb and forefinger, the very picture of a philosopher, while my brain turned to mush at all the complicated mathematics. Like a true American, he lived off peanut butter and said 'Y'all' a lot.

Chris and Hugo had gotten into a routine when it came to putting the anchor up and down, so I watched and learned from them. Sailing a catamaran, it turns out, is not that different from sailing a yacht. There are the same lines to pull and sails to hoist but they have slightly sillier names, like reacher and screecher. The main difference is that when you have the sails up you don't heel over, so your drink stays where you put it on the table and you can walk from A to B without holding on to anything. There are two engines, and so two throttles to control, and a V-shaped bridle – a rope with a hook on the end – has to be attached to the anchor chain to keep it in between the two hulls, but that is about as tricky as it gets. Being on deck on a cat is fabulous – there's all that cockpit space for lounging around in and you don't have to sit with your face inches away from someone else's feet. On *Gillaroo* there was plenty of shade if you wanted it and plenty of sun if you didn't. And I haven't even got to the best part yet, my home away from home – the trampolines. On the bow were two large nets made from strong woven nylon webbing. Despite the name, they aren't for bouncing on; they are strong enough for crew to walk on while working but help reduce the overall weight of the catamaran and its windage. As long as it wasn't too wavy, which made the water splash up through the nets and drench me, I would lie for hours on those tramps, reading, listening to music, watching dolphins swimming underneath me and getting a wicked suntan. I can't explain to you how wonderful it was and how happy I was. In photos from that time I have an almost beatific glow (or maybe that was sweat and salt water?). Despite being in the sunshine the tramps were the coolest place on the boat, much cooler than inside, where the daytime temperature in the saloon resolutely sat at 36°C. The only downside to them – and it never put me off – was that if I dozed, I'd end up with a criss-cross pattern imprinted on my face/back/bum, depending on what position I'd been in when I'd fallen asleep, and two dead arms.

We stayed only one night in Langkayan before we started our passage straight to Kuching. I got the impression that Tyrone and the boys weren't overly enamoured with Borneo and were keen to leave Malaysia behind. I thought it was a shame they'd not had the chance to enjoy everything that I had, but maybe if you've just come from the tribal wilderness that is Papua New Guinea, everything else pales in comparison.

As the sun set, I did all the preparations I'd been shown for my first night watch, switching on the navigation lights, illuminating the instruments and changing the interior lights to red so they wouldn't affect my night vision when I went inside to check the computer and fill in the log book. As the sky darkened I was able to see lightning going off all around me, which was usual for Borneo. During the passage on *Kingdom* from Kuching to Miri we had seen lightning all night, every night, while we were offshore. I wasn't too worried about it. Until Tyrone stuck his head out to double-check everything was OK.

'Hmm,' he said. 'There's a lot of lightning about.'

'Yeah,' I replied, 'but it seems to be always like that round here.' I watched him watching the sky. It had started to rain. There were more flashes, doing little other than making the sky look pretty and angry at the same time – but then came a fork that speared its way down to sea level. Tyrone's eyes did the extreme widening thing I'd begun to notice and he dashed inside, came out with a rucksack and went on to the starboard bow. He stayed up there, fiddling with something, for what seemed like an age. In the dark, I couldn't see what he was doing but from time to time lightning flashes illuminated his bent back. The storm was getting closer. While I was waiting for him to finish, a bolt struck the sea directly in our path and at what I estimated to be only a few hundred metres from the boat. I stifled a little scream.

'What were you doing?' I asked, trying to sound nonchalant, when he came back into the cockpit.

'Putting up the lightning conductor.' The calmness of his voice was at odds with the agitation evident in his body language. We were both pretending to be cool.

I tried to keep calm as I sat, on my first night watch, on a stainless-steel chair (good conductivity, that stainless steel), by the stainless-steel helm, outside on a boat miles away from land and in the open sea. And with the storm getting closer and the lightning more frequent.

'What happens if we do get struck?' I asked Tyrone, all

casual, like. I was determined not to seem like a big, fat wuss.

'Then it's game over,' he said. Thankfully he was referring to the boat, not to our losing our lives. 'I can't afford to replace all of the instruments. I just don't have the money. So it'd be the end.'

Subtly, I moved my fingers off the steering wheel and lifted my feet from the floor. *Is it better not to be touching the floor when your boat is struck by lightning?* I wondered. *Or should you stand on one leg? Should I be wearing rubber shoes or would that make things worse? And it's a fibreglass floor but a metal chair with a foam cushion on it. So am I better off remaining sitting or getting up and standing? Shall I put my trainers on?* I didn't know enough about the physics of it all. My knowledge was limited to urban myths of parachutists dangling from electricity wires but surviving because they were mid-air and something vague about trees and golf courses. Chris would probably have known what to do but Chris was asleep and so now was Tyrone, on the sofa in the saloon.

So I sat there, helpless, my feet lifted and my hands tucked firmly into my pockets, awaiting my fate. And the storm passed and we were fine. Come 9pm I woke Tyrone and he took over, leaving the conductor dangling in the water, just in case. I went to my cabin and lay on top of the throbbing engine and tried to get some sleep before my alarm went off at 5.30am.

We sank into the easy rhythm of the watch system, each doing our six hours a day on the helm, sleeping when we could, eating, reading, chatting and generally lazing about. There were squalls with 30mph winds and heavy rain to disturb us from time to time – the temperature dropped to a chilly 29°C at one point – but otherwise it was pretty relaxed. *I* was relaxed. All the watchkeeping left a lot of time for contemplation and navel gazing and I could see, now I was on *Gillaroo*, how wound up I'd been on *Kingdom*. OK, so *Kingdom* was a nice boat to look at, with a fair few mod cons, but on *Gillaroo* I had more freedom to do what I wanted to, without the constant fear that I'd done something wrong. I got used to the quiet – no loud music blaring, no man (or cat) demanding to be entertained, pandered to or loved. It was as if I'd moved from a bustling city street into an empty sound-proofed room and it wasn't until the door closed behind me that I realised how chaotic and stressful it had been. With no rent to pay on board the catamaran, money was no longer a worry. And everyone on board was single and seemed happy to be so, so there was none of that pressure I'd felt back home. It was just about living in the moment and only thinking about the immediate task at hand, which was the journey we were making. Plus, with a boat weighing only four tonnes, we were doing a lot of sailing. If the big flappy things being filled with wind weren't a dead giveaway of that, the facts that I hadn't showered for two days, that absolutely all of my clothes were wet and that I was feeling sticky, salty – and gloriously happy – definitely were.

On the fourth morning of the week-long passage I came up into the cockpit from my afternoon snooze to find a couple of guests on board with us. Two egrets, tired of flying, had decided to hitch a ride on the boat and find what shelter they could from winds of 20 knots.

'That's Henry,' Hugo said, pointing to the bird on the coach roof. Henry had hunkered down, his chin into his chest, and braced himself, knees splayed backwards, talons slipping on the solar panel and eyes blinking against the wind. Handily for us, he had a habit of turning his head directly into the wind, so with one glimpse at him we could tell what the apparent wind angle was.

'And that's Morgan,' Chris added, pointing behind me. I looked down on to the steps of the port hull at the back of the boat. There, on the middle of the three steps, stood an identical bird: white, about a foot and a half tall, with a yellow beak and suspicious eyes. Morgan had picked a more sheltered spot so he was more sure-footed and able to extend his long neck and turn his head to get the best view of us.

'Morgan?' I asked. 'As in the Captain's rum?'

'As in the Captain's rum,' Chris nodded. As I watched, we bounced on a large wave and Morgan was flung into the air. But he wasn't giving up his comfortable perch that easily: he flapped his wings, hovered above the boat and lowered himself back into his favourite spot again. Later in the day a flock of six egrets circled overhead, getting a better look at us. Tyrone didn't want any more of them. 'They'll shit everywhere,' he said.

They were both still with us the next morning when I came on watch but Morgan had inched his way forward into the cockpit itself. He was getting braver. Henry, who had an identifying yellow mark on his forehead, remained stubbornly in his precarious, slippery position. We had a go at feeding them, tossing them tuna and bread, but they weren't interested. I tried tempting Henry with a flying fish I'd found on deck. I swear his eyes lit up when he saw it and he took half a step towards me but when he realised it was dead he turned his beak up at it. No one saw him move but Henry appeared in the cockpit, too. Morgan clearly didn't like this encroachment on his territory and attacked him; Henry retaliated and they had a pecking fight, flapping their wings and circling each other. They backed off and stared beadily at each other and then launched into their scrap again, pausing for breath with their heads and beaks entwined, like boxers falling into a clinch after a particularly strenuous bout. They started up again. 'Boys!' I chided them and they stopped immediately and moved apart. They must have declared a truce.

'Where's Henry?' Hugo asked later in the afternoon. We searched all over the boat for him but no joy. Surely he hadn't had the strength to fly away – he'd not eaten or drunk for two days. So had he fallen or jumped overboard, or had he been pushed? Morgan was chilling, his head tucked under one wing, the picture of innocence.

He had moved right up to the helmsman's chair, which was better for us because in his old position he kept standing on the sheets we needed to pull. As time passed he allowed us to stroke him; his feathers were cold to the touch. It was tempting to think we had tamed him but he was probably just too exhausted to put up a fight. Small, brown, sparrow-like birds visited us from time to time, too, struggling in the gusts to cling on to the guard rails with their tiny feet. One canny fellow sought shelter in the galley. Chris picked it up and brought it outside, laying it on a cushion. It rested for a few minutes and then, when his back was turned, flew straight back into the galley again. Tyrone picked it up this time and put it out of the front saloon window. It was blown straight into the sea.

Dolphins were swimming near the boat and snakes and jellyfish were wriggling their way under it. And don't forget the ants and the cockroaches – and a big spider that decided the best place in the whole of the boat to live was on my pillow. ('Ty-ro-one... I know I'm a 32-year-old grown-up but can you please get that thing off of there?'). Gerald Durrell had nothing on us.

By 6am, Morgan was dead. At least, that's what Chris told me.

'Morgan's dead,' were his exact words. There was no beating around the bush with that man. Next to him, on the seat, a feathery corpse lay, splayed in the ungainly position he had collapsed in.

'What are we going to do with him?' I asked Chris.

He rubbed his nose. 'Throw him overboard?'

'I suppose we have to,' I said, sighing. 'But I'm not doing it.'

'What?'

'I hate dead things. Can't touch them. You saw me with that flying fish – I had to pick it up with a piece of paper. Nope. You've got to do it.'

Chris gave Morgan a tentative poke – neither of us knew how to take a bird's pulse – and he twitched. Not quite dead, then. More in a birdy, vegetative state.

'Oh come on,' Chris said, after another ten minutes. 'We've got to put him out of his misery.' He picked up the bird with both hands. 'Ah, dude, we were so nearly in Kuching. If only y'all could have held on a while longer.' Morgan lifted his head a little bit and looked Chris in the eye. The next second he was floating on the water, the South China Sea becoming his vast, watery grave. Apart from all the memories we had something else to remember him by – his poop, which he had left all over the boat.

12

Singapore Fling

It took us a further four days to sail across the South China Sea from Kuching to Singapore, and with good winds our speed topped 9.2 knots. The winds were too good at one point – we ripped the clew clean off the jib and the mainsail reefing lines got caught in one of the wind turbines, breaking the blades. The first few days were choppy and when I wasn't on watch I felt too sick to do anything more than sleep or lie around listening to music. When the waves died down I turned my hand to cooking, whipping up loaves of bread, batches of yoghurt and trays of chocolate brownies. It was all pretty calm until we got closer to land again. With Singapore being an island off the southern tip of the Malay peninsula, it is a very busy place for shipping to converge. Think about all of the goods we buy that are made in China, Taiwan or Japan. They have to get here somehow, and they often do so on the back of container ships. Those enormous lorries you see on the motorway, which create so much turbulence that they try to blast your car out of the middle lane when you overtake them? The steel containers those lorries carry have come to our shores on the back of a ship, piled high among hundreds of identical boxes. The cargo ships are gigantic, sometimes hundreds of metres long, they weigh thousands of tonnes and they shoot through the seas at 20 to 30 knots. That might not sound like much to a land lubber, but consider that the best speed I was doing on *Gillaroo* under full sail was just over 9 knots, and, on *Kingdom*, 7 knots. And then add in the fact that these ships have no brakes; it can take them a mile to do an emergency stop, which they perform by throwing their engines into full reverse thrust, and they can't exactly turn on a dime, either. So they are basically the biggest bulldozers in the world, there are hundreds of them and they are all aiming for the same small gap, slingshotting around Singapore, at the same time. And we, in our little floaty catamaran, which was made of a bit of lightweight foam sandwiched between a couple of sheets of plastic, were heading for that small gap as well. At night all we could see of them were a few white, red and green lights, from which we were supposed to be able to decipher whether they were heading towards us, away or if they were going to collide with us. It was a mind fuck.

Even the brainiac needed help – Chris woke me up during his night watch to help navigate through the maze of ships that all seemed to be aiming straight at us. We had a gadget called AIS that sent us little text messages telling us which direction the ships were heading in and their speed, and it plotted their positions and courses on a radar screen. You had to be able to understand how a radar screen works to use it, otherwise it just looks like a lot of little sperms wriggling their way across a Space Invaders game machine. Between the two of us we managed to manoeuvre between anchored and moving ships without being sunk. Go, team! The smug, we're-so-clever attitude didn't last long: we hit a reef when coming in to anchor and, after the sun had set, discovered we had illegally stopped in Indonesian waters, rather than Malaysian ones. Indonesia in some places is closer to Malaysia than the UK is to France. Who knew?

By night, the city scape of Singapore was beautiful, all skyscrapers and multi-coloured lights. After weeks of blackest Borneo rainforest views, it was a bit of a shock to the system. Tyrone was eager to move the boat as soon as possible the next morning, first to get out of Indonesia before the coastguard spotted us and fined us, arrested us or chopped off our hands, and second to get across the shipping lane. We needed to be the other side of the straits, closer to Singapore, to get to Johor Bahru on the Malaysian mainland. In theory it was a bit like crossing the road, as there was a straight line of traffic going west straight ahead of us and another line going east just behind that. Except we couldn't see the ships in the dark – the only way we could tell where they were was by watching the buildings on the land and waiting until their lights went out, meaning a ship had passed between them and us, obscuring our view. Obviously there are no road markings in the sea but we knew when we were at the edge of the shipping lane by referring to our GPS, so we motored along, waited for a gap, gritted our teeth and gunned it, maxed out, put the pedal to the metal. At 4 knots. That's about walking speed. And have I mentioned those big ships couldn't stop?

Obviously we made it through (otherwise you wouldn't be reading this now) and safely moored the boat in Johor Bahru, at the southern tip of the Malay peninsula, a stone's throw from Singapore. Danga Bay marina was the Skegness of the Far East, a sprawling site that included a mall of tacky souvenir shops, an outdoor market of food stalls, a couple of bars that no one visited, a fishing area, a theme park and a zoo. Rumour had it that the owners of Danga Bay had bought up an entire amusement park that the Sultan of Brunei no longer wanted and had transported it across the South China Sea to Johor Bahru. At night, particularly on Thursdays and Fridays, the Islamic weekend, the whole place lit up like a Christmas tree and families strolled around, chatting away. The haphazard layout of the park lent itself to dark nooks and crannies and it was popular with courting teenage couples, who sat on the benches and talked. The boys wore their best pressed jeans; the girls heels and headscarves. I never saw any kissing, sitting-on-laps or even hand-holding.

Danga Bay was the place to take stock and knuckle down to some work on the boat. A fridge engineer was called out, the sun shades were taken off and sent away to be patched up, Tyrone changed the engine filters and Hugo, Chris and I spent a dirty day dismantling all seven winches, cleaning the parts in petrol, regreasing them and trying to remember how they all fitted back together. I bought flights to the UK and back so I could make my brother's wedding in six weeks' time. Hugo booked his plane ticket home to New Zealand; Tyrone accepted another Kiwi called Aaron as his replacement. Tyrone and I took our damaged jib into Singapore on the bus and the MRT to be repaired, looking at immigration on the border like we were dragging a dead body in a bag, and I had my first taste of city life in ages – hello aircon, tea and cake and Topshop.

I went back by myself a couple of days later, lured by the appealing prospect of books, a new dress and some tampons (very difficult to find in Malaysia). At first I felt right at home. Singapore's malls, with their escalators, chrome and limestone styling and mix of designer and high street brands, are just like London's. But gradually I became aware of how much I stuck out as I walked among the locals. Ethnic Chinese and western expats alike were dressed in winter fashions despite the 30°C+ heat outside, with pale, made-up faces and conditioned, poker-straight hair. I was unfashionably tanned, I had coarse, sun-bleached hair and my rubber flip-flops were just not appropriate among the leather boots and über-cool trainers. After half a day I had had enough and went back to the boat, where I could kick off my flip-flops, put on my faded board shorts and happily pad around barefoot again.

A wide variety of boats filled the marina. Most, like us, were passing through, although many looked as though they had been 'passing through' for a few months now. Every day there was the sound of drills, planes and other power tools being deployed to plug holes, mend decks and fix rotting interiors. One catamaran had been there so long the occupants had turned half of one of its hulls into a planter. Next to us was a boat called *Incognito* with a young British man on it, Guy, a scuba instructor/computer nerd. He was waiting for crew to arrive before moving north to Thailand. The first thing I noticed about him was his hair – there was a lot of it. He had old-fashioned mutton chops, like Mr Darcy, and wore a pony tail. The second thing I noticed was his devastating good looks – a twinkle in his eyes and a smile so broad and dazzling it could have featured in a toothpaste commercial. The third was that he appeared to have a sort of girlfriend. A French woman, Sylvie, from one of the other boats, was constantly hanging around his yacht.

Our new crewmate Aaron turned up, a few days early, before Hugo had even left, smelling strongly of Nivea suncream – he was a redhead with pale skin (and a lot of tattoos). Sailing on the equator wouldn't have been my first choice if I had been him. We did the round of introductions and Tyrone gave him a tour of the boat. I was going to the supermarket to get more food for us and Aaron offered to come with me.

On his feet were leather sandals held in place by just one strap over the big toe. I noticed them because the front edge ended in a point that extended a couple of inches past his toes and curled up into the air, like some kind of strange gnome footwear. He also had a hat with bells on it. *Hmm, looks like we might have a hippy on our hands*, I thought as we walked to the bus stop.

He was a talkative chap – a welcome addition, in my opinion – and pretty well travelled. He had done his OE (overseas experience) in the UK and the previous year had travelled solo through South East Asia and some of the Arab states. He told me his ex-girlfriend, who he had remained close to, had died of a brain tumour in the spring, and it had put things into perspective for him about what was important in life. He was hoping his current partner could join *Gillaroo* in Thailand and sail to Europe with him.

I liked Aaron immediately and we became firm friends – real friends this time, with no hidden agenda – but I think he was more of a girl's man than a man's man. Not that he wasn't masculine: he had motorbikes and a VW Beetle, he knew his way around engines, he worked out and had the inverted triangle kind of torso that men's fitness magazines have based their industry on. His enthusiasm for travel, for getting the most out of life and not sticking to the well-trodden path just because it was expected of you, infected me.

Some of his theories were slightly too hippy for me, however. One he firmly believed in was manifestation.

'What are you on about?' I asked him as we lounged in the shade of the cockpit, barely able to keep the cynicism out of my voice.

'If you want something strong enough, the universe will manifest it for you,' he said.

I snorted. 'Manifest?'

'Yeah, you know, make it happen.'

'Yes, I know what manifest means.' I closed my eyes and held out my hand. 'Dear Universe, I'd really like a Cadbury's Dairy Milk.' I made a show of opening one eye at a time to peer at my empty palm. 'See?' I needled. Aaron took my scepticism in good humour.

But as time went on some of what he believed, especially about doing what you want to in life, even if it involves going against the conventional flow, started to chime with me and subtly change the way I thought about myself.

In my darkest moments I thought that what I was doing, here in Malaysia, was running away from failing at 'real life' in England. I didn't think this way most of the time but the negativity was buried in my subconscious somewhere. The way Aaron explained things made me think. I wasn't running away; I was exploring. So I didn't have a conventional 2.4 life. So what? I had *this* life – this interesting, ever-changing, free-running, go-with-the-flow, beautiful, calm yet exciting life. And that was no bad thing.

For centuries the Malacca Straits were notorious for pirates. Ships laden with valuable spices bound for Europe had no choice but to pass through the narrow channel between Indonesia and Malaysia as they set sail homewards with the north-easterly trade winds, taking their chances against the fearless cut-throat bugis who patrolled the waters, looking for boats to pillage and crews to murder. Today, piracy in these waters is fairly uncommon – it is the Somali bounty-hunters further west that the shipping companies have to worry about. Nevertheless, the Straits do have their dangers for a small sailing vessel: sumatras, ships and fishing nets.

Sumatras – the fierce, sudden squalls that are thrown up by the steep Indonesian terrain west of the Straits – were unavoidable no matter what route we took. They can bring gusty winds of 50 or 60 knots, fierce enough to rip sails in half (we had had first-hand experience of this, when the jib tore on our approach to Singapore), and downpours of the kind of rain that feels like needles when it is blown horizontally on to bare legs by the wind.

Tyrone opted to take an offshore route, close to the shipping lane, to have the best chance of avoiding submerged fishing nets, which could get caught in our propeller and stop us dead in the water. So that left us with the shipping to negotiate, which was meant to be confined to the designated lanes a couple of miles off our port side. It didn't quite work out like that.

We didn't settle into the easy, rhythmic routine of the other passages I'd done on *Gillaroo*. We started off sailing but the wind was strong and unpredictable and we were constantly putting sails up and down, reefing and fiddling with them to keep our speed high and the chances of damaging the already well-worn sails low. After a short while the wind came round on to the nose and, as tacking would have been a lot of effort in those conditions and with a small sea space, Tyrone decided we would motorsail a very bumpy ride into it, so that we could keep our course. We tried to use one engine at a time, alternating them every few hours, to save fuel and wear and tear, but we found we had a problem with the steering so we had no choice but to use them both, constantly. They got so hot that a part of the exhaust system in the engine under my bed melted and the fire extinguisher went off, filling the chamber with powder and stopping the engine. I began to worry about fire – what if it overheated again, while I was sleeping on top of it, and now without an extinguisher?

And then there were the other boats. The long outlines of container ships, grey rectangles on the horizon, were our constant companions. But, unlike the captains of the bigger vessels, the local fishermen didn't feel that they had to stick to maritime law and when the ships peeled off from the shipping lane to head into Port Dixon or Malacca, it was every man for himself.

I was sleeping in my cabin, waiting for my 3am to 6am watch to start, when shouts woke me. I sat up, straining to listen over the throb of the engine and the roar of the wind. Chris was calling for Tyrone. I scrambled into a T-shirt and picked up my glasses, and as I lowered myself down to the floor I glanced out of the window and saw a green light really close to us. Dangerously close. Outside, because I had been in a deep sleep, it took me a few seconds to get a grasp of what was going on. Chris was at the helm and there were ropes all over the cockpit. Tyrone and Aaron were already on the coach roof, struggling to get the mainsail down in the wind and the dark. The green light belonged to a small fishing boat off our starboard bow and we had narrowly missed it. Just beyond that was a small ship, which must have turned right out of the shipping lane to cut across our path to the mainland. I could see its green light, which was on its starboard side and meant it was heading east, moving away from us.

I glanced down at the winch and struggled for a few seconds with tangled ropes before I could release the main sheet, looked up and the green light was gone. In its place was a red light, which meant the ship had turned 180 degrees and we were now just a hundred metres or so apart, moving towards each other. Everything went into slow motion. Tyrone yelled from the bow: 'Stop!' I froze. Did he mean for me to stop or Chris? 'Go back! Put it into reverse!' he screamed. Chris switched both throttles to full reverse and the engines whined as the propellers struggled against the momentum of the boat. The move slowed us down just enough that we missed the ship by maybe 20 metres. It wasn't as large as a container transporter but it would have caused us serious damage, perhaps even wrecked the catamaran, if it had hit us. Tyrone was furious and tried hailing the ship on VHF but it ignored us. We didn't even know if it had seen us at all.

We were all pretty shaken by the near collision and Tyrone decided we wouldn't use any sail at all from now on, so that we had more manoeuvrability in case something went wrong again. What I didn't know was that it already had.

The next day, while Aaron was sleeping, Tyrone said to Chris and me: 'I think Aaron's going to get off the boat.' Before we almost collided with the small ship, Tyrone explained, there had been another incident.

'Aaron took us into the shipping lane and didn't notice there was a big ship coming up behind us,' Tyrone said, the calmness in his voice at odds with the seriousness of what he was telling us. 'He said to me that he couldn't handle the responsibility of watches and he doesn't think his girlfriend would be able to, either.'

Chris and I looked at each other, stunned. It was a shock – Aaron had flown all this way, with plans to stay for months, and we had only been sailing for a few days. He had done a couple of night watches, with Tyrone awake in the saloon during them, and it was understandable to be rattled by a couple of near crashes. The Malacca Straits was proving to be a particularly horrible crossing for all of us but it wasn't at all typical of the cruising experience.

Aaron painted a slightly different picture of what had happened when we were talking about it later. He said that he had wanted to look at our course on MaxSea but that Tyrone had been using the computer and he hadn't wanted to keep disturbing him.

'And I said we should tack and Tyrone said, "In 10 minutes",' he added. By then, we were already in the shipping lane.

Who knew which was the true version of events? Probably the blame lay somewhere in the middle, but it didn't really matter. And there was no persuading Aaron into giving it another shot. As well as being a bit nervous of the responsibility, he was also majorly bored, and being cooped up on a small boat meant he had no way of burning off his excess energy. He wasn't a reader or a thinker like the rest of us; he needed to be doing things.

'Five days of this is bad enough,' he said. 'There's no way I could handle two weeks of it across the Indian Ocean.' So when he left in Thailand, as Chris would too ('I'm done with sailing,' he said), we would have two new crew to find.

13

What a difference a day makes

Aaron was more than enthusiastic about our imminent crossing of the border from Malaysia to Thailand. It was only half a day's sail north from Langkawi in Malaysia, where we spent a few days before Tyrone checked us out of the country, to the first Thai island, Koh Lipe.

'You're going to love Thailand,' Aaron said. 'The water is clear, the food is great and the beer is cheap. Party, party!' he chanted. 'Whoop, boy!' He danced around the cockpit. 'I'm gonna go insane!' I looked doubtfully down at the greeny-brown, jellyfish-ridden water streaming past our hulls.

'But it's only a few hours away,' I replied. 'How can it be that different?'

'Just wait and see,' he said, grinning at me.

He was right. It was as if the water knew the international boundaries: greeny brown one side, beautiful blue and crystal clear the other. And he was right about everything else, too.

As we pulled into Koh Lipe ready to drop anchor, Chris laughed. 'Hey, y'all. Look, there's Guy's boat.' I looked at what he was pointing to and there was *Incognito* at anchor.

Despite leaving Danga Bay two weeks after him, we'd caught him up.

We were sheltered in a natural channel between the islands of Koh Lipe and Koh Adang. Both islands had white, sandy beaches, dotted with the odd bit of driftwood. From where we were I could see a beach bar on Koh Lipe and a couple of people milling about. How different it was from Malaysia. The sea was clear enough that we could see the bottom. I hadn't seen water like that since Mabul. Chris and Aaron jumped straight in and swam for shore. I followed in the dinghy and even felt inspired enough to have a short snorkel by myself, but there was little to see.

I passed *Incognito*'s dinghy as I walked in my swimsuit to the beach bar, where Aaron had headed to. He had a few Thai baht in the pocket of his shorts and was already sucking down his first beer. I had changed my remaining ringgit before we left Malaysia but I'd left it on the boat. Dammit! I looked longingly at his glass bottle (not a can to be seen!), with condensation running down the sides.

'Is OK,' said the barman. 'You pay later,' and handed me a Leo. I was liking Thailand already.

Guy and his new Canadian crewman, Pauly, emerged from a path between the trees. At the sight of Guy, my stomach did a little flip and I started to feel self-conscious, sitting there in my swimming costume. I tensed my abs, to pull my stomach flatter, realising that my physical reaction to Guy meant that I liked him.

'Yo, Guy!' Chris shouted, beckoning them over. They came to sit with us on the bar stools, made of polished tree trunks sunk into the sand, and we caught up. Now that I knew I was attracted to Guy, I couldn't look at him for long for fear of blushing. I looked at my beer bottle, at my toes digging into the soft sand, out at the boats, up at the palms above, anything to stop that tell-tale red from flushing my cheeks. I sneaked glances at little bits of him at a time – at his deep brown skin, his wide shoulders, his beautiful full mouth, his white, straight teeth, his thick brown hair, until I'd made a mental jigsaw. *He is so good looking*, I thought as I picked at the label of my beer, made soggy by condensation, *but I don't think he knows it*. His friend Pauly was handsome in an I-work-out-a-lot way but Guy obviously didn't really care about his appearance – his shorts were old and holey and he had the beginnings of a beer belly – but that made him even more attractive. He was magnetic to me.

Tyrone had told me to invite them over for dinner and I eventually plucked up the courage to ask. Pauly already had plans with some girls but 'I'm up for that!' was Guy's reply. He threw a huge, dazzling smile my way, holding eye contact for longer than was necessary. *Is he flirting with me? What about the French girlfriend?* 'What time?'

I looked at Aaron, whose turn it was to cook and who was planning a Mexican fajita feast.

'About seven thirty?' he asked.

'Oh, shit, I can't,' Guy said, frowning. 'I agreed to meet some friends at eight and I can't let them down. But you could come?'

We arranged to meet later and I had a grin on my face as I walked back to the dinghy with the boys.

The 'you' in his invitation had been general but I spent extra time getting ready after my bucket wash, leaving my hair down, putting on a short, bright red playsuit I'd bought in Singapore and putting in earrings. I told the boys – and myself – that I was making the effort because I could, now that we were free of the Malaysian modesty dress code, and because we were on a party island, but who was I kidding?

After dinner, Chris said he didn't want to go out and Tyrone wasn't interested, either, not being much of a drinker, so Aaron and I set off in the dinghy, dragging it up the beach and tying the painter to a stranded log. We walked along a jungle path in the dark until we could see lights ahead and emerged on to a cute little winding sand street lined with hut-like shops and restaurants. There were few people around and Thai families were taking advantage of the quiet time to eat rice and fish on the doorsteps of their shops, sitting on the floor and picking at the food with nimble fingers. I looked at everything as we walked along, noticing how everything was prettier than it was in Malaysia, more geared towards tourism. We passed a tattoo parlour where a white guy lay on his stomach having ink jabbed into his back by a Thai woman holding a length of bamboo with a needle sticking out from it. Most of the restaurants were empty and staff stood waiting patiently outside. There were fresh juice stalls and shops selling jewellery. We reached the tourist information centre, where Guy had told me I could buy some more baht, and I copied Aaron as he took off his gnome shoes ('Me jandals,' he called them) and walked barefoot inside. It was pretty low-tech: no computer, just a phone and some brochures for scuba trips and boat tours. They had one of those old-school card-swiping machines that rubs carbon paper over the card to leave an imprint of the information. While I waited for the woman to count out my money, I noticed what looked like a machine gun propped casually against the wall. I nudged Aaron. 'Do you think that's real?'

'Probably,' he nodded. I wondered why a shopkeeper on a

calm, sleepy island like this would need a machine gun.

Guy had told us to look for a bar called Pooh and that his friends' dive shop was behind it. We spotted the AA Milne character illuminated in blue and walked round it to the back.

It's not only the water clarity, landscape and culture that are different in Thailand; the time zone is, too. We were an hour late. But no one seemed to mind, and Guy's friend Neil went out to buy beers for us with his islander's discount. After a beer and within the group scenario I started to feel less tangled up inside around Guy and I was able to relax and talk and laugh with him just as I did with everyone else. Thoughts of the possible French girlfriend held me back from openly flirting with him.

From the dive shop we went to Pooh bar, where we had to leave our shoes outside. There was such a pile of discarded rubber flip-flops that I idly wondered if I'd be able to find my Havaianas again. There were no chairs in the bar, only fold-out mattresses to cushion our bums as we sat on the reed-matted floor or reclined like feasting Romans at low tables. This bar was the busiest place Aaron and I had seen when we did our little recce through the village and yet it was only about half full. The divers left and the three of us walked through the brush again, with our reclaimed footwear on, to a beach on the other side of Lipe, to sit on sun loungers in the dark and drink vodka and Red Bull.

In the humid evening, as a slight sea breeze blew salty air on to our faces, the conversation turned to relationships.

'If it was the right girl, I'd follow her anywhere,' Aaron said. I snorted but Guy nodded. *What was this? Two romantic guys and one cynical woman? Surely it should be the other way round?*

'Hannah wants to teach in England and I'll go with her, even though I've already been there, done that,' Aaron said. 'We'll just have to find another way of getting there now that I'm leaving *Gillaroo*.'

'You're leaving?' Guy asked. 'Why?'

Aaron told him what had happened in the Malacca Straits.

'Shit! That sounds like a nightmare,' Guy said, stretching back in his deckchair. 'Maybe you're better off out of that.'

'And you?' I asked. 'Why would you follow a woman?'

'I followed my ex to Germany,' he shrugged. 'Lived there for a year. Learned German.'

'Sprechen Sie deutsch?' I asked.

'Ja,' he said and followed it with a stream of German words I didn't understand.

'Ich bin elf Jahre alt,' I informed him, using the only German I could remember from secondary school. 'Ich möchte ein Erdbeereis.'

When we could drink no more, we walked back right across the island to our beach and our dinghies. As we got under the cover of trees again, and it was darker, Aaron walked a couple of metres in front and I dropped back to be level with Guy. We picked our way along the path and he took my hand and kept hold of it as we carried on walking. *OK, so he is definitely coming on to me now*, I decided, the warmth from his palm driving any concern about la femme française out of my mind. I had forgotten to pay the beach bar for my afternoon beer when we came ashore so I went off to settle my bill, all £1.20 of it, while Aaron fetched our dinghy. I thought Guy would be doing the same with his but when I turned away from the bar I could see him standing in the shadow of the trees on the path, waiting. Yes – there was a tall, gorgeous, travelling, sailing guy waiting for me under a gently rustling palm tree on a tropical, moonlit night. My stomach flipped again, my breath caught and I walked over to him. He pulled me close and kissed me.

As kisses went, it was a very good one. You can't get much more of a romantic setting than under swaying trees on a sandy beach by starlight. It was the full-on Hollywood works. All that was missing was a camera panning 360 degrees around us. It left my head spinning.

Guy and Pauly had a clear 'no bringing girls back' rule but Pauly was off chasing two Swedish girls that he'd met on the island, even though the one he liked most had a boyfriend, and he wasn't going to be returning to *Incognito* that night, unless he was thinking of making a swim for it.

'Does your boat rule mean no girl *visitors* are allowed?' I asked Guy, stressing the temporary nature of the noun.

'I think visitors are OK,' he said, smiling and turning towards the beach.

Aaron had already pulled *Gillaroo*'s dinghy into the water – the beer must have given him superhuman strength – and it was bobbing gently in the shallows.

'I'm going to go to *Incognito* for a tour,' I told him, trying to sound nonchalant while feeling ridiculously pleased with myself. 'See you later.'

It was tricky climbing on to the back of the narrow steps on *Incognito*'s transom and there were a lot of obstacles lying all over the rear part of the deck and in the cockpit – clothes, buckets, brushes, diving equipment, empty beer cans. It was absolutely tiny compared to *Gillaroo*, probably less than half her width. Inside was cramped, too, although bigger than it had been under the original design, as Guy and the friend he owned the boat with had cut away the front wall, joining the forepeak cabin into the main saloon. He gave me the tour, which took all of ten seconds, since I could see almost everything from where I stood at the bottom of the companionway steps. In layout it was similar to *Kingdom*, but shrunken down and with stuff everywhere. This was clearly a boys' boat. Doris Day had not been round to give it a 'woman's touch'. Saucepans were even – the horror! – left unwashed on the side. There was an aft cabin but it was used for storage, not sleeping, and so was the head.

'So where do you go to the toilet,' I asked, 'if it's full of stuff in here?'

'Over the back.'

'OK but what if, you know, you need a poo?'

'Still off the back,' he laughed.

'What, you just hang on and squat out over the sea?'

'Yeah. I call it the poop deck. And we use the outside shower as a bum gun.' Definitely a boys' boat.

Guy sat down on the sofa by the captain's table and flicked some switches on the control panel. A fan standing on the table sprang to life. He looked at me and patted his lap. I sat on his knee and he pulled me close again.

Kissing is difficult on a tiny boat. Unless you stand dead in the centre of the main cabin and don't move, there's no room for arms, legs, heads. Tables, fridges, spare bits of plumbing, books and cable ties all get in the way. To fit in between the furniture you have to contort yourself into an uncomfortable position that leads to a dead leg or arm or a cricked neck. You can try lying down but the sofas are too narrow to fit two people on and the floor is too hard. We settled on the forepeak bed, shoving tools and junk over to one side, and fell asleep, wedged in on our sides with our legs dangling in mid-air, my shoulder jammed up against the feeder pipe for the anchor chain that rudely cut through the centre of the bed and Guy's head bent back at an unnatural angle.

He ran me back to *Gillaroo* at 4am and I slept for a bit longer before Tyrone and Chris started fixing the rub rail, which was working loose, back on to the dinghy in the cockpit, inches away from my pounding head. I kept looking over at *Incognito* all through the day, hoping to catch sight of Guy so that I could wave or beckon him over, but he didn't emerge from the bowels of his yacht once. I knew he was still on board because his dinghy was tied on at the back. Was he regretting kissing me?

'See?' Aaron teased me when I was making my breakfast, his pale skin reddened from the sun. 'I manifested you a sailing boyfriend.'

'He's hardly my boyfriend,' I said, trying to be cool. 'And I'll probably never see him again.' Nevertheless, I copied down his email address from a piece of paper he'd given to Aaron.

'Are you lefting it now?' Aaron asked me later that afternoon, as we bobbed about in the sea off the back of the boat, holding on to the dinghy hoist pulleys to keep ourselves in one place. I sensed an explanation of another of his life theories coming up.

'Am I what-ing it?'

'Lefting it. Look.' He let go of the pulley hook with one hand to touch his nose. 'Breathe in through your nose. If more air goes in through your right nostril it means you're sad or unfulfilled or something.' He waved at his nose again and inhaled noisily. 'But if more air comes in through your left nostril it means you're really happy.'

I was sceptical but I tried it. 'It's hard to tell.'

'Try again.'

'Both the same,' I said.

'Ha.'

'But surely that means I'm balanced?' I said (and breathing properly, I didn't add). 'In yoga, when we do breathing exercises, we breathe through one then the other nostril to balance them out.'

'Well, I dunno about that. All I know is, it's good to be leftin' it.' He breathed deeply again, as if to double-check his nose was still content with his life choices.

14

My Thai

We had only a week to reach Phuket, where we had to clear into Thailand, and so we had to move on. As we left Koh Lipe the next morning, I felt gutted that I hadn't seen Guy again. It looked like he still hadn't come out of his boat. Could he really be that embarrassed and desperate to avoid me? I took a last, dejected look at *Incognito* as we pulled out of the bay. *Maybe it's better this way, as a perfect, romantic, brief encounter*, I tried to convince myself, *without everyday reality stepping in and spoiling things. Always look on the bright side, and all that*. I didn't entirely believe myself but there was nothing I could do about it.

Our next stop was Koh Muk, for the emerald cave. Apparently, at low tide we could pass in the dinghy through a low entrance in the rock and feel our way through to a beach that was actually inside the island. Low tide was at 7am and we had to zigzag up and down the face of Koh Muk before we spotted the way in. There were no strings of garish buoys to indicate where it was, no signs screwed to the rock, no man waiting to charge us 500 baht to go in. Just a hole in the cliff. Tyrone cut the throttle and we ducked our heads to pass under the overhanging grey rock and felt our way along the passage in the dark with our hands. As we finally emerged, blinking in the sudden bright sunlight, we found ourselves in the middle of a small, circular lagoon. It was stunning, so perfect it almost looked man-made. The water was bright turquoise, lit up by the white sandy bottom. A pristine beach curved in the opposite direction to the wall of rock we had just emerged from, forming an eye shape, and beyond the beach were coconut palms, stretching up towards the light coming from the wide circular opening above us. The rocks formed steep grey cliffs all around. It was absolutely beautiful and we were the only ones there.

After we had whooped and clapped, listening for echoes, I paddled through the water, thinking about how lucky we were to be able to come here by yacht. The emerald cave was a popular tourist attraction and presumably later in the day the peace would be disturbed by the roar of boats pulling up, laden with passengers who would swim through the entrance and fill up the beach. Surely they couldn't experience this in the same way as us? If I had come here with my mates, hungover, on a £30 boat trip with a bunch of strangers, I wouldn't enjoy it half as much as I was doing now. The four of us, Tyrone, Aaron, Chris and I, had fallen into a reverential silence and the high tide had wiped away any traces of the previous day's visitors from the beach. I felt a magical and almost spiritual connection to the natural beauty of the earth.

What Tyrone and Aaron were feeling was not quite as deep. 'Elvis was 'ere', Tyrone wrote in the sand with a stick. Aaron gleefully scribbled, 'Hello, tourists!' We scarpered before anyone else arrived.

The further north up the coast of Thailand we went, it seemed, the busier it got. Koh Phi Phi was a horrible, frantic maze of a place, swarming with boats and sunburned chavs. Phi Phi Don, the bigger of the two islands there, is shaped like an hourglass, with a bay on either side. The first side we tried to anchor in was horribly rocky-rolly with wash thrown up by ferries and tourist boats so we tried Lohdalum Bay: much calmer but with huge coral bommies sticking up almost to the water's surface, so we had to anchor quite a way out and Tyrone said no one could go ashore after sunset because it would be too complicated and dangerous to try to navigate through them in the dark. Not that I minded much: the place was a nasty seething mass of tattooed, semi-naked people looking to get drunk, high and laid. I took one trip ashore in the daytime, to get cash from the ATM, and that was enough for me. The narrowest part of the island had been rebuilt after the tsunami as a warren of alleyways lined with restaurants, clothes stalls, dive shops, internet cafes. It was poky and bewildering and easy to get lost. As I waited for the ATM to dispense my notes, a group of drunk Scousers came up behind me. 'Fookin 'ell, warra cunt,' one said. Nice. Especially at three in the afternoon. Flying the great British flag abroad.

I stuck to the boat after that, trying to ignore the hideous human aspects of the island (difficult when house music is being blasted out on the beach from dusk to dawn) and concentrate on enjoying the natural beauty of Phi Phi instead. We were anchored off a small beach that was supposed to have monkeys on it. At least, that was what we cleverly assumed: it was called Monkey Beach. At dawn, Chris, Aaron and I took the dinghy ashore to try to catch them at play, even taking some apples and longans as gifts, but they were in hiding. On the dinghy ride back to *Gillaroo*, though, we spotted something much more exciting.

'Is that dolphins?' Chris asked, jerking his head seawards.

'What? Where?' I asked. Surely they wouldn't come this close to land? We often saw them when we were well offshore but why would they come here, with the noise and boat traffic and snorkellers everywhere?

And yet come they did. A school of about eight of them surfaced a couple of hundred metres away. I gunned the throttle and sped over to where we'd seen them, dropping us into neutral as we approached so that I wouldn't damage any protruding fins with the propeller. They popped up again, back where we had just come from. And so began a five-minute game of cat and mouse, or dolphin and dinghy, as we dashed to and fro. We got pretty close to them in the end, about 10 metres or so away, before they vanished.

Aaron and I decided to take the third boat in our collection, the canoe, for a spin. Well, with my spindly arms, a slow paddle was more accurate. Each time I'd been in the canoe before, Chris or Aaron had been in the front seat and I had sat in the back. For some reason this time we got in the other way round and it was a complete disaster. With the strength coming from Aaron in the back, his paddle acted like a rudder, steering us to one side with every stroke he did and, no matter how hard I tried to dig mine into the water, I couldn't counteract it. We were a long way off from the boat before we worked out why we weren't able to go in a straight line.

'There's some rocks up there,' Aaron said, indicating an outcrop at the foot of a cliff. 'If we can get there we can switch seats.' Easily said; not so easily done. Canoes are not stable things to stand up in, even less so when waves are crashing up against the rock you are leaning on with one hand, and you're afraid of falling into the water in case you're dashed against the near-vertical cliffs. Somehow, wobbling a lot, we managed it and it was so much better. Off we paddled, scanning the rock face for a gap I thought I'd seen when we'd been coming in to anchor. I had had a funny feeling that there would be a sheltered lagoon beyond the gap, like at Koh Muk, but it was just a hunch. For all I knew, it was just a brief, natural indentation in the hundred-metre-tall cliff. The waves were big rollers, lifting us up and down a good metre or so every few seconds. We were a long way from the beach and the drivers of the engine-powered tourist boats that came shooting around the corner towards us gave us quizzical looks when they saw we were so far from the allocated areas – and not wearing lifejackets. But we persevered and, just when I was beginning to think I'd imagined it, we found the gap and, inside, a sheltered long, thin, natural harbour that hooked backwards and had a very small beach at the far end of it.

Dragging the canoe up the sand, we stood to take stock of our surroundings. The remnants of hammocks, half rotted away, hung from a couple of trees and there were some wooden platforms built into the rock face, like hideaway huts. It was decrepit but all the more picturesque for it. A circle of blackened stones and ash on the beach told of campfires and secret parties. There was a red and white sign screwed into the rock but it was in Thai so if it was telling us we were not allowed in this place, then we were blissfully in ignorance. (Later I found out it was a protected area for swifts to settle without fear of humans stealing their nests and turning them into soup.)

It was the peaceful beauty of places like this that started to attract people to these Thai islands in the first place. The Leonardo DiCaprio movie *The Beach* was filmed on Phi Phi Lay, the neighbouring island, and that beach's remote loveliness had led to Phi Phi Don's overcrowded tackiness. People came here expecting to find an empty paradise like in the film and what they got was boat- and hotel- and beach-loads of others all coming for the same thing. And the more that came, the worse it got. Little pieces of paradise, like the one Aaron and I had found, were still left and I hoped they would remain that way.

It was forbidden to anchor at Phi Phi Lay, Guy had told Tyrone, but if you were lucky you could take one of the mooring buoys after the daytripper boats had left for the evening. I was curious to see this famed beach and judge for myself if it was all it was cracked up to be. We planned to reach the bay in the late afternoon and keep our fingers crossed that there would be a mooring free.

In the movie the secret beach is surrounded on all sides by cliffs, like a bigger version of the emerald cave we had seen at Koh Muk. In reality, it is a sharply concave bay but open on one side to the sea. That made our entry easier – no jumping off waterfalls. There were no moorings free when we got there so we sat tight, the engine idling, watching people from the daytrip boats swimming and larking about. By five o'clock they had all gone and, apart from two other cruising boats, we had the bay to ourselves. To be fair, it was a breathtakingly spectacular place, with a deep beach, jungle at the back and high, sheer cliffs all the way around. And the Thai authorities had done a good job of recognising what they had and holding on to it. The only development was a small campsite hidden behind the jungle, where people could stay on closely supervised overnight trips.

It took me all of five minutes to explore the campsite, following the sandy path that had been cut between the trees, and then I was back on the beach again. Tyrone was sitting on a wooden bench, talking to an older man with neat, short white hair, sensible round spectacles and a grey moustache. The man was wearing only a pair of shorts and the skin of his naked upper half was well weathered.

'Hello,' I said, going over to join them.

'Hello,' the man said. 'Would you like some rum?' He passed me a flask of neat Bacardi. I took the tiniest sip and it burned the back of my throat.

The tan, the rum and the overall weathered look led me to presume he was on one of the other cruising boats and the conversation turned to the usual yachtie talk: where have you come from? Where are you going? How was the weather? The tide? Current conditions?

'Oh, the tide is a big problem for me,' the man said. 'If it is stronger than two knots I go backwards.'

I frowned, looking at the boats on the moorings and then back at the stranger. *Gillaroo*'s 4 knots under engine was the slowest I had come across before.

'Your yacht can only do two knots?' I asked him, confused.

'Oh no,' he laughed. 'I am not in a yacht. It is just me and my kayak.'

Detlev, it emerged, was a German who lived on Koh Samui

with his Thai wife and children and ran a resort. For his holidays he liked to fasten his kayak on to the roof of his car, drive it somewhere and paddle off.

'This is it,' he said, proudly, walking us over to a small kayak parked high up the sand.

'Where do you stay? Where do you sleep?' I asked him, slightly incredulous.

'Oh, I have everything I need. I have my tent, my tea and of course my rum.' He waved the bottle. I looked again at the kayak. One of the seat spaces was empty, the other was packed with his belongings.

'And how long are you away for?' I asked Detlev.

'Oh, about a week. Already I go to Phi Phi Don. Now I would like to go to Phuket. But I think it is a long way. Perhaps you can kindly let me see your charts?'

'You don't have charts?' Tyrone asked.

'So how do you know where you are going?' I wanted to know.

'I have my compass,' he said, pulling an old-fashioned compass from his pocket, 'and if I know how far away the next island is, I know if I can get there in one day.'

I don't think my eyebrows could have risen any higher on my head. 'So you just point in the right direction and keep going until you reach land?'

'Yes. It is good fun.'

This had to be one of the craziest things I had ever heard. But at the same time I felt a deep admiration for this little old man, who looked like he weighed barely more than eight stone. He was an adventurer proper, doing it old school.

'So I come to your boat in the morning and you show me the charts?' he asked. We agreed.

He turned up while Tyrone and Chris were still out canoeing the whole circumference of Phi Phi Lay. I heard his greeting and went outside to see him paddling on the spot alongside the starboard hull. He had brought his own tea with him and I brewed a pot and showed him the computer.

'Hum,' he frowned, peering at the screen. 'I think maybe it is too far to go to Phuket.' He finished his tea and shrugged. 'So, OK, I go again to Phi Phi Don. Thank you for showing me this. You save me a lot of trouble.'

And with that he got back into his kayak, taking his jar of tea leaves with him, consulted his compass, and paddled off into the distance.

15

Close encounters of the turd kind

If I thought Phi Phi Don was bad, it was nothing compared to Ao Chalong in Phuket. So far we had been in Thai waters for a week without stamps in our passports or visas and we had to check in in Phuket with customs, immigration and the harbour master. The harbour was vast and absolutely chock-a-block with anchored boats: cruising yachts and catamarans, dive boats, tourist boats and, worryingly, the odd wreck. Because Ao Chalong was the main port of call for visiting yachts, some clever government official had set up a one-stop shop with all the various checking-in authorities housed in one building. It went very smoothly and quickly until I saw a sign on the wall that said anyone who arrived in Thailand by boat had to leave Thailand by that same boat or, if they wanted to leave by other means, have to forfeit a bond of 20,000 baht. I had to fly back to England for my brother's wedding and Aaron and Chris were going to leave under their own steam. None of us wanted to pay £400 to leave the country. 'You go main immigration office,' the man behind the counter said. 'Talk them.'

The immigration office was in the town centre so the following day we set off in the direction of the main road the official had roughly pointed out to us to flag down a taxi. To get there we had to walk along a decrepit street lined with seedy bars and massage parlours. Thai women in tiny clothes shouted hello to us as we passed, trying to persuade us to go in for a drink. They looked nothing like the beautiful and elegant air hostesses I'd seen on my flight out to Borneo and instead had bloated bellies forced into cheap polyester vest tops and brightly-painted faces that looked squarely masculine in the harsh morning light. Every bar we passed on a street maybe half a mile long was like that. There were no customers at 11am.

I dreaded a huge queue at immigration but we went straight in and were seen immediately. I explained my problem and a woman official told me, yes, there was this bond to pay. And I could only pay by cash. It was a fair way to a bank, apparently, and I wasn't really sure if I could withdraw £400 in one single transaction.

'I speak my boss,' she said, and picked up her mobile, said something in Thai and passed the phone to me.

I must pay the bond, the man on the other end told me, who spoke good English. I could claim it back after I left Thailand the second time. *But how would I do that?* I wondered. *I wouldn't be in the country any longer to get the cash.* Or, he continued, I could pay an agency a fee to put up the bond for me. The fee, which worked out at about £30, was non-refundable. I opted for definitely losing out on £30 rather than possibly never seeing £400 again and they gave me a pile of forms to fill in and stapled some paperwork into my passport. Chris and Aaron decided to take their chances at the border when they left the country. If they were blacklisted and banned from entering Thailand again it didn't matter, they shrugged. But I had paid for flights and I was due to get back on to *Gillaroo* after the wedding so I needed to be sure I could return.

Aaron left that very afternoon – I think the draw of some partying friends in Koh Phangang was too strong to put off for a moment longer. 'Remember – keep leftin' it,' he called out over his shoulder as I waved him off into a van. Chris went the morning after, leaving me his broken guitar to bury at sea in the Indian Ocean. And then *Gillaroo* was down to a crew of just two.

I hated Ao Chalong so much that I was itching to get away but I still had a week to go before my flight back to England. I dug out the piece of paper that I had written Guy's email address on. I knew that he was due to be in Koh Lanta now, renting an apartment on land for the winter season. I turned the paper over in my hand, wondering if I had the gall to email him and invite myself over for a while. I got out my laptop and stared at the screen, biting my lip. He had reassured me on Koh Lipe that there was no French girlfriend, so that wasn't the problem. My fingers hovered over the keys, poised to write, but the fact that I wasn't sure how he felt about our evening together stayed me and I shut the lid sharply. I got up from the saloon table and made myself a drink, staring into the depths of the cup. I desperately wanted to escape being stuck on anchor in this shithole, I reasoned with myself, and I could use that as an excuse for a 'friendly' visit. I could tell myself that until I was blue in the face but the reality was that I wanted to see Guy again and this might be my last chance. I fired off a brief email in a brave moment.

'Sure,' he replied after a couple of anxious hours. 'Come for a visit. I'll have an apartment sorted by tomorrow and you can stay with me.' Excellent news – he apparently wasn't avoiding me after all.

It took a mini van and two ferries to get to Lanta. The first ferry, from Phuket to Phi Phi Don, was jampacked full of foreigners who stripped off to their bikinis and stayed outside on the deck for the fast, windy ride, efficiently using every available second of tanning time. I went inside, to sit on the chairs in the air-conditioning, and watched touts clambering through the stretched-out legs of the sunbathers, showing them photo albums of hotel rooms, offering them the best rates, free taxi rides, their first-born children. They pushed and pushed to get a sale or even an agreement to just take a look at the proffered photos. But they didn't give me any hassle. 'I am staying with my friend,' I said and they smiled and moved on. Perhaps the tan made me look like a long-termer – there was precious little money to be made from the semi-permanent farangs.

'I'll pick you up on the bike,' Guy had texted. 'Let me know when you get in.'

He pulled into the car park looking every inch the Easy Rider in his shorts and T-shirt, sunglasses on, hair tied back and with his wide smile. I climbed on casually, trying to look as cool as him.

'Emma, don't lean when we go round corners or you can tip the bike over,' Guy shouted backwards over his shoulder to me as we went along. Seemed I wasn't all that cool. I tightened my grip on his waist.

We went straight to his apartment – which turned out to be one room and most of that was taken up by a bed. He had a little fridge, a desk and chair and a TV and little else. *Looks like we'll be sharing, then*, I thought. *Maybe he does like me too*. I tried to get a grip on my giddiness and act normally.

'Beer?' he asked. I took a can of Skol – the cans were back! – and we sat on the bed, drinking and talking about what we'd been up to since we'd last met. He told me he'd felt really ill the day after we went out on Lipe and had been laid up in bed for a few days, worried that it was a second bout of the dengue fever he'd had earlier in the year. *Yay! No avoiding!*

'They call it break-bone fever,' he said, 'and now I know why. It really does feel like your bones are breaking. It was so painful. And apparently it's even worse the second time round. I was lucky it wasn't that.'

Dengue fever, dengue fever. It sounded so tropical, so colonial. 'Oh no, I'm sorry, I can't come to luncheon today. I've been struck by damned dengue fever.' I'd never met anyone before who had had it. Was it worse than malaria? And if you could get dengue round here, did that mean malaria was prevalent, too? I'd stopped taking my lariam a few months earlier because I wanted to save my remaining tablets for when we got to places where hospital care was less reliable than in Malaysia or Thailand: Sudan, for example. Or Eritrea.

The phone rang and Guy spoke to someone for a few minutes and then asked if I minded if he just popped out to pick up his friend Ross, the guy he owned the boat with, from the ferry terminus.

'Have a shower, watch some TV, use my computer to check your emails if you want,' he said, logging on for me. 'When I get back we'll go out. There's a few parties on tonight. I won't be long.' And he closed the door behind him.

What I really wanted, after the hot, sticky travelling, was a long shower – my first in weeks that didn't come from a bucket – and to use the toilet. I hadn't been to the loo all day.

The bathroom of Guy's apartment had a normal, Western-style toilet, not a squatter, I was relieved to see, and although there was no toilet paper, there was a bum gun. After hours of holding it in it was a relief to sit down and relax. I gunned my bum, stood up and flushed, glancing at the bowl. *Oh*, quite literally, *shit*. I looked on in horror as, instead of emptying, the toilet filled with water. *It'll be OK*, I reasoned with myself, *maybe there's a trick to flushing. I'll just try again and hold the handle down for longer this time*. I waited for the cistern to refill and flushed a second time. Water rushed in, but not out, and now my poo was swirling around, dangerously close to the top of the bowl. I started to panic properly. Guy could be back any minute and I could imagine fewer things less romantic than having to tell him I had blocked his toilet with my turd.

I looked around the bathroom for a bin, a drain, anything. There was a covered drain on the tiled floor and I lifted off the grate and looked down it. *Could I throw the poo down there?* I wondered, wildly. I looked from toilet to drain, from drain to toilet. But I couldn't do it. I had another idea and went into the bedroom, looking for a plastic bag. There was an empty crisp packet in the bin and a small plastic bag. I grabbed them both, checked the plastic bag for leak-prone anti-suffocation holes and went back into bathroom, praying that Guy wasn't about to open the front door and catch me red – well, brown – handed. There was nothing else for it. I had to poop-a-scoop my own shit. I took a deep breath and lowered my hand into the bowl.

So now I had a bag of poo in my hand to dispose of and time was running out. I ran, panicked, back into the bedroom and opened the door to step out on to the small balcony. The apartment was on the first floor. Could I get away with dropping it over the side? I dangled the bag over the railing and scanned the ground below me. Yes – there was a grassy area. Maybe I could secretly retrieve it later. But then I saw a middle-aged Thai woman cooking at a stall to my right, her washing-up area only a few metres from the bag's likely landing point. What if she heard it thump and, curious, went to investigate? Or – far, far worse – what if the bag exploded on impact with the ground, like a water bomb? I turned and went back inside. There was only one place I could put it – and that was back in the bin. I pulled the knot of the handles even more tightly, moved the other rubbish out of the way and buried the bag of shame underneath it all. I sniffed the air cautiously – would he be able to tell? I didn't think so.

I did a Lady Macbeth on my hands, showered, changed and was checking Facebook, pretending to be calm, when Guy arrived back. 'Everything all right?' he asked.

'Yes, fine, fine.'

He went into the bathroom and I heard the toilet. I braced myself for any surprised shouts, in case anything had been hiding halfway round the U-bend and had decided to worm its way back out. But there was only the sound of the shower starting. Crisis averted.

As we left the apartment, I pointed nonchalantly at the trash. 'Your bin is pretty full now with all these empty beer cans. Shall I empty it on the way?' I asked, and swept it up and out.

The weather in the UK, of course, has a lot of to do with it, but when you see bikers in England they are invariably clad head to toe in leathers, with stiff boots protecting their feet, gloves covering their hands and sturdy helmets cushioning their heads. If they come off their bikes at speed and slide along the ground, the leather gets ripped off, rather than their skin and muscle. But in South East Asia it's not like that. It's hot and sticky, the laws and approach to health and safety are laxer and, well, it's just not cool. In Malaysia, at least, everyone wears a helmet. And their coat on back to front if it's raining. But in Thailand, with their laidback approach, which I was loving, it's shorts, flip-flops and hair flowing free in the wind. And drunk driving all the way. I was very lucky that Guy is a good, well-practised rider and we never had an accident, not when it was raining, when it was dark or when we were drunk, and especially not when it was all three at the same time.

We flitted from bar to bar, from birthday party to dive masters' graduation ceremony, from snorkel tests to transvestite fashion show. At our final stop of the evening, I climbed wobbly off the bike in the car park of a pub. Although we had been getting on well, talking and laughing, Guy hadn't made a move on me, or even touched me, and I had decided, with the clarity inebriation brings, to lunge at him and kiss him. As I focused my eyes on his gorgeous face, I was dimly aware of Toni Braxton's 1997 hit 'Un-break My Heart' playing in the background. I started my offensive.

'No!' he yelped and jumped back, further away.

'What?' I demanded, hands on hips. 'Am I not allowed to kiss you?'

'Oh,' he said, moving back towards me a little bit. 'I thought you were trying to slow dance with me.'

'In a car park?' I laughed, finding it funny but also a little bit hurt that he'd leapt away from me so abruptly.

He let me give him a quick peck, a bit awkwardly, given that the moment was lost, and we went in to drink buckets of samsong (very strong Thai whisky) and Red Bull, and meet more of his friends. Later he led me to some sun loungers on the beach for some proper kissing, sans Toni Braxton.

I stayed on Lanta with Guy for four days, meeting his friends, who were all divers, or training to be dive masters, or ran dive shops or taught diving or owned diving companies or were on holiday to – you guessed it – dive. We went out drinking every night, starting from about 4pm or 5pm, and carried on until the early hours of the morning. In the afternoons, while we were recovering from one pub session and steeling ourselves for the next, Guy entertained me with tales of island life, filling me in on all the gossip and drama. And there was a lot of it – *Lanta Life* could easily have been a soap opera, and a multicultural, incestuous one at that. Everyone went out with everybody else and even those with a boyfriend or girlfriend back home joined in with the sleeping around pretty much the minute after they had waved off their beloved at the airport. Those people who had done more than one season on the island seemed to have their own moral code and completely lived for the moment. They didn't worry about the expectations and values of the wider world, about their futures, their bank balances or pensions, whether they would find a husband or wife and settle down. They worked for a pittance, just to pay for the rent on their one-room flats, and as long as they had a beer – or 10 – in their hand each night, and they were diving, they were happy. Although I admired their carefree spirit, I couldn't help but worry on their behalf about what they would do when they got older. A hand-to-mouth, party-led existence is all well and good while you are young and beautiful, but later on? I was curious about whether people eventually become so detached from normal life that they are unable to go back to it. But maybe they didn't want to 'go back'. Maybe this *was* normal life, doing what you loved, with no stressing over anything other than who had pinched your latest boyfriend. Perhaps I should try it for myself.

After a lunch-time breakfast of sticky rice and spicy som tam papaya salad each morning, Guy and I climbed on to his bike and he showed me his favourite spots on the island. During mid-afternoon chats over first beers I picked up on his back story. He'd been to uni and got a job in computer programming, earning good money, but he'd seen it as a means to an end – and that end was travelling, teaching diving to fund himself as he went. He'd never settled or even stayed in one place for long enough to put down roots, it seemed, except here in Thailand, where the monsoon season drove the divers away every spring and drew them back again before Christmas. He had lived out of a bag for years, visiting remote parts of South America and Asia. I got the impression that he was very happy to continue his itinerant lifestyle for ever. A girlfriend would fit into that only if she went with him.

'It's harder for chicks, you know?' he said one afternoon while we lazed in a couple of hammocks on a beach, the smalls of our backs just inches from the sand, his toes hooked around one edge of my hammock, rocking me slightly. 'It's more natural for them to want to settle down, have a home, friends around them. So it's difficult.' He was talking generally, not about us – if there even *was* an us – but I found myself wondering if I could be that kind of woman, never settling, constantly moving. I always liked to have a nest to go back to, to feel secure in – as a kid I'd turned our garden shed into a mini house, making pretend bunk beds out of cardboard boxes, and baked beans and sausages from orange beads and brown wax crayons. I wasn't sure I could be literally homeless, however much I liked someone.

I was having a good time with Guy but I was finding it hard to read him. He wasn't very touchy-feely or affectionate, especially when ballads were playing in car parks. In fact, in looks and personality and in terms of his and my 'relationship', he was the exact opposite of Steve. The only thing they had in common was that they were both boat bums. Guy would say confusing things like 'I'm no good at relationships,' and leave me wondering whether that meant he thought we were in one, and he was apologising for his behaviour, or if he was telling me he didn't want one. But then the next minute he would say, 'I'll miss you when you're gone,' 'Why don't you come sailing with me to Indonesia?' or 'I find you much more attractive than those beautiful Swedes over there.' (Actually, that last statement mainly just left me unsure whether he was complimenting me or telling me I was ugly.) I was really, really attracted to him and it could well be that the fact he wasn't throwing himself at me was making me keener. The thrill of the chase, and all that. I ordered myself to stop worrying about it, in my new spirit of letting things be. I had to leave both Lanta and Thailand anyway and get back to England for my brother's wedding.

You would think that, having been to an actual official immigration office, had a conversation with two immigration officials, paid money to an immigration agency and had some official immigration papers stapled into my passport, getting on to my plane to fly to the UK would have been straightforward. Oh no, my innocent friend, not in Thailand, where the bribe is king. On second thoughts, the king is the king in Thailand and it's a criminal offence to disrespect him and probably not even an offer of a substantial bribe could get you off the hook for that – but that's another issue entirely, and one that, having written this sentence, I am likely to have to deal with if this book is published in Thailand. But anyway, as I was saying, bribery rules in Thailand, OK? But I didn't know that. Then.

I stood in the immigration queue at Phuket airport, ready with ticket in hand to fly to Kuala Lumpur and on to Stansted. When I reached the front of the line I handed over my passport to the official. He opened it at the stapled-in pages, frowned and told me to go to the immigration office. Red faced, I left the queue and followed the signs to the office. A woman official beckoned me to sit at her desk. She grilled me on how I had arrived in the country: by what boat? Where to? Where from? Why did I have this form in my passport? Why had I not posted the 20,000 baht bond?

'I went to immigration,' I explained, 'and they said I could pay an agent to put up the bond for me. Then they gave me these papers.'

'Who is agent?' I didn't know – the male 'boss' on the phone had sorted it all out for me.

'Where is receipt?' I didn't have one.

The woman, in her sharp military-style navy uniform, eyed me sternly.

'The people at immigration arranged it,' I tried again. 'I come back Thailand two weeks. I go England my brother wedding.' Now I had resorted to pidgin English to try to get my point across. 'They say OK.'

She read through my papers again and took them off with her. I looked around the office while I waited, finding some solace in the fact that it was open plan. Less chance of my being locked in.

The woman came back with my passport. 'I must send copy to immigration office. You pay 500 baht for taxi.'

Why, I wondered, *does the immigration office need copies? They were the ones that had signed the forms in the first place. And the copy is unlikely to get there before my plane leaves in 40 minutes, anyway and... Ah.* (Ting! went the lightbulb in my head.) A bribe. I was relieved that she had dressed it up as an official fee to pay, saving me the embarrassment of taking some notes out of my wallet and wafting them under her nose, adding to the wad until we reached an agreement. To be honest, I was so green at this stuff that I wouldn't have had a clue how much to make my starting offer for, anyway. I handed over the 500 baht 'administration fee', which was all the cash I had in my wallet, and walked through to the departure lounge – without a receipt, naturally.

16

Epiphany on the slow train from Stansted

It was effing cold in England. There was even snow on the ground. The UK was in the grip of one of those record-breaking cold snaps and I'd heard it had reached minus 18°C in Derbyshire one night, near where my brother was getting married. I was coming from 30°C in Thailand. That's a temperature difference of nearly 50°C.

It was so cold, in fact, that the doors of the hold of the plane had frozen shut and they couldn't get them open to unload our suitcases, so it was another long wait at the carousel in the pre-dawn hours of the morning. I tried to get water from a vending machine but it kept spitting out my money rather than a bottle of Hildon. Next I went to fetch a trolley, to save carrying my bag (just the one this time) on my back, and it charged me a pound.

There were posters all around the baggage reclaim area advertising different ways of getting into London. There was the Stansted Express, which took only 45 minutes to Liverpool Street but it was a ball ache to get from there to Clapham, where I was headed, and, besides, as one of the most expensive train journeys in the UK by the mile, it cost far more than I was willing to pay. The better option, I decided, was to take the National Express coach. It took longer but put me in Victoria and cost only a few pounds. Plane hold crowbarred open and luggage retrieved, I trudged off towards the coach stand. They had a timetable on the desk and I realised that the next bus wasn't for two hours. The millionaire's limousine service – sorry, Stansted Express – was going shortly but at a price I really couldn't bring myself to pay. In Malaysia, I was living off that amount of money for a whole week. Then I remembered I'd been to Stansted before on the local, stopping train service. I walked over to a ticket machine – of course, half of them were out of service – and put in my destination details. The price came up for an adult single – £17.70 for a half-hour ride to Tottenham Hale in north London. I blinked at the screen. Surely there was some mistake? I cancelled it and tried it again. No mistake. So it was wait in the cold, empty airport for two hours or pay up and put up. Reluctantly I slid my card into the slot, cursing 'I fucking hate this country' under my breath. Gold-plated ticket retrieved, I was on my way to the platform when I passed a vending machine and realised how hungry I was. I stuck in cash for some chocolate – and neither it nor money came out. I didn't have time to argue it out with anyone so I left it and got on the train, which was dirty, covered in graffiti and the heating was broken. Welcome to England, Emma!

My stiff upper lip and British pride deserted me completely then. They had already been weakened a bit by the free and easy style of living abroad that I had been witnessing. The realisation of how ridiculously expensive everything was –

why would that £1.50 I had lost in the sweet machine only get a me quick sugar fix over here when it can buy an entire fresh, healthy meal in Asia? – and the grubbiness and crappiness of everything broke me. Nothing worked – they couldn't even get a door open in a country where it is winter for about eight months of the year. The UK was grey, grey, grey. The people were grey-skinned and ugly. They wore grey, ugly clothes, lived in grey, ugly houses and had, judging by the scowls I was seeing on the train (and this was a Saturday, so they didn't even have the excuse that they were stressed-out commuters), grey, ugly personalities. *Why does everyone in this country let themselves be bullied into working more and more hours, slogging away in their grey offices and factories, just to earn a bit more money to buy more useless crap that they don't need in the first place,* I wondered. The people I had seen and met in Malaysia and Thailand – the locals, that is, not the tight-fisted yachties or the drunken holidaymakers – seemed much more content with their lot. Yes, they had less, but they wanted less. They worked at a slower pace – much to the yachties' chagrin when they needed a job doing – but they chose to do so and weren't made to feel ashamed about it. They smiled hello to strangers, they dressed in colourful, beautiful clothes, they were polite and they didn't go around scrawling on the sides of trains with magic markers. And don't even get me started on the weather. *I've had it with England*, I thought.

Thinking back, I like to imagine that a ray of yellow sunlight cut through all that negative thinking and greyness to shine down on me, and me alone, on that train, illuminating me with a golden glow, bathing me in a wash of warmth and filling my ears with the sound of angels harmonising as this next thought popped into my head. Sadly, I don't think that actually happened – but what I did have was an uncommonly clear moment of thought. A realisation. An inspiration. A eureka moment. I had an epiphany.

It came to me all of a sudden, a complete idea downloaded into my brain in a millisecond. If I could slow it down and reproduce a transcript of that lightbulb moment, it would go something like this: *'Sod this. I'm off to live somewhere hot and sunny. I'm going to get a job to do with boats, save a bit of cash, and buy a house – in the Caribbean. It will have a beautiful green garden full of flowers, an outdoor pool and a spare room for family and friends to stay in. I'm going to get a ute, like in* Neighbours, *and I'll drive happily through the dusty roads to the airport to pick up my constant stream of visitors. We'll eat barbecued fish – only not catfood tuna – and they can have the run of the house while I have to pop out for a few hours to see to my boat/tourist business. I won't have any money worries because it'll be miraculously cheap to live on my Caribbean island, I'll never wear grey or black again and I'll be tanned, happy and healthy. All the time. It's going to be ace.'*

In case you haven't already noticed (not likely), I have a very overactive imagination and I even filled in the smallest of details of my daydream: the colour of my house – yellow – and the positions of where my friends would ride in the ute – adults in the front, with the air-conditioning, kids allowed in the truck bed, because I'm cool. I even went so far as to think about whether my parents would come to visit – they aren't fans of hot climes.

And it didn't really occur to me that that couldn't be my life. For the past 32 years, if I had wanted something, I had just applied myself and gone for it and usually it worked.

I wanted to be a journalist on a national newspaper, even though I was a sheltered kid from northern suburbia. I wanted to be able to run long distances like a gazelle, even though I couldn't limp along for more than 10 minutes without having to stop. I wanted to own a property in a decent postcode, not somewhere that was so far out of London it gave me a nosebleed just thinking about it. I don't mean to sound big-headed; I prefer to think of myself as determined. If I had a goal, I just applied myself to it, found ways of working with it or around it, and eventually, many breathless training sessions or village fete reports later, I got there. Why should this be any different?

It was with this thought in my mind that I returned to Thailand and to *Gillaroo*. My fortnight in the UK had been a blur of shivering coach and train rides up and down the country, from London to Derby to the New Forest to Brighton and back to London again, seeing my little brother say 'I do' to his fiancée (now there are two Emma Bamfords in my family), catching up with friends, rebuffing countless queries about when I was going to come back home and boring senseless absolutely every single person I met about my epiphany, my Caribbean house and my ute. The odd one was excited at the prospect of cheap holidays in an exotic location; most just looked at me kindly, nodded and patted my hand.

Tyrone had been busy while I was away, finding not just two but four new crew members. Pablo and Libertad, a Spanish couple in their early twenties who had been cycling around Malaysia and Thailand, had already moved into my cabin when I returned, their bikes wrapped in multiple layers of clingfilm to protect them from the rust and stored in the hold. I decamped to the front cabin that had been Hugo and Aaron's – the one that was on the cockroach superhighway.

Pablo and Libertad had never sailed before and Tyrone decided that I should help him teach them. We got a Spaniard each – Pablo was mine. They looked like typical, black-haired southern Europeans: Pablo was small and skinny, with a toothy grin and good-looking features that reminded me of Noah Wyle, who played John Carter in *ER*. Libertad looked a little like a boy – she wore men's clothes and had very short hair – but had the sweetest, loveliest personality, always checking everyone was OK, laughing and finding fun in everything.

The other crew, an English couple, Ben and Vicky, who were a couple of years older than me, were to arrive later in the week, Tyrone said, and we would leave for a four-day passage to the Andaman Islands on 23 December. Christmas Day would be at sea, hundreds of miles from any land.

I had just enough time for another quick visit to Lanta. Guy picked me up again and I was bursting with excitement to tell him about my epiphany. We lounged on beach chairs, staring out at the sea over the tops of our bottles of Tiger, as I explained. I was fairly confident that, unlike people back home, he would understand where I was coming from, that he would see it as a realistic aim, that he would be as excited for me as I was for myself.

And he did understand, and was excited for me. But there was a but.

'The Caribbean wouldn't work for me,' he said, digging the bottom of his empty beer bottle into the sand. 'The hurricane season.'

I don't remember inviting you, I thought, although not unkindly. Once again I wondered whether he thought we were in a relationship. If we were, it was one doomed to failure. I was about to set sail for the Andamans, Sri Lanka and the Arabian Gulf, swiftly to be followed by yellow-house-hunting in the Caribbean.

Why, then, did I have a lump in my throat when we parted at the ferry harbour? Despite how wrong I thought he was for me – he didn't want children, he would be happy with an itinerant lifestyle, he was so laidback he was horizontal, and, don't forget, the hurricane season 'wouldn't work' for him – I still really liked him. He was so very, very different from previous boyfriends – no rugby-playing, blond-mopped hooray Henry here – and the strength of my attraction to him caught me off guard. Was I so desperate to like someone that I was willing to turn a blind eye to some fairly basic-level incompatibilities? Or were all the new things that I was experiencing changing me?

17

Happiness is ...

Gillaroo was full of shit on my return. The starboard toilet had broken and the other crew had had to pull it to pieces and clean it. Tyrone picked me up from the jetty in the dinghy. 'Ben's here,' he said, 'and Vicky's coming tomorrow.' A nice welcome for Ben – less than two hours on the boat and he was unscrewing toilet pipes blocked with excrement and having to scrape them clean with a screwdriver and a few steel nuts tied on to the end of a piece of string.

'It is the calcy deposits,' Libertad informed me. 'They have built up over the time.' Apparently when faeces mixes with seawater it can form a substance as hard as cement. Layer upon layer of it had built up inside the pipe between the toilet and the holding tank until our poos were left trying to squeeze their way through an opening the diameter of a knitting needle. Strong chemicals and a chipping action were our weapons of choice against this blockade. It's a wonder Ben didn't leave there and then. But he wasn't a quitter; he was a stoic. A stoic full of sarcasm and northern humour, which is exactly what is needed when scouring a toilet pipe. He gritted his teeth, cracked a joke and got on with it. By the time Vicky arrived the next day the boat was back together again and we lifted up the anchor and set a course for Port Blair in the Andaman Islands.

Tyrone and the Spaniards (or The Spanish, as Ben referred to them in a jokily xenophobic fashion, as if they represented their entire nation) had been busy while I was getting drunk in Lanta. The galley had been cleaned and completely reorganised (what was it with new crew and the need to clean the kitchen?). Even the herbs and spices pots had been relabelled. 'Curry powder', 'Curry powder', 'Curry another more' were written on white stickers with black marker in Pablo's cursive hand. They had been to a cash-and-carry and restocked the boat with a lot of provisions and there were some weird Spanishy things in there – a whole gallon of olive oil, a kilo of paprika, extremely short-grain rice and 90 eggs. *Ninety*.

Within a few days it became clear that it was going to be the English (and Irish) vs The Spanish when it came to food. Pablo and Libertad were not big curry eaters. 'Is it spicy?' they asked waiters in Thai restaurants. 'Is it spicy?' they checked with Tyrone when he served up vegetable curry for dinner. 'What is this? Is it spicy?' they said, poking at a bowl of coleslaw with their forks. They couldn't understand Asians' and English people's love of hot food. And we couldn't understand their love of oily, bland food. Everything Spanish seemed to taste of oil: tortilla, vegetable paella, flan. Ben took to pouring chilli sauce on to everything, much to Pablo's disgust. The only thing they cooked that wasn't bland was cakes – and they were so sugary they made my teeth hurt. But a cooking rota is a cooking rota and we stuck to it.

Christmas Day I was on dinner duty. I started at 11pm on Christmas Eve, cutting up sausages and wrapping them in streaky bacon before I went on night watch. I made a loaf of raisin bread with cinnamon butter for breakfast and a traditional English Christmas lunch. I couldn't afford a turkey in Thailand but I had got hold of a chicken for the others and I roasted that and served it with potatoes, two types of stuffing, carrots, the pigs in blankets and even Brussels sprouts. With one small oven and only three hob burners, it was as much of a juggling act on the boat as it was at home. I reheated a stollen cake and poured custard over it for pudding. I had managed to find crackers and we sat around the cockpit table, 200 miles off the coast of Thailand, in some of the bluest water I had ever seen, tucking into our gravy-smothered dinners in 35°C heat, paper crowns on our heads. In keeping with the festive spirit, I wore a red bikini and white shorts all day. Pablo and Libertad had never experienced a traditional English Christmas dinner and they were more than a little bemused by it. If you take a step back and look at it – flimsy hats and crappy toys inside a shiny wrapped firework, types of meat and vegetables you wouldn't normally touch with a bargepole the other 364 days of the year, three gazillion calories in one sitting – it is faintly ludicrous. But I like to mark an occasion and I think everyone enjoyed it, even if it did make them sweat even more heavily in the strong sunshine.

The wind politely waited until Boxing Day to come in – and thank God it had, for I wouldn't have fancied doing that seven-hour cooking and washing-up marathon in rough seas. For the first three days of the passage we had been motoring along, so there was only a small amount of new information that Pablo and Libertad had to grasp, on how to check the chart to make sure we were on course and monitor the instruments. Now the sailing lessons were to begin.

'OK, so this is a boat,' I said, drawing a kind of curvy triangle on a piece of paper as they sat facing me at the cockpit table. 'If the wind comes from here, straight ahead,' – I drew an arrow pointing towards the peak of my triangle – 'we can't sail. It has to come from at least 45 degrees for that.' I drew arrows coming from all directions to spear my little boat, as if Robin Hood and his Merry Men had let loose against it. 'Following so far?' I looked up and they nodded at me. 'If the wind comes from here,' I said, pointing at one of my arrows, 'we call it a close reach. From here it's a beam reach or on the beam. From this direction it's a broad reach or on the quarter or sailing downwind or…' I'm sorry to say I bamboozled them with information that first sailing lesson. They did really well, especially considering that English wasn't their first language and that sailing terms aren't really English at all anyway. They were very keen students and took notes and asked questions and everything. I was proud of them.

But, over time, I noticed Pablo's attitude towards me starting to sour. I wasn't sure whether it was because he was getting frustrated with himself over the language barrier, was not happy with being taught by a woman or just plain hated me. Because there were six of us, we had to do only two two-hour shifts each in every 24-hour period. Tyrone and I also worked Libertad and Pablo's watches with them. With Pablo's deteriorating attitude, the crew started to noticeably split into three camps: The Spaniards in one corner, the English in another and Tyrone by himself in the third. It was subtle to begin with and no one seemed to mind too much: it was tricky to involve all six people all of the time, anyway.

Ben and Vicky became good friends of mine that trip. They had been together for so long that they didn't make me feel like a gooseberry. While Pablo and Libertad would be kissing and cuddling, Ben and Vicky didn't really go in for PDAs. They had met at university and were still together, 17 years later. Ben had tried one year in a normal, London office job after graduation and soon quit. They were divers and had worked all over the world, running their own dive company in Mozambique for a few years. When they sold that they bought a home in Malta and Ben had been driving boats for a watersports company and Vicky had been teaching English there. He had landed himself a job for the summer being a paid sailing buddy to a rich businessman in America; Vicky was going, too, and the businessman was throwing in a house for them to stay in as well. They were a very good-looking couple, tanned and slim. She was as southern as he was northern, she was fair to his darkness. We all three shared a love of reading and an English sense of humour. But what I liked about them most was that they were proof that it was entirely possible to live this kind of life, long-term, make money from it and still stay sane. You didn't have to turn into a freeloading hippy if you decided to make a warm, sunny island your home. Ben and Vicky were the most normal people I'd met so far. I don't know if they'd ever owned a ute, though.

There were dolphins, dolphins everywhere on that four-day sail across the Andaman Sea. Tyrone wrote a note in the log that more than a hundred of them had been following the boat on Boxing Day morning during his watch, when I was sleeping. He said there'd been whales, too. I didn't get to see schools as big as that or any whales but I did witness a particularly spectacular acrobatic display by some spinner dolphins. We had the usual group swimming in our bow wave, weaving in between each other as they kept pace with the boat, and we'd all gone forward to get a good look at them. Then we saw a smaller group following the boat a way off our starboard quarter. One dolphin leapt completely clear of the water by a good 10 feet or so and threw himself into a horizontal corkscrew spin through the air. He did this a few times, until he had our undivided attention, and then he pulled out his party trick: he did three backwards somersaults in the air, tail fin over bottle nose, all in a row before hitting the water. I wanted to applaud, it was that impressive.

Our destination, the Andaman Islands, together with the Nicobar Islands further south, make a long, thin chain of dots of land extending north to south in the Indian Ocean, about 400 miles off the coast of Thailand. Originally inhabited by indigenous tribes, they were commandeered by the British, and on the main island, South Andaman, the Brits built a prison to contain freedom fighters campaigning for independence. If you were Indian and you were caught plotting to overthrow the Brits, you were tossed into the Cellular Jail, your hands and feet shackled and fettered, and you were forced, on a daily diet of just two cups of rice gruel, to turn a wheel to press oil out of coconut husks and reach a quota that even a water buffalo would barely be able to manage. Only Indian nationals are allowed into the Nicobars now. They are so far from India and undeveloped that I doubt they get many visitors. But a handful of the 330-plus Andaman islands are open to foreign visitors in possession of an Indian visa and, luckily for us, they welcome yachts.

Welcome is perhaps too strong a term; allow is more like it. I thought rules and regulations were bad enough in the UK but that is mere child's play compared to the Andamans. We spent 36 hours dealing with the authorities – customs, immigration, the coastguard and port control; we'd been warned to expect it to take at least two days. There was an unbelievable amount of paperwork to complete. We had to list every food item on the boat and each piece of equipment and at one point I seriously thought I would have to itemise every loose screw and nut in the tool box but – lo and behold! – a 'gift' of a bottle of wine was requested by one of our visitors and after that the paperwork all went smoothly. We were informed that we could only stay for a maximum of 30 days; even if our engine failed we still had to leave once our time was up. We had to provide the authorities with a strict itinerary of our route, listing which anchorages we would use on which day. We were warned that it was strictly forbidden to deviate from this programme once submitted and that random checks would be carried out. On the crossing we had done our research, all reading the pilot guide and having a meeting to discuss which islands we wanted to go to so that we could draw up our itinerary. Some places were out of bounds to everyone, particularly those where original tribes still lived. Just one or two were geared up for tourism, still on a basic and small scale, and the rest were uninhabited. It was these islands that we were the most interested in. Because we had our own boat, we were fortunate enough to be able to go where no wily backpacker had boldly gone before.

The plan was to restock in Aberdeen Bazar, the main

shopping town of the Andamans, and then sail off, moving from island to island for just over three weeks. Then we would come back to anchor at nearby Port Blair and provision up again before sailing for a week to Sri Lanka. With six people on one boat, everything had to be strictly rationed: food, electricity, even drinking water. We were lucky that we had a big fridge and freezer (big in boat terms but about the capacity of a standard domestic fridge-freezer) but six people get through an enormous volume of food when they are eating all three daily meals on board for three weeks. Tyrone called a crew meeting to explain how it would work. Whoever was on cooking duty would have to use up the fruits and vegetables that were likely to go off first, he said. I made a shopping list of fresh foods that I had learned from experience would keep the longest, especially in the heat and humidity: pumpkins, cabbages if we wrapped them in newspaper, potatoes covered in dirt, yams, onions, green apples, very green tomatoes. Stacks of carrots, which wrinkled within a couple of days, were a no-no; the same with peppers. Pablo volunteered to turn over the 90 eggs each day to help keep them fresh.

We had enough water, Tyrone calculated, to last two and a half weeks. If it didn't rain, we'd have none left for our final week. For drinking, cooking and cleaning teeth we had 5 litres per person per day. Five jerry cans of tap water, holding 90 litres, sat in the cockpit for washing six people's bodies and their clothes. One bathtub back home contains more than that. Obviously we were hoping it would rain but it was the dry season, so we had to be prepared. I became paranoid we were going to run out and I used probably 500ml of water to wash my entire body the first day and didn't shower at all the second. My hair, despite the sweat and salt, went three days between shampoos. It was always tied back and it matted up nicely with the wind and dirt, so it stayed easily in place.

It was a week since any of us had set foot on land, last in Thailand, and *Gillaroo*, despite her generous size, was starting to feel claustrophobic. We were all dying to get off once the bureaucratic procedures were completed. But I don't think any of us were prepared for the sheer chaotic lunacy that was India. First came the people, great crowds of them – mainly men – wanting to look at us, shake our hands, drive us places. Next came the traffic – constant streams of tuk-tuks, motos, cars, vans, lorries, buses, trucks. And all of them, every single one, were beeping their horns. Next to the little landing platform at the harbour was a car park full of lorries, all with a hand-painted sign across the back: 'Please sound your horn'. So everyone did. They sounded those horns when they were overtaking, turning left, turning right, when a pedestrian crossed in front of them, when a pedestrian didn't cross in front of them but stayed on the pavement, when they sped up, slowed down and sometimes just because they hadn't had a good old toot for a minute or two. We walked along the side of the road and they beeped at us – *'Why are you walking?' 'Where are you going?' 'Hello, white people!'*

Everyone's skin was a deep brown – far darker than British Indians' – and the moustache was a very popular look for men. The moustaches weren't the only hangover from the 1970s; the tuk-tuks were all painted brown and yellow. As we walked along the road, moving out of the path of families of goats and stringy-looking cows, and staring in wide-eyed wonder, taking everything in, a huge, old-fashioned car slid past us. It had curves everywhere, a long bonnet and shiny hub caps: an Ambassador, the classic car of choice for Indian government officials and, presumably, ambassadors. Had we accidentally set off *Gillaroo*'s flux capacitor during our trip over the Andaman Sea and jumped back in time?

I've never been to the Scots' Aberdeen but I can't imagine it bears even the slimmest of resemblances to this town on Great Andaman island. Built on a hill with shops and stalls lining the main road, it was so chaotic that the pavement just stopped, suddenly, in places, to form holes big enough to eat Gloucester's Dr Foster for breakfast, and we were forced out into the traffic. Cows stood idly around, not caring that they were blocking the highway. Even the sounding of loud horns couldn't budge them. What pavement there was was half filled with tables laden with the shops' best wares. For some reason, their best wares were almost always enormous underpants or hand-woven floor mats. If I'd been after a pair of belly-warming Y-fronts, I'd have been spoilt for choice in Aberdeen Bazar. Everything was shabby but buzzing and alive with colour, bustle and noise. The streets, all three of them, were teeming with women in saris and gold jewellery and men in black trousers, shirts and leather sandals spitting on to the tarmac. There were 'Spitting strictly prohibited' signs everywhere but no one seemed to take any notice. Nothing was new – possibly not even the underpants – and buildings, pavements, railings and road were crumbling. Unlike Malaysia, there was little plastic to be seen. Shop signs and billboards signs were painted on to wood, with modern brand logos painstakingly copied by hand.

'It's just like mainland India,' Tyrone said, 'only smaller. It's India Lite.'

As if to prove the similarity, a beggar approached us. He was a middle-aged man, with neat, grey hair and didn't look especially thin or dirty. He spoke fairly good English and at first we didn't realise what he was after. We thought he just wanted to chat to us. He said something we took as a joke and we all laughed politely. The man was furious.

'I have not eaten for three days,' he said, his eyes burning darkly. 'This is a joke to you? You have money.' He tapped Ben's watch. 'I have no money.' He paused. 'God is watching.' Just as we were starting to feel so uncomfortable that we were willing to go through our pockets, he walked away, shaking his head in disgust.

Havelock island was our first stop. The main tourist island of the Andamans, it was just as popular with wealthy Indian holidaymakers as it was with backpackers and Europeans seeking an exotic getaway. It was a long, slow sail to get there, with the wind on the nose. We were mindful of our limited supply of diesel for the three weeks so we persevered with the sailing, making long tacks and taking 10 hours to cover the 20 miles. A large, yellowish, spotted fish swam past the boat as we crawled along, snaking its body in a distinctly recognisable way.

'Leopard shark!' Ben yelled out, pointing at the water. It was the first shark I'd ever seen in the wild.

Crocodiles worried Pablo and Libertad more. They had read in the pilot guide that crocodiles lurked in the waters around the islands, including Havelock.

'Don't worry about it,' Vicky told them, the morning after we'd dropped anchor, when they were discussing whether or not it was safe to swim. 'There's no mangroves or mud here. It's just sand. There won't be any crocodiles.' Reassured, they put on their masks and fins and swam the third of a mile to shore. Neither of them was suddenly clamped between a giant set of gnarled jaws and pulled below the surface. But it looked an awfully long way to the beach, I thought, as I followed the progress of the tips of their purple and blue snorkels. It took them an age.

'Do you fancy taking the dinghy?' I asked Ben and Vicky. Thankfully they were with me on that one.

The beach we had anchored off at twilight the previous evening was called, poetically, #7. Its Indian name was Radha Nagar but by convention the beaches on Havelock were all hashed and numbered: #1, #3, #5, #6 and #7. The villages were also numbered, for the convenience of the tourists, although the locals knew them only by their names, so asking for directions was doubly difficult. And, to make enquiring after the correct way even harder, questions were invariably answered Indian-style, with a sideways rocking motion of the head, a bit like a nodding dog stuck to the parcel shelf of a Ford Fiesta parked on a slant. I never knew whether it meant 'yes', 'maybe', 'I don't know' or 'no', so it got a bit confusing. But within a few days I found myself subconsciously mimicking the movement.

Beach #7 was a deep expanse of soft, clean sand and breaking waves and that made it the most popular beach for the vacationers. Indian holidaymakers were standing right by the surf line, fully clothed, bracing their bodies against the power of the breaking waves and letting the water soak them to the skin. And not just the children; mums, dads, aunties, uncles and even grannies stood waist deep in the water. Few people swam – perhaps they didn't know how – and everyone, always, was fully dressed. The women wore their saris in the sea. They are heavy enough dry on the hanger. Imagine what they are like full of salt water.

Dodging between Indian waders, Ben skilfully guided the dinghy on to the beach, managing not to let any waves break over the stern to sink us. Pablo and Libertad came over to help drag it up the steep beach and a passing backpacker, a Danish guy, stopped to lend a hand, too. As we staggered under the boat's weight, he dropped into conversation that there had been a crocodile attack fairly recently at the end of this beach and an American girl had been killed. I caught Vicky's eye. 'Yes, they captured it and it's in Port Blair zoo,' the Danish guy said. How very humane of them. Pablo and Libertad didn't swim to shore again.

Apart from a couple of changing huts, a posh resort that was out of bounds and the odd food stall, there was nothing there so we took a van across the island to beach #5. The interior of the island was a mix of beautiful, undulating jungle, palm plantations and a few farmhouses dotted around. There were oxen in the paddies and egrets by the oxen. It was a travel photographer's dream.

Beach #5, which merged into #3 (what happened to #4?), was very different. There were no bathers, no soft sand, no breaking waves. This was the backpackers' side of the island and they had their pick of small beach bungalows in low-tech resorts run by hippyish diving fans. Dead coral dotted the beach and the shallows and, broken down, made a rougher but still beautifully white sand. Trees overhung the edge of the beach and wooden fishing boats, painted as turquoise as the sea, rested their bellies on the shore. I lagged behind as the others walked on. *This*, I told myself, *is what the Caribbean must be like. It's stunning.* I pushed my toes idly into the sand and smiled. I felt so lucky to be able to come to places like this. A peaceful stillness settled on me and I took a deep breath. *Happiness*, I thought. *This is all it takes to feel happy. This is all I need.* And I remembered my epiphany on the train and I grinned.

18

The curious incident of the dogs in the night time

Before I left Thailand for the UK, Tyrone had asked me what I thought about recruiting a couple as crew.

'Why not a couple and then another single person for the small port cabin?' I had replied. 'The more the merrier, as far as I'm concerned.'

It was good in theory but what I hadn't anticipated was how much more claustrophobic the boat seemed with six on board rather than four. It meant that there were more people to talk to and have fun with, sure, but there were also more people just getting in the way. Whenever I went to the galley, to get a drink or to make some breakfast, there was someone else already there. The tramps, which I had come to regard as my own private territory, since Tyrone, Hugo, Chris and Aaron hadn't been interested in sunbathing on them, suddenly became overrun with other people. Tyrone's favourite place on *Gillaroo* was the sofa in the saloon. He liked to stretch out along it, aligned with the centre of the boat, the back of his head being cooled by the breeze coming in through the window. With six people around it became more difficult for him to do so. If it was sunny, he was OK, because everyone else liked to be outside, but if it was raining he'd find himself hemmed in by three or four crew members all wanting to sit down. I think having so many people around overwhelmed him a bit. Already a quiet, contemplative man, he retreated further into his shell. At times it felt a bit like he was the tired social worker resigned to keeping watch over a rowdy youth club. When the rest of us went ashore to explore Havelock, Tyrone stayed on the boat by himself for three days in a row. No doubt he relished having some peace and quiet.

Libertad had noticed the change in him. As we walked through the jungle area at the back of Beach #7 on our way to the tuk-tuk rank, she turned to me. 'Emma, can I ask ju something? Is Tyrone angry with me and with Pablo?'

'Oh, Libertad,' I said. 'Neither of you has done anything wrong. If you do, Tyrone will always, politely and gently, mention it.'

She looked at me, concern still plainly written on her face.

'Trust me,' I said. 'The way he is acting is not your fault.'

Tyrone wasn't the only one who was being affected by all six of us being crammed in together. As we continued to sail around the Andamans, Pablo's anger grew. He stopped listening to me when we were on watch together, not making eye contact when I tried to explain sailing concepts like side slipping. I got the feeling he wasn't enjoying the sailing at all. I tried to spark some enthusiasm by showing him more things, like how to drive the dinghy, but it made him even angrier with me. I started to think that I must be the nastiest, bossiest person in the world, judging by the way he was reacting to me. But then he snapped at Tyrone, too, when he tried to helpfully make a suggestion about the dinner Pablo was preparing. 'I do know how to cook lentils,' he snapped, practically adding, 'Ju imbecile!' at the end. So I knew it wasn't just me. Probably he didn't like being told what to do by anyone. Libertad did her best to placate him, murmuring softly in Spanish as they sat on the trampoline at night.

We were at Havelock for New Year's Eve and we saw in 2011 at a beach party, watching excited Indian men disco-dancing to techno music, doing, oddly, the white man overbite and pumping their shoulders up and down, elbows cocked. There were no women dancing and the men were getting very touchy-feely with one another.

I flopped down next to Tyrone in the cool sand, where he sat with his arms loosely circling his long legs, which were crossed in front of him. He was still and seemed relaxed.

'It was like this in India,' he said, watching the dancers. He'd told me he had spent a year there in his twenties. 'The unmarried men would hold hands with each other in the street, put an arm round another man's shoulders on the bus. It was strange to see.' By strange, I guessed he meant worrying, to his 20-year-old straight self. Indeed, in a culture to which homosexuality is anathema, it was doubly odd to see such close physical contact between men and for that contact to raise eyebrows only among nations more comfortable with gay people.

Everyone on the island had come to the party. The organisers had set up a beautiful wooden bar in the sand, decorated with strings of paper feathers. It was all very ecologically sound. Near the water's edge, groups of people let Chinese lanterns fly up into the air, cheers and claps breaking out with each one released. Some wrote their names on the paper sides of their lanterns and by midnight the black air was filled with dozens of tiny, flickering orange lights, disappearing high over the Indian Ocean.

There was very poor phone reception on Havelock, although it was the best we were to get for the rest of the trip, but I persevered in sending Happy New Year texts to friends and family. A reply came through at about 2am from Guy in Thailand, sent just before midnight: 'Happy new year baby... have fun x.' *Blimey – a 'baby' and a kiss. It must be love!* Despite my sarcasm, it was wonderful to hear from him, and so affectionately at that. But I still found him confusing. I am rarely confident enough to trust in what a man seems to be feeling for me and I even – for a split second – imagined he had meant that text for someone else, possibly because it was so out of character. Then I caught myself being negative, thought again of my new philosophy of letting things be what they are, and shook myself out of that. *Don't over-complicate things*, I ordered myself. *Just be pleased that he contacted you.*

The next morning more messages started to trickle through, with the usual best wishes for the year ahead. And then came one from Steve. I stared at his name in my phone's message inbox. I hadn't expected, or wanted, to hear from him. I pressed 'open'. 'You were the most important thing that happened to me last year and I still love you,' it said. It left me cold.

We were off a day later to visit my first bona fide deserted island, North Button, and I was really excited. *This is real adventure*, I thought as we shot through the water at 9 knots. *How many people can say they've actually been to a real desert island?*

Within a day I was bored. I was in paradise, a perfect

desert island of a paradise, where we were anchored in clear water off a small, sandy outcrop dotted with brush and the odd coconut palm and surrounded by rocks and coral, and I was bored. The bleached coral and rocks, combined with the waves, made landing the dinghy too dangerous and swimming ashore looked like an equally foolhardy – and scratchy – option. So we were stuck on board and, with nothing to do, I ate. Pablo baked cakes, Ben made bread and I ate. Bread with butter and honey and bread with peanut butter for breakfast; bread with chocolate ice cream syrup (yes, it was as disgusting as it sounds) as a mid-morning snack; pasta, veg and beans for lunch; a teatime snack of coconut biscuits and an ancient, slightly rusty can of bitter lemon; a bag of cashew nuts; a curry dinner. Having read back through the previous day's journal entry, which consisted of little but a list of various things I had put into my stomach, I decided I could not go on like that. I was already reading and this place was a bit too wild for swimming. What else could I do to entertain myself? Putting my thinking cap on, I had it – I would plan my future.

So much for letting it be. Old habits die hard and I am a list-writer by nature. I find great satisfaction in scratching a line through a needed item bought or an objective achieved. And I didn't see why my future could not be condensed, ordered and bullet-pointed in exactly the same way. I came up with this:

What to do:
1.   Get off *Gillaroo* mid-May, wherever we are, fly home and get a job on a boat in the Mediterranean for the summer season and the Caribbean for the winter.

2. Stay on the *Roo* 'til Spain in late spring, as planned, then go home and settle down.

3. Get off the *Roo* in Spain and go and find another boat going off on adventures.

4. Get off the *Roo*, go find Guy.

Chewing on my pen lid, I surveyed my work. Options 1 and 4 were the most appealing. I wasn't that enamoured with the idea of another six months of cruising, option 3, and the settling-down part of option 2 I was never really serious about.

It's funny, I thought. *Two years ago, settling down was all I wanted*. I had yearned for it. Cuddling other people's children actually made me physically hurt with the need for that kind of life for myself. I got upset when friends told me they were pregnant. But how things change. Now I was mainly putting option 2 on the list to pad it out a bit.

For inspiration and guidance, I re-read *Working on Yachts and Superyachts*, a book I had brought with me in case I wanted to stop somewhere and find work. I had my timings off with option 1, it emerged. I'd need to be in France in April, which was when captains looked for crew. That meant getting off *Gillaroo* in late March, when we were expecting to be in Yemen or Eritrea. The more I read of the book, the more excited I got. I started to daydream: I'd get a job as a stewardess or deckhand on £2000 a month, rising to chief stew in a few years, save an awful amount of tax-free cash, marry a captain, have a baby at 38, do the odd yacht delivery and set up a training school of some kind… in the Caribbean, naturally. Sorted.

I let myself run away with this daydream and option 1 became the favourite over option 4. As lovely an idea as it was, I couldn't really take number 4 seriously. Being a boat bum traveller for the rest of my life was just a step too far. It was best to think of my time with Guy fondly as a happy holiday romance and leave it at that.

The crew had been 50/50 about visiting Narcondam, a dormant volcano 100 miles north-east of the main archipelago, when we were drawing up our itinerary. Tyrone, Ben and Vicky weren't fussed, but the rest of us voted in favour. It went on the list. And boy, as I sat outside now in absolutely sheeting rain, struggling with the jib in 44 knots of wind, wearing full oilskins and feeling sick after bouncing sleeplessly for two days straight on a hard close-hauled tack, I really wished I hadn't raised my hand.

It was the north-east monsoon season for the Indian Ocean so it made no sense at all to deliberately go in that direction but Narcondam was on the list, and the authorities had been very clear about having to stick to the submitted itinerary, so here we were, wet and miserable and hours and hours away from anywhere.

Visibility was poor but once we got near enough to the island to see it, it was very impressive. Narcondam had steep sides reaching up from the sea to a flattened-off point wreathed in mist. There was very little land at its base; it *was* just a volcano. I was relieved that we would soon be able to stop. But no.

'We can't stay here,' Tyrone said. 'It's too dangerous. We could easily drag anchor offshore.' We had had 30 knots on our approach and very deep water at the one recommended anchorage. He went off to consult the pilot book and came out bearing bad news. 'We have to go back. I'm sorry, Emma.' Not as sorry as I was, thinking about the dreadful conditions out to sea. He said we could do a circuit of the island, so I motored us slowly in a clockwise direction around Narcondam. On the north-east side I spotted a small green hut and some wooden boats pulled up under the bushes. We had read in the pilot book that Narcondam was an abandoned police outpost but it turned out that people actually lived here, on this rock 100 miles from anywhere, and they came, six of them, including a woman, to stand shoulder to shoulder in a line on the beach and stare at us. Two men lifted a hand and waved at us slowly. I wanted to stop, to go ashore and talk to them, find out their stories, how they came to be here, how they got their food, their water, what they did for shelter. But we couldn't. So I kept going until I reached the point at which I had started my circumnavigation and then set a course back to where we had come from.

When I got up for Pablo's night watch, it was to find Libertad sailing downwind under the reacher at 9 knots from 20 knots of wind, in much calmer sea conditions and with no rain. Hooray! The rain hadn't been entirely unwelcome, since we had topped up our tanks, but we hadn't needed two incessant days of it.

We were to deviate from the itinerary, Tyrone decreed, and go instead to Long Island, which wasn't on the list at all. Everyone was tired, the food stocks were running low, although they hadn't reached dangerous levels yet, unless you count having to eat Supernoodles for lunch as a crisis (I kind of do), and we could all do with a break.

We anchored by a crumbling jetty and went ashore just after dark in search of dinner. As I had suffered the most with seasickness, no one was as glad as I was to step on to land. Until I saw the dogs.

I have never liked dogs. If a new acquaintance notices me acting weird in a pub garden or a park, I tell them that I 'don't like' dogs. But 'don't like' in no way encompasses the sheer awful, uncontrollable panic that sets in when I see one. It's something I've always suffered from and, while no one I have met really understands what it feels like for me, close friends and family know what is expected of them – basically, they need to throw themselves between me and the animal and selflessly sacrifice their lives for mine. It is an uncontrollable physical reaction on my part. From nowhere an enormous burst of adrenaline gives me a punch in my stomach. My eyes open wide, my head spins and I start to panic. I absolutely, at all costs, no matter where I am, have to get away from the dog. I have no mental control over my body. Sometimes my adrenal system and legs react before my eyes and brain are aware that I've seen a dog. Even something that sounds like a dog leash – a person jangling their keys, for example – will trigger it. Friends are left, mid-conversation, wondering why I am suddenly on the opposite side of the street. One day I'm going to end up dead, sprawled in the centre of a busy road, after I've dashed out carelessly, just because a Jack Russell has looked at me. I joke about it, but it's serious. And sad. And excruciatingly embarrassing.

On the rocky beach where we were coming ashore was a pack of wild dogs that started barking and running around excitedly when they saw us. I froze, looking around for another way through to the road. The others were barely even aware of the pack. Up to this point, no one, not even Tyrone, who I had spent the longest time with, had witnessed my fear. Malaysia and Thailand had been relatively dog-free. I spotted an alternative route – it meant going right out of the way and climbing over some rocks and walls. I didn't stop to worry about what my crewmates would think of me; I just went. The main road, once I reached it, gasping because I had been holding my breath in a panic for so long, was mercifully clear and I relaxed a bit. When the others reached me we walked along, talking, looking for signs of a village where we could get something to eat. When the road – and the street lamps – ran out, we turned off down a path in the darkness. Ben, who had the only torch and so was leading the way, asked the next people we met if they knew of a restaurant, and they said 'hotel' and pointed diagonally off from where we were. We continued, following the path. It was so dark now that all I could make out was the occasional light-coloured stone peppering the hardened mud we were following. Then the barking started.

The dogs were somewhere ahead of us, in the direction we were headed, and they were getting louder and more frenzied as we got closer. Panic rose up again and I fought to get it under control, digging my nails into the palms of my hands. I was at the back of the group and had slowed down, afraid of going any closer to where the barks were coming from. As we neared a couple of houses, whose gardens we had to pass between, the barking reached, to my ears at least, deafening proportions. It sounded like there were so many, all around me. It was so dark I couldn't see them. I didn't know how far away they were. I didn't know if they were about to leap out at me. I couldn't physically take another step. I stood, paralysed, on that path, with every muscle in my body trembling and my fists, still with my nails driving into my palms, lifted up to my ears to protect my head. And I wept.

Vicky realised something was up and came back to find me. Ahead, the guys were shouting things like 'Come on! We want to get to the restaurant. What are you doing?' They couldn't see me in the dark. Vicky rubbed my arm.

'I'm sorry,' I sobbed, my voice wobbling. 'It's the dogs. I've got this stupid phobia and there's so many of them and I can't see them.' I cried some more. She put her arm through mine and started to slowly walk forwards, towards the others, taking me with her.

'Keep looking straight ahead,' she said, in calm tones. 'Keep walking. Don't look at them. They're just marking their territory, they won't come over.' She was right, of course, and she kept repeating these things to me until we were past the worst of it and standing outside a hostel called Blue Planet.

In making this unscheduled stop at Long Island, and enduring the Dog Walk of Death through the woods, we had unwittingly stumbled across one of the only other places in the Andamans, apart from Havelock, where backpackers could stay. The ones camped here were fully fledged crusties. All eight or so of the hippy men sitting around the dirt-floored courtyard were bearded; the two women wore shapeless long sack dresses they had evidently chosen for their authentically ethnic vibe. (Funny that we never saw any local women wearing them, though.) They had their own tiny travelling paraffin camp stoves with them which were so inefficient that, in the time it took for us to order our 'Is it spicy?' curry dinners from the hostel's kitchen and eat them, they had still not managed to finish boiling pasta. They were not the friendliest bunch of people, either. Tyrone, always keen to make new pals, tried to start a conversation with a few of the men but they were not interested, giving him single-word answers. I got the feeling they weren't happy to discover other Europeans – Europeans without matted beards or dreadlocks, who didn't have multiple piercings and who were wearing high street clothes – had turned up at their little camp. The Indians who ran the place were much more welcoming.

There was a wooden shelf wedged between two trees that served as a library of sorts. It held mainly German books but, as I rifled through the stacks, I found some loose pages about the Andamans that had been photocopied from the *Lonely Planet* guide to India, and some printouts of articles posted on the website of an NGO called Survivor. I looked over the printouts while Pablo and Libertad, black heads bowed together, studied the *Lonely Planet* and a map someone had hand-drawn of the island. The article was about the Jarawa tribe of the Andamans, who were part of the first successful wave of migration out of Africa and into Asia 30,000 years ago. About 250 Jarawa remained today, it said. They were a black-skinned hunter-gatherer people who lived in the jungle in the same way they had done for millennia: they built communal thatched huts, wove baskets, hunted for fish with spears or bows and arrows, and wore no clothes apart from headdresses or a thin string belt around the waist and biceps. They only first came out of the jungle to 'mix' in 1998. I was fascinated. I read on.

Diseases like measles could kill them easily, I learned, so reserves had been set up that were no-go areas to outsiders

– until the government built a trunk road right through the centre of one reserve on Middle Andaman. Now various unscrupulous tour operators had been discovered, the article proclaimed, offering illegal 'human safaris' to see the Jarawa and take pictures. Some Jarawa, having been given a glimpse of modern-day civilised life, begged by the road or tried to entertain the tourists for money. There were two other surviving tribes in the Andamans, I read, the Onge and the Sentinelese. The last Bo man died a year or so ago, bringing his tribe to an end.

I was enthralled. In 2011, there were people in the world who were still hunter-gatherers, who continued to live as our ancestors did 30,000 years ago. I wanted to know everything about them: Where did they sleep? Did they make bread or cultivate rice? What did their language sound like? How did they celebrate? Did they believe in romantic love, in the way we did? Who were their gods? Were they happy? The article had no more information for me. Mainly it was designed to expose and shame these evil 'human safari' operators. I wanted to – whisper it – go on just such a human safari. But at the same time I respected the Jarawas' decision to, in the main, remain cut off from the world. And yet to meet one, to have a discussion, to learn about a world so far removed from my own it was difficult to comprehend we were of the same species – well, that would be beyond words, a once-in-a-lifetime experience.

19

Bringing order to the chaos

Since we had already deviated from our 'strictly enforced' itinerary and not been thrown into an Indian prison, we decided to take a chance by visiting out-of-bounds Interview island, which was said to be very beautiful, with fantastic coral and fish to see, and hope that we weren't caught.

It was a long sail, past mile after mile of jungle, beach and rock, and we saw not one house, nor one road, electricity pylon or telecommunications mast. Even in the remotest South Pacific islands Tyrone had been able to visit villages and barter for fish or buy meat preserved in freezers powered by electricity generated in some kind of civilisation. Here there was nothing.

At only a couple of hundred metres wide, Homfray Strait, a narrow channel between two islands that we had to navigate, looked more like a river than a stretch of sea, not dissimilar to the entrance of the Kinabatangan. Finally there was an indicator of human life: power lines strung across the water and a small ferry. We were unsure how high the power lines were and whether we could pass safely underneath them or would be zapped by a huge zing of electricity straight down the mast. Tyrone had asked the harbour master back in Port Blair what the height was but he hadn't known. Ever the maths teacher and problem solver, he donned his going-ashore khakis and he and Ben went over to work it out. He did something tricksy with the sextant and pacing out distances. What was Pythagoras's theorem? The sum of the square of the hypotenuse is equal to the force with which your head implodes under the pressure of trying to recall complicated maths equations you haven't used since you were 14 years old? I think we all uttered a little silent prayer that Tyrone's careful calculations, otherwise known as an educated guess, would be correct, as we squeezed underneath.

We were through and then – bang! – we hit a reef. The strait had widened into a circular bay that narrowed ahead of us, with a small gap between rocky outcrops to get out to sea again. Tyrone had been heading straight for the gap – and so was the coral growth. The water was clear but with the low angle of the gleaming sun we couldn't tell where the reef was, and we needed to find a path through. Ben and I got into the dinghy and I drove ahead of *Gillaroo* while Ben checked the depth, dipping an oar into the water to see how far down he could push until he crunched into rock or coral. The catamaran's draft was 1.8 metres. Feeling our way blindly like this, we traced the outline of the reef and crossed to the other side of the bay to do the same thing, until we had mapped out a clear area and Tyrone could motor through. As I zapped along, going fast enough to make the dinghy rise up out of the water and plane along the surface, I felt fantastic, really sure of myself and with – quite literally – a steady hand on the tiller. I thought again about option 1 – getting a job as paid crew on a superyacht. *Surely this is the life for me?* Half an hour later, back on the yacht and in open sea, I was having hot flushes and feeling shaky: seasickness. *Maybe this isn't the life for me.*

Sunset was fast approaching and I left the others doing the anchoring while I went inside to make a dinner of aubergine stew, flat breads and rice. For the first time in ages, we had company: two small fishing boats were at anchor near some rocks. Tyrone, Libertad and Vicky went over to talk to them and returned with a gift of four small fish: a grouper, two snappers and a coral trout. Vicky cleaned them off the back steps and I sprinkled their descaled and gutted bodies with olive oil, salt and pepper, wrapped them in foil and put them in the oven, keeping my fingers crossed that they wouldn't turn out to be as horrible as the tuna Steve had caught in Borneo. Like a gentleman, Tyrone removed the head and spine before handing me the plate so that I only had a pile of innocuous white meat to look at. It actually tasted nice.

Libertad, Pablo, Tyrone and I threw caution to the wind the next morning and went ashore, even though we weren't allowed to. There was nowhere to land the dinghy so Vicky dropped us off and we arranged for her to come back to meet us two hours later at the same place. Interview island had a steep bluff on one side of it and a rough beach made of exposed, dead coral. So much for the beautiful underwater coral gardens we'd been expecting; El Niño had wreaked its havoc here. Millions upon millions of spiralled cone shells, each about 3 inches long, covered the ground so thickly that we couldn't see the sand beneath. Beyond the beach was dense forest. It would have been very easy to lose our way so we stayed within sight of the boat, picking our way through the dead detritus of the sea.

A couple of days later I was sitting in the cockpit, reading, when Ben, who had been in the water trying to catch lobsters but had so far only managed to surface with one sacrificial antenna, shouted my name.

'Emma? Where's Tyrone?' he said, a funny tone having entered his voice.

'Inside, I think,' I called, putting down my book and standing up so that I could see him. 'Why, what's up?'

'You'd better tell him he's got a problem. Actually we've all got a problem.' He pulled his rubber mask off his face and tossed it on to the step. 'We've got no port rudder.'

Tyrone, after he had jumped in and swum around, confirmed it. 'We've lost our port rudder.'

I was sitting sideways in the helmsman's seat, facing the back of the boat, staring at him in disbelief as he climbed up the ladder and on to the port steps. 'What do you mean we've lost it? How?'

It had sheared off somehow, right through the vertical steel shaft that held it in place. The rudder had completely vanished. It wasn't bobbing along on the surface a little way off from the boat; it wasn't sitting on the bottom, waiting to be picked up. It was gone. And we couldn't figure out how it had happened. When we hit the reef in Homfray Strait it was with the front of the starboard keel, not the port keel or rudder. Tyrone hadn't noticed a difference in the steering between then and Interview and neither had Ben, who had been at the helm when we anchored. Since then we'd been in calm waters for three days with barely any waves. How could a 2-inch wide, high-grade stainless-steel pipe just snap off without anyone noticing anything? It was a mystery.

When I was little – and, actually, even now – my dad used to crack one of his many repetitive jokes whenever my brother, sister or I hurt a hand or a foot and went to him, howling for sympathy. 'What are you complaining about? It doesn't matter,' he'd deadpan. 'You've got a perfectly good one on the other side.'

'Oh Da-ad,' we'd moan, desperate to appear cool in front of our mates, while secretly thinking he was funny. Whether it is nature or nurture, now I'm getting older, I find myself turning gradually into my father, so here it comes: the thing about being on a catamaran was, we had a perfectly good rudder on the other side.

Gillaroo had sailed several hundred miles before, in the Pacific, with one working rudder, Tyrone said during a team meeting he called in the cockpit, and we could use the two engines to help steer, so we could easily make it back to Port Blair. But if we couldn't get a replacement made there, he wasn't sure he wanted to sail on to Sri Lanka, across 800 miles of open ocean. We'd have to look at going back to Thailand instead to get a replacement, which was four days away and in the wrong direction.

The mood was subdued, to say the least, as we started our journey back to Port Blair. We still had ten days of our allotted Andaman permit time left and, Port Blair and Aberdeen being as backward as they were, we couldn't see how we'd be able to get a rudder made fast enough to give us time to continue to cruise the islands, if we could find someone capable of manufacturing one at all. No one wanted to spend over a week in Port Blair, at anchor in the dirty harbour alongside the oil tankers. Ben and Vicky had to be back in the UK by mid-February, so a delay made things awkward for them. And our leave to remain in the Andamans expired soon and everything we had read said there were absolutely no extensions to be had. Ever.

Depressed, I looked through the pilot guides that night for Oman, Yemen, Eritrea and Sudan, working on my big plan. It sounded like the Red Sea was a horrible upwind trip with short, steep waves and very cold water. The guides were quite old, dating back to before the days of cheap flights, and they made it sound very expensive and difficult to fly to the UK from Sudan and virtually impossible from Eritrea. We had no internet signal so I couldn't look for more up-to-date information online. I started to think that maybe I should be aiming to leave the boat even earlier, in Aden in March, pretty much as soon as we arrived there, forgoing any sightseeing I had planned.

Our route to Port Blair was to take us back through Homfray Strait – avoiding any coral reefs – allowing us to stop overnight at anchor by Passage island and then to sail on in the morning to reach the harbour by nightfall. No one was speaking as we motored into the strait, keeping our port side closest to land, only about 100 metres offshore to avoid the uncharted reef, everyone lost in their own disappointment. I was sitting at the table, chin in my hands, staring idly at the passing trees.

'Is that a boat over there?' Vicky asked. 'With a man in it?'

Coming across other people was rare so I was intrigued enough to stand up and look at where she was pointing. Ahead of us and to the left were a few rocks jutting out of the sea, then a short beach that was quickly swallowed up by thick, tall jungle. Vicky offered me the binoculars and I looked through them as we moved closer. It was not a boat but a long, flat rock, with someone sitting on it, and another person squatting just behind them. We got closer still, expecting it to be a couple of Indian fishermen casting hand lines into the coral. But we were wrong.

Vicky took back the binoculars. 'They're black.'

And so they were – three Jarawa youths, crouching on the edge of the rocks, one in orange shorts, the others naked except for narrow black bands around their waists. They had dark, dark skin, short, curly black hair and were definitely not Indian. I was so excited that I forgot we were supposed to be leaving them alone and, not even considering whether such a gesture would be universally understood as a friendly greeting, waved. After a pause, the one in orange shorts waved back, slowly. The second man hurled a stone in our direction and the third just watched us pass by. I don't know who was the more surprised – them, at seeing a large floating box drive past on the water with six gurning pinky-white men and women on top of it, or us at being so easily and quietly able to catch a glimpse of some of the most elusive people in the world.

I didn't really believe that we would be able to get a replacement rudder in Port Blair. We needed the highest quality stainless steel, for one thing, and someone who worked with fibreglass, and most of the local boats were wooden. But within a day Tyrone had found someone to weld a new rudder frame for us. A tuk-tuk driver took him to a rusty, falling-down shack, with a scrawled sign outside declaring its business as 'Island Fibre Glass'. The helpful men inside were delighted to see Tyrone – they hadn't had any work for three months. The steel rod was bought, measured and cut, a frame of the blade was welded on to it (upside down, but we won't talk any further about that, apart from to note that it made no discernible difference) and the blade was coated in fibreglass. Four days' worth of labour and materials came to a grand total of about 6000 rupees, or £90. The Doubting Thomas was happy to be proved wrong.

The Doubting Thomas also had a pretty fun time in Port Blair and Aberdeen Bazar. There were some tourist attractions to visit: the Cellular Jail, a park, an outdoor Olympic-sized lido (I had to buy a swimming cap and try not to swallow too many drowned bugs as I breast-stroked my way along) and, a short ferry ride away, an old British government settlement, whose buildings, once independence was declared, had been abandoned and had crumbled into ruins in less than 70 years. At the anthropological museum we positively identified the black men we had seen as Jarawas.

I paid 50 rupees (60 pence) for a haircut, making sure to check with the 'stylist' at the Pony Saloon that he understood what I wanted: just a trim, a few layers around the front. He waggled his head – Yes? No? – picked up some rusty shears and chopped six inches off the front, working his way unevenly around my head. A pile of sun-yellowed hair sat on the floor. He wasn't finished – I had the head massage to come. Given the standard of the haircut I'd just received, obviously this was no relaxing scalp rub. No – there was slapping, there was pummelling, there was neck manipulation and, to finish, he braced one forearm against the side of my skull, gripped my right ear with the fingers of his other hand and pulled and pulled, until the place where my ear joins my head cracked loudly. That procedure he repeated on the other side. My ears recovered pretty quickly but that haircut took months to grow out. I was only relieved I hadn't asked him for a colour, too.

At an internet café I checked my emails. Apart from the texts at New Year, I hadn't been in contact with anyone for nearly a month. The connection was slow and it took a long time to update my inbox. There was the usual spam, some 'where/how are you?' messages from friends and – what was this? – an email with the subject 'Offer of employment'. I vaguely recognised the name of the sender, Carlo Giordano, and decided it was safe to open it.

Ever the cynic, I hadn't subscribed to Aaron's theory that if you want something enough the universe will manifest it for you. Hard graft can get you there, I believed, but not some spooky higher-power-influenced coincidence. Yet here, on this flickering, boxy computer screen, was the option 1 choice I had picked as my life's new direction: an offer of a job, as a deckhand, on a superyacht, in Italy this summer. It was mine, Signor Giordano wrote, if I was interested. Oh, and by the way, the salary was 1500 euros a month.

'Couldn't believe my eyes' was an understatement of an understatement. How did this Carlo Giordano even magically know that I had picked option 1 and wanted a job on a boat in the Med for the summer? An image of Aaron's face, his mouth forming the words 'the universe will manifest it for you' over and over, swirled around my head. Carlo was a captain of a superyacht who had once stayed at my sister's guesthouse in Southampton. She had told him I liked sailing; he gave her his business card to pass on to me. He stayed with her not long after I'd first decided to go off travelling and only a few weeks after I had done a low-level professional crew course to give me the option of picking up work while I was away. I had sent

Carlo an email, with my meagre sailing CV attached, asking him if he wouldn't mind taking a look and giving me any suggestions he might come up with. He replied, saying kindly that my CV was 'quite good, for a beginner'. I thanked him and we had no further contact. That was more than a year earlier. And now here he was, offering me a six-month paid position on his boat, starting in April, without even needing to interview me. And did I mention the 1500-euro-a-month salary? Of course I said yes.

Excited, I Facebooked Guy to tell him. He soon congratulated me.

'So glad you got your epiphany and you go for it!' he wrote. 'That's what life's all about, follow the epiphanies! The job in the Med sounds great experience on a posh boat. Shame as I was hoping I could convince you to spend a few months on *Incognito* for a trip to Indonesia, maybe PNG.'

Argh! What was this? Option 1 and option 4 both manifesting themselves but inconveniently at the same time? Bloody universe and its tricks. I was dying to visit Papua New Guinea – and Guy knew that. But I was still not sure if he was being serious.

'I'd have loved to,' I replied, 'but I've already accepted the job.' I hedged my bets. 'Some other time?'

'I will keep trying, maybe next year,' he wrote. 'I think we would get on well on board together. It would be easy and fun.' Sadly, but pleased that I'd been asked and that he still seemed to like me, I signed off. *Maybe he will ask me again, I hoped, if he really does mean it.*

While I'd been sorting out my summer, Ben and Vicky had been booking flights to the UK, now that we knew we were going to make it to Sri Lanka, and Pablo and Libertad were doing a little internet project of their own – on pirates. The night before we left Port Blair for Galle in Sri Lanka, they brought up the subject.

'Are ju not scared about this pirates?' Pablo asked, casually, after dinner, looking intently at us each in turn through his glasses. 'Because I look on the internet and it says the ships are being attacked.'

Obviously we were all aware of the risks of sailing across the Gulf of Arabia, from Yemen up into the Red Sea. The area was a notorious target zone for Somali pirates and the threat was being taken so seriously by foreign governments and shipping companies that a patrolled 'transit corridor' had been designated in an area where pirate activity was historically at its highest. I used my journalistic skills in weighing up all the evidence and to cut through the hype. Usually, the pirates were after container ships or tankers with valuable cargo and large crews that they could hold hostage. Yes, the British cruisers the Chandlers had been captured, but that had been widely recognised as an almighty cock-up on the part of the pirates. There were tactics that we could use – as Sexy Josh had done, and he'd been absolutely fine – to pass through the corridor safely: go as part of a convoy of at least five boats, run without lights at night, turn off the radio. All of this Tyrone had been aware of for years, from when he first began to plan his round-the-world voyage. He had already loosely arranged a rendezvous in Salalah in Oman with two other boats in order to set up our convoy group. It was a worry but not a major one: the Somalis were after rich, insured ships, not poor cruisers, and they were confined to an area fairly close to the Somali coast. By the time we got anywhere near, there'd be foreign navy ships and aeroplanes keeping an eye on us, anyway. It was exciting, rather than frightening. As Tyrone tried to reassure Pablo when he waved at him a sheaf of pages about pirates he had printed off the internet in Port Blair, 'The biggest danger to us is the weather.' I agreed with him, and Pablo and Libertad said no more about it.

20

On a sticky wicket

Acrossing is a crossing is a crossing. Sorry to sound so blasé about it but sometimes there's just sea, sky and precious little else. I love the peace and the rhythm, when the wind isn't kicking off, but a blow-by-blow account, in either sense of the word, doesn't necessarily make for the most interesting reading. There is one thing that stood out about the one-week crossing from the Andaman Islands to Galle in Sri Lanka: it rained. But you didn't come to me to hear about the *weather*, did you?

In Sri Lanka yachties can only take their boats to two places: Galle, a colonial fort town in the south, and the capital, Colombo. Galle was the closest, and the most popular place for yachts to pull in, and we arrived in the early evening, just as we were beginning to worry about losing light. Two boys in a little metal launch shot out of the harbour to smile and wave at us as we approached, white teeth gleaming in their mahogany faces. This was by far the friendliest reception we had received. Our designated parking space was a tight squeeze against a high concrete wall, with boats in front and behind us. The harbour authorities had hung black car tyres over the side of the wall to fend us off from the concrete. They would have to do as ladders at low tide, too. Using an old car tyre to clamber up a sheer concrete wall – it's all glamour, yachting.

Packs of feral dogs roamed the harbour, making me nervous. A week at sea had generated a reasonable amount of rubbish and I was the one carrying it when we went ashore. One dog broke away from its group to follow me closely, attracted by the smell coming from the black sack. I tried to keep in mind the tips Vicky had given me about dog behaviour during that horrible night on Long Island. *It's only interested in the rubbish*, I repeated to myself as my new mantra. *Just keep going and don't look at it.* I managed to keep my cool long enough to reach the bin and toss the bag inside it. The dog stopped following me and stayed by the bin, sniffing at the plastic. I breathed out, relieved.

The Cricket World Cup – partly hosted by Sri Lanka – was due to start in a few weeks' time and the place had gone cricket crazy. Boys and men set up a game on any piece of spare garden, yard, car park or wasteland they could find. Everyone we met – Navy security guards, fruit sellers, waiters, people in the street – wanted to talk cricket with us. They were out of luck with me. The best I could manage was to smile and cry, 'Freddie Flintoff! Stuart Broad!' loudly and with enthusiasm. The Sri Lankans humoured me. 'England team very good,' they said. 'Maybe win. Or maybe India.' No one fancied Pakistan's chances and surprisingly few were backing their own team for the top slot.

Galle was, we found, a town of two halves. By the sea was the quiet, preserved old fort with narrow, seventeenth-century streets lined with grey stone Dutch colonial houses that had been turned into art galleries, restaurants and hotels for foreign tourists. At the fort's centre, the narrow lanes widened into a peaceful cobbled courtyard and lawyers on their lunch break chatted about court business under the shade of huge banyan trees. Tyrone and I – the crew had broken off into two couples and the two leftovers – meandered about, going into jewellery shop after jewellery shop. Gemstones are big business in Sri Lanka and tourists come to gaze wistfully at the beautiful sapphires, rubies and moonstones on display in every other window. As we continued our tour we found – at last! – a museum and went in, keen to learn something about Sri Lanka's cultural history. But there were no labelled cards, no information boards, no instructive displays. One step into the next room and we found out why: the 'museum' was a front for another jeweller's, a cheap trick designed to get customers through the door. I admired some milky moonstone earrings but reluctantly handed them back. You can't exactly sport dangly earrings when you live on a boat – one wrong move and you'd find yourself hoisted six feet in the air by your ear.

The other half of Galle was for the locals. Every second shop here seemed to be an imitation of Claire's Accessories, the windows filled with pink and black sparkly handbags and hair scrunchies. No one has worn scrunchies in England since about 1992. In Sri Lanka they remain popular, probably because they are the only hair ties strong enough to get a firm grip on Sri Lankan women's hair. Hair growing is practically a competitive sport in Sri Lanka and you're no one if you can't sit on your plait. It must be the one country where the usually feeble excuse 'No, I can't come out with you on Saturday night because I'm washing my hair' is accepted as fair.

With lunchtime approaching, Tyrone and I looked around for a restaurant to try some authentic Sri Lankan food but all we could find was a one-stop-junk-food-shop, a rip-off combination of McDonald's, Pizza Hut and KFC. We were starving hungry but we couldn't bring ourselves to go in there for plastic cheese and reconstituted potatoes. A local man noticed us hesitating in a dingy-looking alleyway and asked us what it was we were looking for.

'Something to eat,' Tyrone said, towering over the tiny man.

'That is easy. You can eat here,' the man said, straining to look up. 'Where you are standing.'

We turned a full circle, confused. We'd been trying to find a restaurant for half an hour and hadn't seen anything apart from the fast-food joint.

'Here,' the man said, gesturing at a doorway. 'See?'

We peered into the darkness beyond. Inside it was tiny, little more than a corridor. 'Here you can eat Sri Lanka food. You like rice and curry?' We nodded and stepped into the room, our bodies taking up all of the available space. We sat at a shelf covered with newspaper. Beneath us the floor was also papered over. When our lunches arrived (there were no menus, we were just handed two plates piled with food and two Cokes) it became clear why: rice and curry (never curry and rice), the national dish, is a messy business. We ate with our hands and, despite our best efforts, rice, curried vegetables, bits of deep-fried chilli, slivers of coconut and shards of poppadum went everywhere – up the walls, on the floor, all over the table. Our fingers were stained yellow with spices and so were our chins. We were given a yellow curry, a green curry and a beetroot red curry, which added to the rainbow effect of our splatterings. Honestly, it looked like someone had involved a six-month-old in a self-feeding experiment using food colourants. What we did manage to get into our mouths was delicious and cost only 100 rupees, or 60p. Our plastic plates were covered in a layer of clingfilm and when we left, one of the teenage daughters peeled the clingfilm off the plates while her sister ripped the top layer of newspaper off the shelf and floor, saving both washing and sweeping up. Pure genius.

The six of us spent a few days in Galle, sightseeing and reading the *Rough Guide to Sri Lanka* to work out what we wanted to do with our two weeks there. Ben and Vicky and Tyrone and I were going to travel upcountry to see the tea plantations and mountains. Pablo and Libertad wanted to go to the north of the country, but that was as much as I knew of their plans because they were rarely around, staying out late each evening. *They must be keeping normal Spanish hours*, I thought. *After all, they'd usually be having their lunch at the time of day we serve up dinner on* Gillaroo. But it turned out it wasn't eating they were doing 'til the wee hours, it was research. They were scaring themselves silly about pirates.

Nothing more had been said about piracy after Pablo had raised the subject on our last night in the Andamans and neither Tyrone nor I had thought any more about it. Then one afternoon the Spanish came back to the boat and asked to talk to Tyrone and me. They were, they said, very worried. They had found reports that the pirates had strayed further away from Somalia, moving east towards the coast of Oman, which was to be our next stop. More ships were being taken, Pablo said, trying to show us research in Spanish that we didn't understand. The pair of them were quite worked up. Ben and Vicky, who were leaving the boat in Sri Lanka, listened quietly but said nothing. Could we sail up the coast of India and underneath Pakistan instead? the Spanish asked. Tyrone said it would take too long – four weeks instead of two – and we wouldn't have enough fuel and we'd miss our convoy rendezvous date in Oman. Then they said they had spoken to other yachties in Galle harbour and had found a man who was organising a convoy of boats all the way across the Indian Ocean, not just through the safety corridor, and would Tyrone consider joining it? Softening, Tyrone said he would be willing to speak to the man to find out more.

Both he and I thought that they were overreacting, that they had allowed themselves to be whipped into a frenzy by this convoy organiser, who undoubtedly stood to make a buck or two from the venture. Nonetheless, we looked into it ourselves, finding websites of various acronym-heavy organisations – UKMTO, EU NAVFOR, MSCHOA – which listed the names and locations of the ships that had been attacked, and how many crew they had that were still being held hostage. It made for frightening reading when faced with pure statistics: more than 800 crew being held to ransom in Somalia. But these were professional ships, major targets and serious money machines – no recent attacks on sailing vessels were cited.

The four of us went to see the TTT (Thailand to Turkey) rally organiser, Hans, a Dutch man who had his partner and two small children on board his boat. *Surely he wouldn't be risking their lives if it was bad as he was making out?* I told myself. He sat spread-legged in the cockpit of his expensive-looking yacht, spelling out the dangers to us and breaking off from his scaremongering to take important phone calls.

'This year,' he said on the phone to 'the media', as he made sure to inform us after he'd hung up, 'will be the first that not all ninety boats will get through to the Red Sea.' It was an impressive soundbite.

'Why aren't you going round the Cape instead?' I asked. He replied that it was just as dangerous. I had to agree with him on this point – almost definitely dire wind and weather conditions as opposed to the remote possibility of being approached by pirates. I looked at Pablo and Libertad, who were hanging on every word. Tyrone was silent, letting Hans have his say, but I could tell he was not impressed.

It was like being given the hard sell by someone who had rung our doorbell with a very good deal on some new windows. Hans had the solution to our problem, he said. We could join his rally and be reassured by safety in numbers. If we joined, he would give us a series of waypoints to head for and other yachts would be there. All we needed to do was hand over US$250. We asked what would happen if one of the 30 or so boats in the convoy had a problem, for example with their engine, and fell behind. No one would wait for them, he replied, they'd be on their own. *So much for sticking together and helping each other out*, I thought. *If the strong don't stop to help the weak, what on earth was the point?* I was disgusted. I felt he was preying on people's fears.

Pablo and Libertad had told us that Hans had informed them he practically had a guarantee of a military escort from a Spanish commander. As we sat in the cockpit of his yacht, his phone rang again. It was one of the acronyms.

Hans's voice rose with anger. 'These are frightened people,' he said into the phone. 'All they want is an escort for three days.' So it was a convoy that wasn't a convoy and he was promising an escort that wasn't yet assured. Those setbacks didn't stop Hans from making a final push for a sale: we must hurry. There were only three spaces left and when they were gone, they were gone.

Pablo was all puppy dog eyes at Tyrone when we got back to *Gillaroo* but Tyrone wasn't remotely interested. He clearly thought Hans was a fool and that his 'convoy' was a waste of time. With 1900 miles to cover, we would only be able to motor at our most economical speed of 4 knots so if we were to join Hans's scheme, once the wind died we would be the ones being left behind.

Ben and Vicky and Tyrone and I were getting ready to leave the boat to spend the second of our two weeks in Sri Lanka exploring the island. We had all agreed to be back in Galle by 10 February, ready to leave on the twelfth. The night before us four were due to catch an early morning train to Colombo, Pablo and Libertad came back very late and were extremely subdued. I thought I knew then what was coming and I waited for them to tell us they wanted to leave the boat, but when they said nothing, I assumed I must have gotten the wrong end of the stick.

Early the next morning we were climbing up the harbour wall, passing up our bags on to land, when Libertad ran up to Tyrone. Pablo was nowhere to be seen.

'Tyrone, can we talk to ju?' she asked. She didn't actually need to say anything; her face told us all we needed to know. Tyrone and I looked at each other. Now was not the time to have this discussion – we were on a tight schedule to make our train. Tyrone started to stride off towards the harbour entrance – it was a good five minutes' walk away – and I turned to follow him.

'Tyrone, wait!' Libertad called out. He kept marching, not turning back to look at her. Tyrone, Ben, Vicky and I walked on in silence, getting almost to the gate before Libertad caught us up, with Pablo. They were sorry, they said, they hadn't planned for this to happen, they were scared of the pirates and they had talked about it between themselves and thought it was the right thing for them to do. Still Tyrone said nothing. He looked straight ahead. I took my cue from him and stayed silent, too, although I did make eye contact with Libertad. When I did, she started crying.

'Tyrone! Say something!' she begged.

He stopped and sighed.

'What can I say, Libertad?' he asked in a calm and measured way. 'You've obviously made your decision and that's it. If you want me to say OK, then OK.' His tone was not angry, not accusing, not laced with spite. If anything, he sounded resigned. We said our goodbyes there, in the street, with hugs and handshakes. Libertad was still crying. She was genuinely upset. *Did she really want to leave because of the pirates,* I wondered, *or had Pablo convinced her to do it? Was the truth really that he just didn't enjoy being on the boat and was using this as an excuse to hide behind?* Tyrone and I continued to walk towards the tuk-tuk rank and I waited for him to speak first.

'It's not the fact that they want to leave the boat,' he said eventually. 'It's the way they've done it. They've known for days and they tell us now? When we're just about to go upcountry? I need to find more crew and we've got to make Salalah by March the first and we don't have a lot of time. They could have given me more notice.'

Later, in our hotel, we discussed our options. Tyrone didn't really want to do the trip just two-handed, and neither did I, but we could if we had no other choice. He couldn't abandon the boat in Sri Lanka; he needed to get it back to Europe to sell it. We would try to find replacement crew for the passage to Oman at least. He said he would send a round-robin email in the hope someone knew of somebody else who would be interested. I texted a couple of sailing friends who I thought might be at a loose end and up for a challenge. Tyrone renewed his online advert and we crossed our fingers that that would work, even with the very small timeframe we had in place – a week and a half.

21

Under my umbr-Ella

I half expected live chickens and goats and bedraggled children clinging to the roof for the train ride from Galle to Colombo. Instead, in this lasting legacy of British colonialism, we got five passengers to a three-man seat and countless more in the aisles. It was just like the old Connex service from Sevenoaks into Charing Cross, except the hair and faces of all the other passengers were dark brown, many with a crimson dot dabbed on to their foreheads. The men, smart in their uniform of polyester slacks, collared shirts and manicured moustaches, paid no heed to their proximity to each other. Small children stared at us unabashedly while their mothers allowed us polite smiles through lips pressed together as tightly as their knees.

'Wadi! Wadi!' came cries from turbaned men who forced their way through the packed antiquated carriages with baskets of deep-fried prawns and sweetcorn fritters served in pages ripped from children's used exercise books stapled together along the edges. I unfolded the paper my breakfast – a sugar roll – had come in. It was someone's maths homework and they had been awarded eight out of ten. My lunch, a banana-leaf-wrapped serving of stringhoppers (rice noodles and spices) cost me just 6p, by far the cheapest meal I have ever had. I copied the locals and tossed the empty leaf out of the train window. I can see why littering is such a big problem in Asia, if everyone is used to letting drop their biodegradable wrappings. It doesn't quite work with plastic bottles and crisp packets, though.

I didn't think it was possible but the second train, from Colombo to Kandy, was even busier. And apparently having a first-class ticket didn't make any difference – it was every man, woman and child for themselves. Getting into the spirit, I managed to squeeze on to the end of a row of young British Sloanes, all pink cheeks and clipped accents, who passed the journey reading their Kindles, rather than looking out of the window at the scenery.

And what a sight they missed. It was absolutely spectacular. As we climbed for hours, screeching and clanging, the crowds thinned, the cockroaches feasted on dropped crumbs and the land fell dramatically away from the rails, dropping into steep valleys of a deep green, punctuated by villages and waterfalls. The names of the villages on the station signs reached improbable and unpronounceable lengths. The heat, the rocking and the steady rhythm were soporific between the alarm-clock calls of the whistle announcing each station's approach. I rested my forehead against the cool glass of the cracked window to try to keep awake. I didn't want to miss these views.

Yet another stop, proudly informing us of its height more than 1km above sea level, and finally we had a sight of the tea fields. Juicy, verdant, vast… but not fields; rather, choppy little steps cut into the hillside. The train struggled with the terrain, snaking a zigzag so tight we could see the Harry Potter-style carriages further ahead curling back towards us.

As we rounded another bend we passed two women working. In their saris and bindis, with hessian sacks looped around their foreheads and backs stooped, they were the epitome of the Sri Lankan tea picker, straight from the illustration on the side of a box of PG Tips.

Unfolding ourselves at last from our seats at Kandy, Tyrone and I shared a taxi van with Ben and Vicky. They got in at their first choice of hotel but Tyrone and I made our poor driver ferry us from place to place, looking for a room with twin beds and internet access so Tyrone could start looking for new crew. The search went on for ages, up and down the narrow lanes on the steep hill of Kandy, in the rain, until we eventually settled on the Thilini Guest House. It was little more than the spare room in the house of a widower and his daughter, with dead mosquitoes stuck to the untiled bathroom walls, and very hard beds, but it was cheap and a hotel next door let us pay to use their computer.

Despite our crew problems, we were determined to enjoy ourselves and see some of this wonderful country, and we arrived at the Pinnawala Elephant Orphanage just as the elephants were having their daily bathe in the river. There were dozens of them, being watched over by handlers, wallowing in the water and climbing up the opposite bank to have a roll in the mud. Hundreds of tourists lined the river's edge, watching and taking photos. A few of the elephants were brought on to flat rocks near the water for people to feed. The handlers weren't very friendly – I think they were frightened that things could get out of hand easily as the animals were effectively free to go wherever they wanted.

'Be careful,' our van-driver-slash-tour-guide, Jagath, had told us. 'Last week they break a woman's arm.' A family of frightened Germans tried to feed pineapple chunks to a young elephant but whenever the tip of its extended trunk came near their outstretched hands they freaked out and dropped the fruit, leaving the creature to scrounge around in the dirt. As soon as the elephant walked away, out came the antibacterial hand gel. I smiled. I had long since abandoned all the hygiene practices the guide books advise you to adopt. I had thrown caution to the wind and ordered salads, taken ice in my drinks, eaten at tables covered with flies, drunk rainwater: basically done all the things you are told you shouldn't do. Not once had I gotten ill and my antibacterial hand gel was gathering dust in my cabin somewhere. I was a different person from the one back in London who had packed syringes, a woolly hat and high heels 'just in case'.

Next, at a spice garden, a guide pointed out the different trees and shrubs and explained their medicinal properties as we went. There was a cinnamon tree with peeling bark, which I recognised, and a vanilla vine, which I did not. I wasn't even aware that vanilla grew on a vine. Like the 'museum' in Galle, the main purpose of the tour was to persuade us to buy some magic lotions and potions. I looked down the list of products we could buy and sniggered when I came to number 22. It was a kind of herbal Viagra, the list said. I think maybe the application process – rubbing an oil into the balls – might have had more to do with its efficacy than the potency of the herbs. Tyrone was the guinea pig for the demonstration of an amazing hair-removal cream. Use this on your body just twice, the guide said, slapping some on to Tyrone's shin, and you will be hair-free for seven years. True, Tyrone did have a little bald patch on his leg when we left the spice garden, but he had the beginnings of stubble a few weeks later.

In Ella, a village high up in the mountains, where the climate was unbelievably different from that of roasting Galle, I had to wear all of the clothes I had taken with me at once to keep warm in the 18°C temperature – I must have acclimatised to the tropics if I was feeling cold in what is not far off the average British summertime thermometer reading. We were so high, at 1000 metres above sea level, that we were level with the clouds and constantly wet. My umbrella had its first outing in months and was up most of the time. It was refreshing and it made a nice change to not be sweating.

Ella was a one-street village, with nearly all of the hotels cut into the hillside to make the most of the views. A grey-haired man with no front teeth, tiny as a pixie, barefoot and wearing a plastic poncho, trotted alongside us as we walked from the train station. He could show us a hotel, he said, and we followed him through a maze of car parks and steep steps – there were no side roads here – to one of the highest in Ella. It had a beautiful garden of lush grass and a terraced restaurant; also wifi. We snapped it up. Tyrone got straight on to the computer to see if he had any replies from potential crew. There was one, from a Canadian called Moe.

'Moe has some concerns about civil unrest in Egypt and pirates,' Tyrone told me. 'I can't tell if she is definitely interested or not. What do you think?' I read the email over his shoulder. It seemed to me that Moe was making polite excuses and I told Tyrone that. We tried to remain positive that our crew problem would get sorted.

The hotel kicked us out the following morning, even though

we'd booked in for two nights – I think they took umbrage with me for having the gall to ask them for an extra blanket. We found another place at the other end of the village on the edge of the woods that was a cross between a guest house and a hotel, Nelly's Forest Paradise. It rained all morning but cleared enough in the afternoon for us to take a walk up to Little Adam's Peak, a lookout point on a ledge in the middle of the tea plantations. We passed two tea pickers as we followed the path and they asked us for money to take our photo. No thanks, we said, and they bent to their work again.

That was one of the great things about Sri Lanka. The locals would make a gentle attempt at making money out of us but their hearts weren't really in it and if we said no they always backed off immediately, not in the least affronted. In many towns and villages the tourism industry is still in its infancy, being stunted by years of civil war, and the people haven't had a chance to grow hard-nosed and cold-hearted.

When we returned, drenched, from our walk, Nelly, the Sri Lankan owner/manager of our guesthouse, knocked on our door. He wanted to talk to me about yoga, he said. I followed him through to his private sitting room, wondering if he was about to launch into a spiritual discussion of enlightenment and becoming one with the universe. I'm not really into that aspect of it; I just like the stretches and the promise that I'm going to get a smokin' hot body if I do enough downward dogs. Nelly invited me to sit in an armchair and ordered one of his two 'Tamil boys' to bring us some tea. I waited for him to settle into his chair and begin. He didn't want to talk chakras at all – he needed help with a business plan.

He had two guest houses, he said, one at the beach in Unawatuna and one here. He wanted to build a yoga centre on some spare land here in Ella, next to the guest house, and hire a live-in yoga teacher. The two of them would split the proceeds – Nelly would have the income from his rooms and dinners and the teacher would get to keep what he or she charged for the classes. What did I think?

'This one Ireland man came last week,' Nelly said. 'Ireland man said people would only want to go Unawatuna for yoga.' In his hoodie emblazoned with the logo of an Evangelical church, which he wore every day even though he was a Buddhist, and with his short hair and glasses, he looked, despite his 50 years, like a little boy who had just been told he couldn't have the puppy he had been promised for months.

I thought it was a fantastic idea. The climate was cool enough here to do exercise, those bendy types love the outdoors and there was plenty of hiking to do around Ella between their yoga sessions. There was also an ayurvedic clinic with a good reputation in the village, so they could sign up for some treatments as well.

'I don't see why people wouldn't come here, Nelly,' I told him. 'It's so beautiful. I would, if I wanted to go on a yoga holiday.' His eyes lit up and I became his best friend after that. He invited us to have dinner with him and his Tamil boys served us rice and curry – what else? – all steamed together inside a banana leaf. Tyrone left for the south the next day because he was sick of the rain but I stayed on, helping Nelly with some research on the web. All I did was use Google to find yoga websites where he could advertise for a teacher but he thought I was the cleverest person alive.

'You come and be my yoga teacher,' he said. 'I give you free apartment, my Tamil boys cook you free food.'

'That's very kind, Nelly,' I said. 'But I'm not trained as a yoga teacher. And I've already signed a contract for a job on a boat for the summer.'

'That's OK,' he said. 'You come in October after boat. I will give you free apartment to live. I will buy you a small car so you can go Unawatuna, too. Good life for you, England lady.'

I have to say, it was tempting. The next morning, as I walked to get the train to the tea plantations, I thought about his offer. It could be a good life. It was beautiful here and if I charged just £5 per yoga session and offered two sessions a day, with no rent or food bills to pay, I'd be able to save good money in Ella. But I'd be lonely, I knew, in this tiny village hours from anywhere. Its tranquillity appealed to me now but I doubted that it would always. Still, it was nice to have an option 5 to add to the list.

Back at *Gillaroo* Tyrone had, at last, some good news: Moe had agreed to come. She was in Colombo with a friend and would arrive in a couple of days. She was interested in staying on the boat until Egypt.

This was a fantastic result. Sailing two-handed would have been quite difficult, having to be on watch for 12 hours a day each and having no long stretches in which to get a good night's sleep. Lots of cruising couples do it, and indeed prefer to have their boat to themselves, but after sailing with a crew of six for six weeks, to be just two people would have been a bit of a shock.

Moe's arrival at the boat – she seemed to materialise from nowhere, her professional photographer's camera tucked into one bag on her back, her MacBook into a second and her clothes into a third – was the quietest thing about her. She was one of the funniest, most confident and most interesting people I had ever met. A 41-year-old freelance photographer, she had been based in London until she left the city with her boyfriend, who had bought a boat with the aim of living the dream in the Caribbean, but their relationship had soured and she had flown off to Asia to travel solo. She was hilarious, gregarious, blonde and beautiful and very, very tanned. We hit it off immediately, swapping tales of woe from our tough times with our skippers and doing a lot of female bonding.

Tyrone warmed to Moe instantly, too, and his personality underwent a change. I don't think he fancied her – 'She's too old for me,' he told me. 'Too old!' Moe protested when I passed on the information. 'Well that's nice!' – but she seemed to bring him out of his shell. The computer games and monosyllabic replies were gone; in their place came smiles, jokes and flirting. He even got a tan from spending more time outside with us. He made a comment about how it was easier to get into the galley and that confirmed my theory that having six people on board had overwhelmed him. Tyrone and I had grown closer during our time upcountry in Sri Lanka. I think the seriousness of what we were about to do, sailing across an ocean non-stop for two weeks, and the way we had had to draw up a plan of action after Pablo and Libertad left, had pulled us together as a team. In the event, it was a very good job the three of us liked, respected and trusted each other. Because we were about to be tested to our limit.

22

A passage through the Indian Ocean

The brightest of blues, the Indian Ocean stretched flat and calm all the way to the full circle of a horizon around us. Nothing – no other boats, no birds, not a breath of wind and not even, for once, any floating rubbish – disrupted the smooth, silk-like surface of the water. It was just mile upon beautiful, calm, isolated mile of space. The engines, behaving themselves (unusually), hummed as they pushed us along at a steady 100 nautical miles a day and the blissed-out crew of *Gillaroo* had no cares in the world.

The first night out of Galle had been very windy and I knew as soon as we hit short, steep waves just beyond the harbour wall that I was going to be seasick. I had started taking anti-malarials – this time, doxycycline – and they added to the disgusting churning sensation in my stomach. I managed to fight down the nausea for my first watch, keeping my eyes on the horizon, but sure enough, as soon as the sun went down and the line between sea and sky vanished, I started up-chucking. I sat in the dark at the helmsman's seat, a bucket wedged between my knees, waiting for the next build-up of nausea to reach its peak so that I could be sick and feel human again for five minutes before the cycle repeated. Five times in one three-hour watch the pattern went like this: I would start to sweat, shake and feel bad and the metallic taste would grow stronger in my mouth until I threw up, noisily, into the bucket. Then, feeling momentarily better, I would tip it over the side, rinse it out with salt water ready for the next round and brush my teeth. It was one of the worst seasickness episodes I've ever had and all the more unusual considering I was sitting outside in the fresh air, which normally helps. But I didn't accept any offers of help from Tyrone or Moe to take over my watch from me. *If I'm going to make a career out of yachting*, I told myself, *I've got to learn how to deal with this.* Then I yacked again and counted down the minutes as they ticked away, achingly slowly, towards bed and freedom from this feeling that I was dying. Seasickness is weird in that way; it has a deeply depressing psychological element to it, quite different from being punished by your body for drinking one too many on a Saturday night. Thankfully, after a few hours' rest between watches, my body had reset itself, the wind had dropped and the waves had calmed.

For two days we motored on, filling the off-watch hours with jobs like polishing the steel, gluing patches on to the sorry-looking shredded mainsail and varnishing the wooden fixtures. We had adopted a rota of two three-hour watches each during the day and one two-hour watch at night. With a new person on board, there was an expanded repertoire of meals and we ate everything from freshly baked cinnamon buns to hand-cut chips. Food, water and electricity supplies were plentiful with just three people for a two-week crossing.

On the third day the wind grew steadily to 10 knots, still

with a flat sea, and we had the most perfect downwind sailing conditions a sailor could ever wish for. With a new spinnaker up that Tyrone had bought in Thailand, we fairly shot across the ocean. That morning a school of young tuna swam alongside us for hours, matching our speed and staying within a couple of metres of the port beam. Later in the afternoon we realised why – they were using *Gillaroo* to hide from a team of dolphins that was hunting them. No sooner had the dolphins appeared in our bow wave than the tuna disappeared, abandoning their cover and taking their chances in the wide blue yonder. With the dolphins came a sail fish, a magnificent giant that swam to the surface of the water just in front of the boat to get a better look at us. As Moe and I stood on the bow, watching the dolphins play, we saw a flash of iridescent purple as the fish's huge back fin broke the surface. The sail fish tilted slightly to one side to raise an eye to see us, weighing up what danger we posed, and, clearly deciding we were likely to win in a fight, it was gone, curling its body sharply to shoot off in a flash far, far away.

It was almost a magical time, that first week of crossing the Indian Ocean. Once the sea sickness was over and done with, it was perfect. Even the weather was sunny and steady and the only frightening thing we had to face was the flying fish. They actually do fly, spreading their fins and soaring right out of the ocean to heights of two or three metres. They might be good at flying but they are hopeless at direction – they will smack into anything that gets in their way. One sailor I know got whacked in the face by a flying fish when he was steering a boat across an ocean. And they stink to high heaven. 'I was scrubbing my cheek for a week, trying to get the smell off me,' he said.

For some reason known only to the underwater world, the flying fish of the easternmost reaches of the mid-Indian Ocean decided to unleash an attack against *Gillaroo*. They bombarded us. In the mornings, the deck was littered with their stiff, shining bodies. At night, I'd hear the thwack of them hitting the fibreglass. One watch I was sitting at the helm in the pitch blackness, minding my own business, when something landed with a thump on the canvas awning above my head. It had been so quiet and the thump was so loud and unexpected that I jumped out of my skin. A foot or so above my head, the noise continued. Thump! Thump! Thumpety-thump! *It sounds like a large bird walking around*, I thought. *It must have landed on us for a rest.* I punched the underside of the awning with the side of my fist, expecting to scare it off. But it carried on bouncing loudly around. I was just getting out of the seat to go and shoo it off when – bam! – a fish came leaping through the open window space in front of me, rebounded off the chair and landed on the floor. If I'd still been sitting at the helm, it would have landed slap in the middle of my lap. I let out a girly yelp and skipped backwards. The flying fish, having recovered from its shock landing, writhed, flipping and jittering, around the footwell. *It's OK*, I told myself, while waiting for my heart to resume its normal rhythm, *it'll suffocate in a minute and I can chuck it back into the sea*. But the slippery sucker wouldn't die. It bounced and flounced and did the hokey cokey for what felt like hours.

One of the tasks Moe had signed up for was the daily radio net. Any sailing boat crossing from Sri Lanka, Cochin in India or the Maldives to Salalah or Muscat in Oman could tune into a certain SSB frequency at two set times of day. Using a kind of code, each boat reported its distance from and bearing to an agreed waypoint, which all yachts held the co-ordinates for. It was relief to hear each crew checking in – or, even better, arriving safely in Oman – and a gentle kind of camaraderie grew from our sharing little bits of information: what the wind conditions were like, who had celebrated a birthday, how long until you reached your destination. It helped break the feeling of isolation. In addition to that, Tyrone had registered *Gillaroo*'s passage plan and crew details with various maritime organisations, who had promised to track us and pass on any information they had about pirate activity. Two cargo ships had been hijacked on 8 and 9 February, a few days before we left Galle, and we had received no notifications since. We were running without any lights at all at night – if a sail needed changing, we did it by starlight. We continued like this until we reached the halfway point of the crossing, a week or so away from land in either direction. And then the news came.

I got up from my morning sleep, ready for my 10am–1pm watch, feeling slightly groggy. Tyrone and Moe were at the saloon table, as usual for this time of morning, finishing off the SSB net and a round of checking the emails and trying to get hold of a weather forecast. Moe was the first to tell me.

'We've had an email,' she said. I was only half listening as I concentrated on making a cup of tea. 'A BBC report about a boat that's been taken by pirates.' Tyrone started to tell me about the article, mentioning 'SV *Quest*'. My stomach flipped and I stopped what I was doing to look at Tyrone and Moe.

'SV? Sailing vessel?' I asked. They both nodded, their faces set into grim expressions. *Shit. It's happened.*

I moved from the galley to the saloon and asked to read the article. An American-flagged sailing vessel, it said, called *Quest*, had been taken off Oman two days earlier, on Friday morning. It was now Sunday morning and this was the first we'd heard of it. I read on. The boat had been hijacked just 400 miles from where we were now, according to the report, and only 200 miles north-east of our intended track. There was an older couple on board and two crew, the story said. There was no further information about what had happened to the crew, boat or pirates since.

I looked up from the computer. Tyrone and Moe looked as panicked as I felt, although they were both trying to be brave and remain calm.

'Where did this email come from?' I asked Tyrone. He explained that a friend of a friend, Lucy, was keeping track of any pirate reports on the web and sending them to him while we were on passage. There had been nothing from EU NAVFOR, Marlo, UKMTO or any of the organisations who had promised us that they would let us know if anything had happened, so that we could alter our course if needs be. Two whole days had passed since the *Quest* hijacking and we'd received not once piece of information from any of them. Tyrone was furious.

I clicked on the MaxSea window and opened the chart so that I could understand where we were and where *Quest* had been when it had been taken. I drew a straight line from the boat icon that represented *Gillaroo* to Salalah; about 800 miles. Tyrone had already marked the co-ordinates of the attack with a shipwreck symbol. With the whole of the Indian Ocean on the screen, the hijack seemed horribly close to our line.

'What if the pirates cross our path?' Moe said quietly. 'Or what if they hang around in the area, waiting to see if any other yachts come past? We'd be a bonus then – two for the price of one.' I didn't answer her. The pirates could travel at 20 knots or more, I knew. If they were 200 miles off, they could be just 10 hours away. We wouldn't know whether or not they were in the area until we saw their skiffs on the horizon and, by then, it would be too late to do anything about it. We were closer to Oman than we were to Sri Lanka now, Tyrone said, especially with the wind in this direction. Our only option was to carry straight on and just hope that nothing happened. We were helpless.

It was 10am and I went to sit outside for my watch, scanning the horizon first for any sign of boats. There was nothing, only clear sky, bright sun and blue sea. It felt so surreal. *This can't be happening*, I repeated to myself, over and over. After a short time the disbelief passed and the shock set in, sending my whole body into fits of tremors as the adrenalin went to work. I caught a glimpse of movement in my peripheral vision and leapt out of the seat, my heart racing. It was just a bird. I worried about us but, more so, I worried about family and friends back home. If they had heard the news they would be terrified for us, and probably more than we were – at least we knew we were safe so far. As the three hours of my watch ticked by, I gradually began to calm down. There was nothing we could do. We just had to carry on.

One of the main principles of journalism is revealing unfairness and wrongdoing. So, despite moving away from newspapers, it was to them that I turned for help. In an unjust situation they can help garner a solution. In stressful times, we all resort to the familiar. To me, that meant writing.

I wrote an article about the situation and Tyrone emailed it, via the SSB link, to my contacts at the *Independent* and the *Daily Express*. We were hoping that my critical remarks about how we had had no information from any of the authorities might shame them into action.

Apart from that, the three of us didn't talk much about it at all. For the rest of the day we were very quiet, I think because we all recognised that if we started to verbalise between us all the 'what ifs?' then we would hype ourselves up into a seriously frightened state. So we read and ate, we checked the email for any other reports, and we sailed *Gillaroo* onward towards safety.

An email came through from Lucy making mention of a 'situation' in Aden but not what it was. Apart from that there was nothing. We continued our duties, ignoring the simmering tension on the boat, until we heard an engine.

We all freaked out for a second before realising it was an aeroplane. Tyrone switched on the VHF while Moe and I dashed out into the cockpit. The plane was pale grey and flew over us twice, low.

'Sailing vessel overflown, sailing vessel overflown, this is coalition forces airplane, over,' came an American man's voice over the VHF.

Tyrone grabbed the mike and replied. 'Coalition forces plane, this is sailing vessel *Gillaroo*, over.'

They wanted our boat name and our last and next ports of call.

'Can I ask you,' Tyrone said, after he had reported the information, 'is the area clear?'

'Yes, all clear, as far as we can see, sir, over,' came the reply. So we knew we were safe for a while at least.

'And do you have any information about Sailing Vessel *Quest*, over?' Tyrone asked.

There was a pause. Then: 'I do not have any information, sir.' I thought that the pause meant he probably did but that he wasn't allowed to say. 'Have a safe trip,' he said, before signing off. Never before had those innocuous words meant so much to me. It was such a comfort to know someone was looking out for us.

Moe reported back to me what had come from the afternoon radio net. 'Obama has made a statement on the situation,' she said, relief evident in her voice, 'about taking action against the pirates.' She spoke to *Senang*, a Dutch boat with a couple and two young boys on board, who were 60 miles away from us, about the possibility of a rendezvous. Tyrone and the *Senang* skipper agreed to monitor each other's progress for now – we could sail faster; they could motor at higher speeds. The wind was due to die that day or the next and one would have to wait for the other if we wanted to team up and waiting was not ideal – everyone wanted to get to port as quickly as possible.

Tyrone made an English breakfast for dinner, which proved a big morale booster, and we went into our night watches, which were even more frightening. Every time I saw a dot on the radar, my heart skipped. After a while, I turned it off. If they came for us, there was nothing we could do anyway. We couldn't outrun them – they could do 20 knots + to our 7 knots under sail or 4 knots under engine – and we had no weapons. They would have machine guns and rocket-propelled grenades. I started to fantasise about what I could do – drop the dinghy into the ocean and speed off; hide in the small storage space underneath my bed. But I realised they could easily outrun me in the dinghy, I couldn't get very far with just a couple of litres of petrol anyway, and they would search the boat thoroughly, perhaps hurting Tyrone or Moe to find out where I was hiding. From what I had read during my research in Galle, the Somalis were often wildly high and hyped up from chewing a narcotic plant called qat. There would be no reasoning with them. If the worst came, I would just have to accept it.

Ironically, I slept the best I had in days that night, both from 10pm to 2am and from 4am to 9am, although I woke myself up sobbing in my sleep. The next morning there was no news other than that the US had asked permission from the Somali government to land their planes in Somalia. We were more than 500 miles from Salalah, I worked out when I checked the chart, and doing 7 knots or 8 knots, so we should arrive about four days later.

'*Quest* are dead,' was the first thing that Moe said when I got up for watch the following day. I expected to be sad or shocked but mainly all I felt was a weird detachment. I hadn't known these people; it was just like hearing something terrible on the news. That was all we knew and we carried on pretty much as normal, gritting our teeth and concentrating on the task of getting ourselves to Salalah. It took a while for the details to come through about what had happened. Lucy forwarded articles from the BBC. They were pretty jumbled but it seemed the American forces had approached the pirates and given them an ultimatum. Discussions had broken down and the Americans heard the sound of gunfire coming from the pirate boat. When they reached it, the four crew of *Quest* were dead. Some of the pirates were also dead and several Somalis had been arrested by the Americans. Although it was frightening to read, it was also surreal. I still had a bit of an 'it won't happen to me' mentality.

We arrived at Salalah port in the early morning three days later and I have never been so happy to see land. We motored past huge cranes waiting to load and offload container ships and into a narrow harbour packed with sailing boats. Almost as soon as the anchor was down and the rear lines tied to shore, the bad memories started to recede. It was just like any other arrival in a new country: sort the paperwork, find some money, go to the shop and locate the nearest bar to celebrate the end of a successful passage. We were all land giddy and raced off to explore the harbour. It was another military and industrial complex but far bigger than Galle. At one end were the docks, at the other, space for military vessels. In between, in a man-made pool of sorts, were 30 or so foreign sailing yachts and catamarans. And everything was beige: the roads, the steep rocky hillside, the buildings, the cars. All were covered in a fine layer of sand. There were no plants. We followed the dusty road past a jumble of dented cargo containers to the shop, where we laughed at the funny foreign drinks – anyone for Pocari Sweat? No? Then how about a can of Thumbs Up? – guzzled down ice creams and generally dispersed the remaining stress of the trip by acting like a bunch of kids. If I'd known that more bad news was just around the corner, I certainly wouldn't have felt so carefree. But at that point I was ignorant and just happy to concentrate on being home and dry – and safe.

23

Tough decisions

To celebrate being on land we met Tony and Helen from the Irish yacht *Crazy Bear*, a boat we were going to go in convoy with to Aden, for dinner in the Oasis expats' club, a short, dusty and beige walk from the harbour complex. The Oasis, run by a couple of South Africans, was to become our home from home for the next week. It had air-conditioning, it had carpet, it had tables and chairs, a giant TV, a beer garden (well, this being an arid Arab country, it was a beer yard), a pool table and – oh joy of joys! – alcohol. Lots of alcohol. Beer, wine, spirits, cocktails. It was like a little slice of back home.

Tony and Helen were a happy-faced, middle-aged couple from Ireland who Tyrone had met in the Pacific islands. It was good to have a normal, relaxed conversation, to drink a glass of wine and not to have to think about putting on a brave face. Yes, we still had to go out there and run the gauntlet again but for now we could stop worrying about it. Tony and Helen introduced us to Tom, a 79-year-old American whose yacht, *Albatross*, was also going to join our convoy.

Most of the other yachts in the harbour were part of the Blue Water Rally, the same collection of round-the-world cruisers that *Quest* had belonged to. All were friendly to us, especially the Kiwi family parked next door, but the sadness and worry was plain to see in their faces. We heard through the grapevine that a memorial service for the murdered *Quest* crew was being held the next day at the Hilton hotel and the three of us decided to go along.

I didn't have any black long-sleeved clothes with me so I dressed conservatively in a white shirt and sun-bleached linen trousers, reasoning that they were the most sombre things I owned. As we took the dinghy the few metres to shore, Tom, the American, was clambering up the wall pretty nimbly for someone fast approaching his ninth decade.

'At least one of you is wearing the right colour for a funeral,' he called out. I looked at Moe, who was in black. 'They wear white for mourning in Arab countries,' Tom said. His comment helped me relax a little – I was already feeling a bit weird about going to the memorial service, as we hadn't known any of the four dead people and it seemed a bit like we were rubber-necking.

One of the function rooms at the hotel had been given over to the memorial and rows of plush, padded chairs faced a giant screen and a lectern. Tyrone, Moe and I sat near the back, trying to be as inconspicuous as possible.

It turned out to be a full-blown funeral, with music, eulogies and prayers from an American priest who had travelled down from the capital Muscat. *Quest* had been a relatively recent addition to the Blue Water Rally and the two crew, Bob and Phyllis, were on board for only a few weeks. Before *Quest*, they had crewed for many different boats on the rally. One by one, people stepped up to share their memories of the pair. Through their stories we learned that Bob had taken part in the previous two-year rally on his own boat and Phyllis had crewed for him. She had loved it so much that she decided to crew again this time round and Bob had left his boat in France to join her.

Photos of them on beaches at sunset, enjoying a sundowner in a boat's cockpit and larking around on tropical islands flashed up on the screen. Phyllis looked so full of life and always had a big, beaming smile. Bob, often in a pink T-shirt and with his long silver hair tied back, came across as quieter but utterly devoted to her. They were no different from Moe and me, really, just people who loved the sea and the cruising life, who were travelling around the world by hitching rides with boat owners kind enough to take them on board. Looking at those photos, so similar to my own memories of my trip, a huge lump bubbled up in my throat and stopped me from joining in with the hymn. My perspective on the pirates changed then: if it had happened to Phyllis and Bob (and Scott and Jean Adam, the owners of *Quest*), it could happen to me, too.

An announcement was made at the end of the service that a representative of Marlo, one of the acronyms who had promised – but failed – to advise us of pirate activity, would like to speak to the skippers. Tyrone went along and Moe and I headed for the hotel's pool to talk things over.

Moe had already decided that she wanted to leave *Gillaroo*. But I was torn. If I left as well, Tyrone would be stuck. There was no way he could sail singlehandedly in a five-day convoy to Aden. Guilt, plus a little bit of a gung-ho feeling that I didn't want to let myself be cowed by these Somali pirate idiots, was making me want to continue. Yet fear loomed large.

Moe and I were going over it for the millionth time when Gemma, a young rally crew member, came over.

'They've asked me to come to talk to you,' she said, indicating a group of older skippers and wives sitting in the shade. 'They want me to tell you not to go on. It's too dangerous.'

She told us how, on the approach to Salalah, her parents' yacht and a few others had been approached by small boats they believed were carrying pirates. The yachts grouped together in a tight formation, she said, and that seemed to have put off the attackers.

'So we know it is a real threat,' she explained.

I plucked at a few blades of the tough grass growing under my sun lounger. If I made eye contact I might cry.

'What are you going to do?' I asked Gemma. Every single boat in their rally was now going to be transported by ship to Turkey, she said, and the crews would fly out there to meet them. I knew full well that Tyrone didn't have the kind of money required to join them.

A few minutes after Gemma had left another woman, Sarah, came over.

'Please, please, don't carry on, we're begging you,' she said. 'You're young girls and I don't even want to think about what would happen if you were hijacked. Where's your skipper? Has he been to tell you what the man from Marlo said?'

We hadn't seen Tyrone yet. We hadn't even known the meeting was over.

Another yacht had been hijacked, Sarah told us. A Danish boat, *Ing*, had been on its way from the Maldives to Salalah. There was a crew of seven on board – two parents, two grandparents and three children. We had heard rumours but this was official confirmation. There was a news blackout to keep things calm and prevent a repeat of what had happened to *Quest*, Sarah said. *Ing* had been moored in our spot in Galle and had left Sri Lanka the day before we arrived. My feelings on the situation shifted again: it not only could happen to me, it actually *might* happen to me.

It was all too much and any bravado I had left dropped away. I fumbled frantically in my bag for my phone. Under the bright Omani sun it was difficult to read the contacts as I scrolled through.

I hit dial and heard the call connect but all I managed to say was 'Dad' before I started crying hysterically.

'Emma?' he said, panic rising in his voice. 'What's wrong? What's happened?'

I had to swallow a couple of times before I could answer. 'Another yacht's been taken by pirates. There were kids on board. They took kids, Dad. I'm scared. I want to come home. I just want to come home.'

I had texted him when we got to Salalah, as I always did, to tell him we'd made landfall but, with the combination of my sobs, a phone call out of the blue and a bad line between Oman and the UK, it was little wonder my poor father was confused.

'WHAT??!! YOU'VE BEEN KIDNAPPED BY PIRATES??!!'

I sniffed. 'No, no, I'm fine.' I was too embarrassed to tell him I was sunbathing by the pool at the Hilton hotel. 'It's another yacht that's been taken. But it's really frightening and I've had enough.'

'ARE YOU OK?' he kept shouting into the phone, until we both calmed down. Even though he's been nowhere more exotic than Madeira, he offered to fly to Oman to come and get me.

'I'll get a visa, I'll get a flight, just stay put and I'll get it sorted,' he said. I started to feel sheepish.

'No, no, don't worry,' I said. 'I'm sure I'll be fine once I get my flight booked. I'll do it today. It's just that all anyone can talk about here, and all we have talked about for the past two days, is pirates. I went to a funeral today and it all got on top of me. I'm OK, really. We're on land and we're safe. I just, I don't want to – I can't – carry on to Aden.'

I felt immensely better once I'd made the decision to leave but I learned later, when I was home in the UK with my family, that my phone call had sent the lot of them into meltdown. They've never been sailing round the world and they had no idea what it was like. I was in the Middle East, a place that at the time was in the news every day during the spring Arab uprisings, with bombs and sexual assaults, riots and governments being overthrown. Dad tried to look up flights for me but his internet crashed; he rang my brother in a panic asking if he could use my sister-in-law's parents' wifi nearby. My sister was in floods of tears in Southampton, imagining the worst, and my brother started frantically ringing round embassies, asking what could be done. ('We advise her to leave the country, sir,' he was told. 'She's already doing that.' 'Well, then, that's about it, sir.'). I had no idea what a kerfuffle I was causing as I sat by the swimming pool for another couple of hours, topping up my tan.

I still had to tell Tyrone. It was one of the hardest things I've ever done, worse even than breaking up with a boyfriend. Broken hearts heal; catamarans and skippers pumped full of bullets and RPGs possibly do not. I stressed all the way back to the harbour in a taxi about what I was going to say, trying to come up with an eloquent speech that wouldn't make it seem like I was cold-heartedly abandoning ship. Moe was remarkably calm and seemed content with her decision. A horrible stone of nausea and trepidation bounced around in my stomach. When I saw Tyrone, any planned speeches went out of the window.

'I want to go home!' I wailed like a five-year-old, started crying again and flung my arms round his neck.

'It's OK, it's OK,' he reassured me, patting me on the back as I gulped out, 'I'm sorry,' and 'I can't,' over and over again.

Melodrama over, we went to the Oasis club for some dinner and to use the wifi to book flights for Moe and me. The club was much busier than usual and full of young, drunk English men. They were the crew of a British Navy ship that had been working in the area and had just docked. Many of the officers were falling-down drunk. Moe, Gemma and I being the only young (well, Gemma was) women around, we were very much in demand. But when the officers heard what we were doing in Salalah they got very angry with us for even daring to venture into these waters in the first place.

'When we left Sri Lanka it was a totally different situation from the one we found ourselves in ten days later,' I tried to explain to one, a posh blond in a pink shirt who under different circumstances might have been the man of my dreams. 'The pirates weren't targeting cruising yachts. And they couldn't even reach this far out from Somalia.'

The lieutenant was having none of it and went on and on about how foolish we were. It was OK for him: even though his vessel wasn't there to fight pirates – it was a survey ship – it had six armed Royal Marines on board to offer protection.

The universe manifested Tyrone a new crew member, in the form of ex-Royal Marine Geoff, who had been crewing for one of the Blue Water Rally boats, *Fai Tira*. The two owners couldn't afford to ship her to Turkey but – one of the skippers, Pete, informed me, with tears of gratitude in his eyes – the other rally members had chipped in to pay the bill. Geoff wanted to complete his circumnavigation. It couldn't have worked out better.

Gillaroo, *Crazy Bear*, *Albatross* and a few other boats formed a council of war and had serious meetings in our cockpit. They issued code names for each to use over the VHF and spoke to the local agent and fixer, Mo, a huge black guy in a white dishdasha robe, about the possibility of an escort to Yemeni waters. At US$8000 per day per yacht, hiring an armed mercenary was out of the question. The promised escort seemed to be the best option until, the night before departure, demands came in for ludicrous amounts of money. The convoy decided to go it alone.

Moe and I thought it best to make ourselves scarce during these negotiations, especially since some people seemed to have taken our 'abandonment' personally. We helped out in little ways – went to the supermarket and provisioned the boat for Tyrone and Geoff, did some cleaning – and spent the rest of our time exploring Salalah with a few other younger crew who were scattered among various boats in the harbour.

Of all the places I visited on my travels, Oman was my least favourite. It wasn't only the barren and dusty beige ugliness of the place – think high piles of rock everywhere – it was also the attitude towards women. By this point I'd spent a fair amount of time in Muslim countries but this was something else. Oman has a small population and takes in a lot of expat workers, European, African and Indian, so the Omanis are used to seeing white Westerners around. But the local men treated us with a lot of disrespect, from taxi drivers ripping us off to a policeman trying to sexually assault one of the female crew to shopkeepers ignoring us and only talking to our male friends, even when we addressed them directly.

The convoy's departure date was two days before our flights so Moe and I were homeless for two nights. Sarah, the lovely woman who owned the yacht *Mystery* with her husband Richard, kindly offered us beds. She and Richard were staying at a hotel with their three children for a couple of days before sending their kids back to family in the UK. *Mystery* was a revelation of what a cruising boat could be like – air-conditioning, a washing machine, stand-up showers, multiple toilets that flushed with a single touch of a button. Pure luxury.

Saying goodbye to Tyrone was just as hard as telling him I wanted to leave. The danger lay, heavy and unspoken of, between us. He told me he was switching off the tracker, just in case pirates were monitoring the website. It meant I had no way of knowing where *Gillaroo* was or if she and her skipper and crew were safe. He slipped lines in the early hours of the morning, while Moe and I were sleeping off our hangovers on *Mystery*. For our last two days in Salalah, the gaps that the seven convoy boats had left in the harbour were a constant reminder that our friends were out there in hostile waters, gambling with their lives.

It was weeks before I heard from him and I worked hard at reining in my overactive imagination. They hadn't pulled into Aden, he said when he could eventually email, because they had had a rough sea state, which would have made it trickier for pirates to board them, so they carried on sailing. It was actually a good job I was no longer with them because they would have needed to break away from the convoy so I could pick up my flight in Aden. After all the worry, they saw no pirates or suspicious boats. They didn't stop in Eritrea, either, because there was a problem with yachts being impounded, so they kept going to Sudan. They were having a great time there, he said, and had helped out at a local regatta, where Tyrone had to keep pulling Sudanese men who couldn't swim out of the water. Soon they would continue their journey up the Red Sea, through the Suez Canal and across the Mediterranean to Spain, where *Gillaroo* had started her voyage three years ago. I was so happy to hear they were fine.

Moe and I flew to Muscat together, then went our separate ways, she to Abu Dhabi to visit a friend and me to Heathrow. After what we'd been through, just saying 'bye' and 'see you later' at the airport seemed inadequate but I couldn't find anything more fitting to say without seeming cheesy. I think she understood, anyway.

It was difficult not to feel sad and slightly regretful about the way this part of my adventure had ended. Circumstances had taken things out of my control, so it wasn't quite what I had planned. *But wasn't relinquishing that control one of the reasons for going away in the first place?* I reasoned as I accepted a stick of chewing gum from the burkha-clad woman next to me on my flight home. *Learning to accept life and whatever happened, instead of always trying to force things into the shape I wanted them to be? Was Aaron's 'universe manifesting' theory so ludicrous after all?* Look at *Gillaroo* turning up in Borneo at the time I needed to leave *Kingdom*, at our bumping into Guy again the moment we arrived in Thailand, at Tyrone always managing to find new crew when it seemed hopeless. And at my being offered a job on a superyacht, seemingly out of the blue. OK, so I had written out my list of options but I had not done anything towards making them happen. And, in a few weeks' time, option 1 would come true and I would be a deckhand in Italy. *It's weird how things turn out*, I thought, as the credits for *Mission Impossible 3* scrolled up the tiny screen and the woman next to me snored lightly. And it didn't even cross my mind that the universe might be sneakily working away behind the scenes, quietly manifesting another one of those options from my list without my knowledge.

Panacea

24

The Italian job

I just about made out someone shouting my name over the din of the electric sander.

'Em-ma?'

'Si?' I asked, not taking my eyes off the door I was grinding back to bare metal.

'Caffè?'

'No, grazie, Imran,' I replied, working the edge of the rotating sanding plate right up to the label on the door, using all of the muscles in my arm to control it, despite the heavy vibrations it was sending up to my shoulders. 'Tè?'

'Oh, sì. Sorry. I forget,' a mix of Indian- and Italian-accented bad English came back. 'You no like caffè.'

I finished sanding the top corner of the door and switched the machine off, waiting for the disk to stop rotating before I placed it down on the teak deck. Pulling the safety goggles off my eyes, I rubbed a damp forearm across my dusty face and peeled off the blue latex gloves to go and fetch my tea.

This was my new life as superyacht crew, the option 1 that I had chosen, and it was about as far removed from my old life back in London as it was possible to imagine. Instead of a 12-hour day sat hunched over a computer screen in a dark and dingy office in London, I worked eight hours in a boatyard. I had swapped an hour-long tube commute for a 15-minute ride in a Fiat 500 through the narrow, medieval lanes of Castellamare di Stabia, English for Italian and journalism for manual labour. My work clothes consisted of a pair of men's shorts, a lemon T-shirt bleached white by the sun and an old pair of running shoes that were swiftly being covered in paint, anti-rust chemicals and grime. I had no electronic swipe card to pass through office security; instead to get into my place of work I climbed four metres up a ladder, holding on with just one hand while in the other I hauled up whatever tools I needed for that day's task. And my crewmates – Carlo the captain, Imran the cook and Daniela the hostess – had become my new colleagues, my family and my friends, as they were the only people I knew in this country where I stuck out like a long, pale, English thumb.

Carlo, the captain who had sent me the recruiting email back in the Andamans, had been waiting for me at Rome Ciampino airport a few weeks earlier. I knew it was me he was looking for because he held a sign in his hands with 'Miss Bamford' written on it in giant capitals. It was a good job he was holding a sign; I wouldn't have picked him out as a superyacht captain from the small crowd of people. I was expecting a tall, suave and rich-looking man, not this small, elfin creature with a heart-shaped face wearing sunglasses indoors. His hair was steel grey and close-cropped and he was dressed in a polo shirt, gilet, chinos and deck shoes – the boaty uniform around the world. I towered over him in my flat shoes as I shook his hand.

The rest of the crew were tiny, too. Imran, who I met the next day after Carlo drove me from Rome to Naples in the crew car – suitably compact and painted red, white and green like the Italian flag – was even smaller. With a bird-like frame, he had razor-sharp cheekbones made more prominent by the way a lifetime of chain-smoking had withered the rest of the skin on his face. An Indian living in Italy for nearly two decades, he had married a much younger wife and brought her and his three daughters to live in Rome. In a bid to keep up with his young family he Just for Men-ed his greys and kept in shape: when he got too hot he had a habit of pulling his T-shirt up, like a teenage boy apeing what he has seen in a rap video, to expose a curiously toned and hairless six-pack.

The hostess, Daniela, arrived a few days after me. Just shy of 40, she had a brunette Mary Quant bob, big brown eyes and a small Roman nose, from which, at night, emerged the most incongruous and startlingly loud snores I have ever heard. We shared a room and, later, a cabin and sometimes it was so bad, in spite of the different types of earplugs I tried, that I would move into the living room or try to sleep on the deck – but I could still hear her through either the walls or several inches of teak cladding.

So here we were, the four motley crew of *Panacea*, grinding, drilling, polishing, scrubbing, screwing, nailing, sanding and varnishing on a daily basis, trying to get the boat ready for a summer season of charter work. It was a steep learning curve: in the six weeks I worked in the boatyard (where Daniela and I were the only women and I was the only foreigner – well, I suppose technically Imran was a foreigner too but he spoke the language and his 18 years had given him an Italian temperament), I sanded, feroxed and painted the bilges and lockers, stretched out, sanded and re-painted nearly 400 metres of anchor chain, filed and painted two 100kg anchors, scrubbed fenders and dressed them in protective socks like furry blue condoms, mixed paints, learned the ratios of resins to hardeners, sanded the deck, serviced the winches, changed the engine oil. The bilges became my office and I climbed, squeezed and contorted myself into inconceivably small spaces on a daily basis, usually with a paintbrush or electric drill in hand. The best job was polishing the chrome fittings to a satisfyingly bright gleam outside in the sunshine. The worst was crouching on my haunches in the main bilge, shielding myself with one hand to protect my face from white-hot sparks sent flying as the captain welded a new pump to the black water tank.

All of it, in its novelty, I found immensely satisfying and interesting. I was learning new things every day, managing to complete tasks I would never have thought I was capable of, and I was using both my brain and my body for once. Every day I would go back to the apartment physically shattered but buzzing.

'Emma contenta?' Salvatore, an electrician who spoke not a word of English, asked Carlo one day, when we were about halfway through our yard work.

I understood enough Italian by this point to reply, although it was one of the few times I could pick out what Salvatore was saying. His Neapolitan dialect was so strong that usually his words all melded into one long, garrulous and high-pitched lump to my ear.

'Sì, Salvatore,' I said. 'Emma contentissima.'

Then, all of a sudden, mid-June was upon us and it was a mad rush to get *Panacea* into the water, cleaned, stocked up and ready for the summer's guests. Like an episode of a home renovation show, our project was over-budget and over-schedule and it was a race against time to finish. While I soaped, scrubbed and rinsed and polished everything above deck, a process which took a good four hours and which I had to do five times over to get rid of half a year's worth of accumulated boatyard dirt and still it wasn't enough, Daniela and Carlo cleaned and tidied away below decks and gradually, as tools were packed away, linens and cushions came out of storage and a thick coating of dust was wiped from surfaces, this ugly duckling of a workman's tool shed was transformed into a beautiful superyacht swan.

Panacea was a 24-metre motorsailer, big by sailboat standards but only just qualifying by length as a superyacht. She had four guest cabins that could hold eight guests, with two master cabins at the back, one in the middle and a twin cabin forward port side. Each cabin had its own shower, aircon and electric flushing toilets. The interior was satin-varnished wood, quite light and modern compared to a lot of the heavy panelling often found on yachts. She had an indoor saloon and bar area and a large outdoor table with a plush, U-shaped sofa curving around three sides. Guests also had a huge cushioned sunbathing area between the mast and the coach roof to lounge on and a further sofa on the bow. A week's charter cost 21,000 euros – and that was before food, alcohol, marina fees, fuel, flights and transfers were added in. In total, a group were looking at a bill of about 50,000 euros for a one-week holiday, depending on where in the world they were flying in from – and what class they chose to travel.

Spirits were high as we took *Panacea* on her first voyage to Naples to pick up the owners and their son – perhaps a little too high. As the autopilot drove us along at 10 knots across the Bay of Naples towards the city, Carlo asked me to stay on watch on deck while he went below to clean. Even though he had two cleaners on his staff – the exterior was my territory, the interior Daniela's – he liked to dust, wipe and tidy things away himself. Countless times in the past couple of days I had offered to help but he had dismissed me. I suspected his emerging obsessive compulsiveness was his way of coping with the stress of the charter season beginning.

I stood by the wheel, keeping a lookout for other boats and playing around with the radar, familiarising myself with the instruments, as Imran came out on to the deck carrying a door that had to be fitted to the bathroom in the crew cabin in the forepeak.

'Em-ma,' he said – Italians always pronounce every syllable, so the two ms in my name became separated, and although Imran was Indian he had a semi local accent – 'You come help me with this door.'

'I'm on watch, Imran,' I said. 'So I can't leave the helm.'

Fury erupted from him and a stream of Italian expletives followed, some of which I understood because I had learned them over the past few weeks. Fuming, he stamped forward down the deck, opened the hatch and threw the door down, climbing down the hole after it.

I tried to make amends when he came stomping back.

'Sorry, Imran,' I started to say, 'but Carlo told me to go on watch and—'

'Is nothing coming,' he sneered. 'I don't want talk you, understand?' He marched off inside. *What on earth is he so angry about?* I wondered. *Maybe I made a mistake not leaving the helm – I suppose I could have done for a couple of minutes*

– but I don't know the protocol here yet. But still, rehanging a door is a job he can easily do himself – even I've done it. So why is he so cross?

Daniela told me not to worry about it. 'He is just nervous,' she said. And once we had arrived in Naples, embarked the owners, transferred them to Salina in the Aeolian islands and disembarked them after a couple of days without a hitch, Imran hugged me and we were friends again. It was my first taste of the volatile Italian temper – and it was not going to be my last.

It brought it home to me that this was not another of my sailing jollies but a job, with stressful situations just like any other. Still, I was confident that it couldn't be as pressurised as a newspaper newsroom. The sun was shining, I was surrounded by sea and I was on a boat – and being paid. The odd little fight was a small price to pay for all that.

25

The first rule of customer service

The three days with the owners on board passed in a blur.
I didn't really have a clue what I was supposed to be
doing so I just did exactly as I was told, as I was told to do it:
Em-ma, take this, give that, pull here, wipe clean, polish
those, rinse these.

From what I had gleaned from my research into the
industry, the role of a deckhand involved cleaning the outside
of the boat, helping with anchoring, mooring and sailing and
driving the guests around in the tender. If it was a big boat
with 'toys' – jet skis, submersibles, inflatable climbing walls
(Google it) – the deckhand had to maintain those, too. Our
'toys' consisted of a few sets of snorkelling gear. I did my
best with them, keeping the fins together in matching pairs
and rinsing and placing them tidily away each day. Cleaning
and polishing was the main part of the job spec for exterior
superyacht crew and I was expected to have a chamois leather
effectively grafted on to one hand. Only now I was being told
that I had more duties than this – I was to be a waitress.

'You will serve the people,' Carlo told me. 'I will teach you.'

This, I was not happy about. My first job, when I was 17, was waitressing in an Italian restaurant in Nottingham. Bar work I did for years and loved it but waitressing I could not stand – I'm just too clumsy. It seems so awkward to me to lean over and between people, picking up and putting down dishes, remembering orders, fetching and carrying and trying not to drop hot food in anyone's lap. And now I was being made to do it on a moving boat. Doubly clumsy. Naively, I had assumed that Daniela, as the boat's hostess, would be the waitress. But, no. I was it.

Some of Carlo's OCD must have rubbed off on me because I did actually take mild pleasure in setting the table. For the formal evening dinner, I had to cover the table with white linen and place silver salvers out for each person, stacking the main-course plates and pasta dishes on top, aligning the boat's name perfectly. There were different glasses for all kinds of wine and real silver cutlery that I had buffed to a sheen. I was never going to win any superyacht table-dressing awards (yes, they actually do exist and taking first prize is considered the pinnacle of a stewardess's career. Imagine. Being praised for your Enchanted Moroccan Evening theme is the thing you covet the most, the next step up after you've already won the Best Coffee Service rosette) – but, with the light from the moon and the candles bouncing off the glass, it did look lovely.

Setting the table is one thing, serving it is another – there are people to factor in. The plates were large and heavy and, with all those candles, salvers and glasses about, as well as two types of wine and two varieties of water, tricky to place. And there was that aforementioned clumsiness. With the configuration of the sofa and table, if we had eight guests on board I had to stand on tiptoes and press my hip bones into the wooden back of the seats to balance myself so that I could stretch far enough forward between two sets of guest shoulders to put a whole dressed 5kg fish on the table. Countless times I dropped knives and forks on to the deck. God knows how I managed to avoid spearing any toes. I could tell which guests had domestic staff at home and which did not. Those used to being served left everything as it was on the table while I struggled to clear around them, while those who didn't have maids or butlers automatically stacked their plates and handed them to me. For that, I was extremely grateful.

My days fell into a routine. I would roll out of bed at 6.45am – well, I say roll, but my bunk in the forepeak cabin that I had to share with Daniela was two metres off the floor, so I had to swing myself sideways on to a vertical steel ladder while simultaneously ducking so that I didn't clunk my head on the ceiling. Next I'd use the loo, perching sideways because there wasn't enough room in the miniscule bathroom to sit any other way, brush my teeth, dress in my day uniform of grey polo T-shirt and blue shorts and clamber up through the hatch on to the deck. Tiptoeing barefoot, so as not to wake the guests sleeping beneath me, I'd creep into the kitchen to make a cup of tea and then start sweeping and rinsing away the crumbs from last night's dinner from the outdoor seating area and wiping and polishing the aft deck and brightwork. I'd check the angle of the sun in our location that morning and climb, standing precariously on the back of the sofa, to zip up shades to protect our guests' eyes. In the saloon I'd unwrap the knives and forks that Daniela had left out on a tray for me (they were individually wrapped in pieces of kitchen paper because a guest had complained that hearing them chinking against each other in the night in the galley as the boat rocked in the gentle waves had kept him awake) and, once the first guests had started to come out of their cabins, quickly set the table for breakfast. I couldn't do it in advance because the summer sun made everything hot. Breakfast could start at any time from 8am to 11.30am, depending on the guests, but I had to be ready in any case and wait until they were, too. I began to see why it is called 'waiting on'.

Breakfast was anything and everything the guests could want: pastries, bread, cereal, toast, hot and cold milk, cheeses, ham, eggs, omelettes, cake, biscuits, fruit, juice, tea, two kinds of coffee – and anything else they requested was made to order, all coming out of a tiny galley that was about half the size of a domestic kitchen. Our first set of guests, a family of eight from Central America, ordered scrambled eggs with sausage each morning for their kids. Every time I cleared their breakfast dishes away, the plate was full of little bits of untouched sausage. Why they didn't ask for just plain scrambled eggs, I don't know.

But I quickly learned that the customer does always know best in this industry. If they want to hire a boat and travel through the night and rough seas to another country, even though they all suffer horrendously from seasickness, then that's what we'll do. If, after a few days, they want to make the return journey from that same country because they've decided the sea temperature is too cold for them, then that is fine as well. You want a special kind of ice cream for your teenage daughter's bedtime drink? Of course, we'll go ashore at 11pm and trawl the restaurants until we find it. The wine is not cold enough? We'll make more ice for you. The wine is too cold? Well, I am very sorry, sir, we will adjust the setting on the fridge. No, of course I don't mind you waking me up at 3am because your child wants a bowl of cereal. What kind would he prefer? You would like six Russian girls helicoptering out to your boat, along with two boxes of condoms (size: large)? Not a problem. You want one more bottle of Cristal? Certainly – I will arrange for it to be brought by speedboat from the mainland. It will be here within one hour. OK, so the last two incidents weren't requests made by our guests but I was told that they did happen. Oh, and the delivery price of a solitary bottle of Champagne from Naples to the island of Capri by speedboat at midnight, in case you are tempted, is a bargain at 1000 euros. We were not just cleaners, cooks, waitresses and boat drivers; we were servants, available 24/7 and ready and willing to do anything our (temporary) masters commanded.

Lunch was more formal than breakfast, with always two or three courses, and there were snacks and drinks between breakfast and lunch and lunch and dinner to be served, too. In one five-day charter alone I served 185 coffees and five litres of ice cream. Cries of 'Em-ma! Un caffè! Em-ma! Un gelato!' followed me around the boat, punctuating my endless stints of cleaning up after one meal had ended and before the next one began.

There was the 'sailing' to fit in as well – motoring really, as *Panacea* weighed 100 tonnes, there was barely any wind and, in any case, we couldn't hoist the sails because the sun shades were obstructing them. 'The sails are there just for looking,' Carlo told me. *I wish he'd made that clear before I'd accepted his job offer*, I thought. What had seemed like the dream position of being a professional sailor was morphing into being a cleaner and a waiter, albeit a waiter with a good tan who didn't have to wear shoes. I lived on a boat and was surrounded by sea all the time but I missed sailing like crazy. Most of the other boats we saw were motor yachts – those Italians sure do love their power, and they especially love driving their motorboats really fast while their white-string-bikini-clad wife/girlfriend/hired companion clings to the bow, trying to look nonchalant while in reality her hair is being whipped into a furious tangle, her skin is being doused every few seconds by salty Mediterranean water and she is clutching on to the cream vinyl cushions for dear life. There were no cruisers' Hawaiian shirts here – it was all Hermès or Gucci linen, invariably white and worn unbuttoned over a pair of black Speedos, the better to show off the mahogany suntan – and the size of the gut.

At least twice a day we moved to a different anchorage or marina. Some of them were so beautiful: in the shallow, turquoise waters of Cabo Pumice, named after the rough, foot-sloughing stones; just 100 metres or so off the black volcanic beaches of the continuously smoking Stromboli; beneath the dramatic cliffs of Sorrento or Positano. Either the captain or I would drive the guests ashore in the tender and somehow, in the middle of all that, I'd have to squeeze in washing the salt off the entire boat, showering myself and changing into my evening uniform of blue polo T-shirt and trousers ready to serve the evening aperitivo drinks and dinner before crashing into bed at midnight, exhausted.

I wasn't the only one who had it tough: Daniela, cleaning up after the children, would find lumps of chewing gum on the sofas, where they had dropped out of open mouths, sticky sweet wrappers and fingerprints everywhere and iPads stuffed carelessly under mattresses. The guests would go into the store cupboards and help themselves to fresh towels, even though theirs were being changed every two days and their pillowcases on a daily basis. The tumble dryer was broken and Daniela spent half her time on her knees in the 48°C engine room, stringing laundry up across the ceiling in an attempt to get it to dry.

Imran was trying to keep up with an always-changing list of demands for meals and adaptations and was constantly having to go ashore to get more provisions. With the 185-coffee guests, they ate so much he had to shop three times a day. Sometimes he'd spend hours preparing a meal, only for the guests to decide at the last minute that they'd rather eat out and, frustrated, he'd pitch half of it into the sea.

And Carlo? Well, Carlo was re-folding the guest towels just so, lining up the water bottles in the fridge so that all the labels faced outwards and stacking the forks in perfect alignment in the cutlery drawer. He was under a lot of stress – the boat was losing money each year and bookings were down, he told me.

'It is the financial creases and the war in Libya,' he said, finishing one cigarette and immediately lighting another (of the four crew, I was the only non-chain-smoker on board). 'Usually we would have maybe ten charter in a season. What is best for us is to have twelve, maybe thirteen charter. But these Americans, they are very afeared of Libya and they think the terrorist will come look for them here in Italy. So this year they do not come. And we have only five charter. It is cupside down.'

Five charters meant not only less money for the business but also considerably fewer tips for the crew – and the

Americans were a sore loss. Tips can make up half of a charter crew's salary and are important because they might only work for six months in a year. Gratuities are not compulsory but in the contract that guests receive it makes it clear that it is expected that you tip the staff for their hard work in, say, getting you your favourite ice cream in the middle of the night or procuring fresh prostitutes. And the Americans are the biggest tippers of the lot.

'This one year,' Imran told me, 'American family is coming. They are just two. Me and American man we are good friends. We sit together on deck, talking, talking, always talking, and look at the stars. They give me 1500 euros. Now I am sad they not come *Panacea* this year.' *I bet you are, Imran,* I thought. *That would buy a lot of school books for your three clever daughters.*

I've never thought of myself as a person motivated by money but I was discovering that when you're being worked into the ground for 17 hours a day, tips start to matter. Our first charter we each received a crisp 500-euro note. I didn't even know they came in that denomination anywhere other than Monopoly. They aren't actually legal tender in the UK and I had to find a special currency dealer in London to buy mine off me. But other times we received far less – 100 euros here, 20 euros there and once, in the case of a group of the owner's friends, who had been given approximately 4000 euros of boat hire, food, alcohol and service all for free – absolutely nothing at all.

Our first charter of the five was a Central American family of eight – they of the seasickness – who had holidayed on *Panacea* before. We were to pick them up in Vieste, on the east coast of Italy, and take them to Croatia for two weeks.

Panacea was in the Aeolian islands, between Naples and Sicily, and we had a three-day delivery trip around the toe of Italy, across its sole and up and round the heel to the mid-calf. The seas were rough and Daniela suffered badly, only just managing to make it from her bed to the toilet in time to throw up. Imran spent his time slumped in the corner of the galley, not really able to stand, and Carlo and I took over his watches, spending stints of up to 12 hours each on deck. Everyone could have done with some time to recover once we got to Vieste but no – we got a call from their driver that the guests were almost there while we were in the middle of our dinner and we had to hastily pack it all away before greeting and serving them and setting off immeadiately for our overnight trip to Dubrovnik.

They seemed a glum bunch when they arrived, varying in age and height from a little boy of five to the patriarch, a grandfather of about 65. *They don't seem very excited to be on holiday*, I thought, *but I suppose if they've just flown all the way from Central America they'll probably be tired.* We offered drinks and snacks and struggled on board with the three suitcases each they had brought with them. Within a few minutes the luggage, divested of clothes, had been dumped in the saloon.

'Where on earth are we going to store all of these cases?' I asked Carlo.

'Don't worry, Em-ma,' he said. 'I will take care of it.' He piled them all up in his and Imran's shower, which meant whenever we needed to wash – mine and Daniela's shower was out of order – we had to take them all out and stack them on the bed and then repack them in the shower cubicle again afterwards.

In the morning, when they came out for breakfast at 11.30, they seemed less rude and sullen, despite the fact that they had suffered from seasickness on the way over. The grandfather, in particular, and his son were especially friendly, but as a whole they were a very quiet bunch who didn't seem to like yachting or the water. I don't think the grandmother spoke much English or any Italian and the daughter was generally busy trying to keep her three kids and niece under control.

Imran filled me in on the family history – they had stayed on *Panacea* several years in a row. 'The totter [daughter, I eventually worked out], she come before with her husband but now the marriage is broke. The son, he come one time with wife. Phew, she crazy! Now he no with her no more.'

The daughter was absolutely stunning, with long, thick dark hair and a beautiful figure. She had had three children and was in much better shape than I was. Her brother, who was a couple of years older but still under 40, had warm brown eyes that twinkled when he smiled and a spattering of freckles across his nose. He was fond of wearing white shirts so I nicknamed him Enrique Iglesias.

'I was in London last year,' Enrique told me. 'I ate the – how do you say? – fish and chips.'

I laughed. 'Did you have mushy peas?'

'What is this mushy peas?'

I described them and he wrinkled his nose. 'No, this I have never try.'

'Son want to ask Golden Lady to have drink with him,' Imran teased me one night after we'd finished dinner. He'd taken to calling me Golden Lady because my hair had been lightened by the sun to a yellow tinge. At first I was flattered – until I found out it was a jingle from a TV advert for tights.

'That why he walking, walking around boat every night.'

'Don't be silly, Imran,' I scoffed. A small part of me was secretly pleased that a handsome, Central American, horse-riding, playboy millionaire's son might have taken a shine to me, especially as I was effectively his servant. But, even if it was true, as a guest he was off-limits. And I've seen *Downton*. I know how these things turn out.

Carlo, to my mind, had some pretty crazy rules about what 'the rich people like' – and don't like. One was about the rubbish. Obviously, if you are feeding eight guests and four crew three meals a day you are going to generate a not-inconsiderable amount of trash. But Carlo didn't want the guests to see it, even when it was neatly tied in black sacks. For some reason he thought it would offend them. So it would pile up during the day in the galley and we'd have to wait until the guests were ashore – or asleep – to drive it over to the mainland and get rid of it. I dubbed it Mission Impossible: sometimes as late as 1am we'd tiptoe across the deck, lower the black bags silently into the tender and drive off to dump them into skips on land.

Other strange 'rich people' ideas would crop up every now and then. One day I walked into the galley to see Imran cutting the ends off every single baby plum tomato in a bowl that must have held 200.

'Captain say me rich people no like tomato ends,' he told me, when I asked. I just raised my eyebrows in response.

Earlier that day we'd been lucky enough to be able to do the rubbish run during daylight hours – a rare treat indeed. I drove the tender up to the Mljet quayside and held on to a rock with one hand while Imran nipped ashore with the black sacks. While I waited for him to come back, a tender for another superyacht pulled up. After one guy leapt had ashore with his rubbish, the driver leant over to shake my hand and introduce himself.

'I am Sven,' he said, moving the wooden toothpick he was chewing from the centre of his mouth to one side so that he could speak. He was your typical Slav – a huge beast of a man, thickset, with a vast neck and overhanging brow. His close-cropped hair was blond and his skin golden. Probably in his mid-30s, some of his muscle was turning to fat but he was not unattractive despite that.

We chatted briefly about the different boats we were on and then he said: 'Perhaps we could have drink tonight, hah? Give me number.' Because I was still in traveller mode – and keen to meet new people – I gave him my number, not really sure if he was being friendly or asking me out on a date. He pulled a small mobile out of his pocket and typed it in, struggling to work the tiny keys with his enormous hands. 'OK, I SMS you,' he said, gunning his tender's engine as his crewmate climbed on board and shooting off.

SMS me – to use the euro-speak term for texting – he did. And he swung by at midnight in his tender to pick me up. Enrique was pacing the deck as I climbed down the side of *Panacea*'s hull.

'I want to walk a little,' Sven said, as we moored his tender. When he said 'walk', he actually meant 'talk', and he regaled me with tales of his life for two hours, barely pausing for breath – or to ask me anything about myself.

Sven had an ego to match his giant stature. He was, it turned out, the owner and captain of a 30-metre charter boat, not the deckhand, as I'd assumed. For 11 years he'd worked on big ships as a chief engineer, visiting dozens of countries around the world but almost never getting to see anything of them beyond the harbour. One time, he told me, he had gotten frostbite all over his body when he had to go on deck in temperatures of –37°C to change a masthead light. He had been in hospital for a month. And a decade of drinking demineralised reverse osmosis water had left him with terrible toothache – which was why he chewed on the toothpick constantly. 'It wreck my tooths.'

I found his tales fascinating – so far removed from the usual date chatter back in London over a beer. So I agreed to meet him the next night as well, since both yachts were due to be anchoring off the same island.

'How was your day today?' I asked him as I clambered into his tender again, using the porthole of a guest's cabin as my ladder down. 'How were your guests?'

'My guests were fine, my beauty,' he said, standing wide-legged to steer us away from *Panacea*. 'You hear about the 35-metre boat?'

'No. What 35-metre boat?'

'The one that was shipwrecked today. It go on the rocks with all guests still on board. Fuck! You didn't see it?'

I bounced slightly on the side of the rib as we accelerated away. 'No. We didn't see anything. What, so a charter boat went aground? Near here?'

'Yes, the fucking stupid captain went straight on to this rocks that was on fucking chart.' The toothpick was switching from side to side as he talked. 'I hear on radio, hah, so I goes over there and fucking captain is doing nothing. So I says, "You! You fucking crazy? Get guests off now."'

'What did he say to that?'

'No matter. Soon all guests gone. And then I says, "Don't worry, my friend stupid, I will get boat off rocks for you." Because this fucking captain, he don't know what to do.'

I had a vision of Sven, like a fat, Croatian Hercules, swimming through the sea, clutching a thick tow rope, dragging a stricken vessel to safety single-handed.

'And you did it?' I asked.

'Yah. I find other ship and we pull and pull and get boat off rocks.'

'And it's all OK now?'

'No. Boat is fucked.'

This man is so ridiculously, over-the-top masculine, I thought, it's like he is a caricature of a man. He probably sweats pure testosterone. If he was a cartoon character, he'd be Sven the Honourable or something. He's practically 'Me man. You woman. Come live in my cave. Uggg!'

It was funny that I thought that because an hour or so later, after he'd caught a fish – with his bare hands, naturally – he effectively threw me the old Neanderthal chat-up line.

'What I want is to find woman,' he informed me, sitting down on a low wall by a darkened restaurant and dipping his feet in the sea to cool them off after a hard 18-hour day standing up. 'Buy house in bay in Croatia, keep my boat in bay in winter. Somewhere near village so she can walk there for shopping. But I am tired of Croatian women. All are the same. All just want money and jealous – so jealous. Too much trouble.' He sniffed and jostled the toothpick. 'Maybe I find nice English woman?' He looked at me sideways. For a second I pictured it: a headscarf, long skirt, wicker basket, a winding path through the woods to the village to buy bread and apples. It was a bit Red Riding Hood, I grant you, but fairytales were my main go-to reference point for eastern European life.

Thanks for the offer, Sven, but no thanks, I thought. *Peeling turnips in a remote farmhouse is not my future. Where are the white Caribbean beaches, the tropical garden, the fun parties and the ute? I think I'll stick with my epiphany.*

26

Language of love?

After we waved the Central Americans off, each clutching a crisp 500-euro note in our hand (actually, we were more subtle than that – Carlo discreetly handed out the tips after they had departed) I had the chance, at last, to take stock of my new life.

That first charter had been hard work, no doubt about it, especially going into it straight off the back of six weeks of boatyard work when my head had been jammed full of new stuff to learn. But Carlo assured me that other guests would be easier to deal with and would keep better hours, not wanting breakfast at 11.30am and dinner at 1am.

'And now you know what you are doing,' he said. 'So you will find much easier.'

I wasn't so sure I would. Being busy and being rushed off my feet meant I had no time to think about my situation but now, with a few days off, I began to notice all the little things about the job that I didn't like. Food was a big issue. Italian food is lovely – if you go out for an occasional meal or if you pop over to Rome or Venice for a few days on holiday. All that lovely pasta, bread, pizza, tomatoes, cheese. But eat it day in, day out for two months and it starts to get a bit bland. Pablo and Libertad would have loved it – no 'Is it spicy?' here. There was fresh fish and seafood available every day, but as I had gone back to being fully vegetarian after my two fish-eating episodes, I didn't eat it. So my diet consisted of bread, bread, more bread, cheese, fruit, pasta and biscuits. Dinner would often be cold vegetables, rice and bread. It wasn't exactly balanced, and I was ballooning by the minute. The fact that Imran put enormous glugs of olive oil into the pasta sauce wasn't helping my men's shorts to fit any more loosely, either. I once measured the bottle after he'd used it and worked out that we were getting 200 calories from the oil alone. Each.

When Enrique had been on the boat, he often tried to make conversation with me and I found myself speaking about my past life as a journalist. For some reason, I didn't want him or his family to think of me as just a servant. I was a little bit ashamed to be seen as just a waitress. I wanted them to know that I was just as intelligent, as widely travelled and as cultured as they were. I needed them to see beyond the uniform. As time went on, I continued to struggle with this. I hadn't even considered, when I decided to change my life and my job, what a change in socio-economic status would mean to me. I was no longer an A/B – as a cleaner and waiter on a temporary contract, I was demoted to C1/C2 or even a D. And that rankled. *Am I really such a snob that this matters to me?* I wondered. *Why am I finding this so hard?* Imran must have noticed that I was having difficulty with it. 'Why you do job this level?' he asked me, when I told him I had been to two universities. 'You higher level. For me, OK. For Daniela OK. Why you not profession?' He came from a culture where education was everything and the idea of someone getting to a senior level in a real career and then jacking it all in to do a menial job, although in an arena they loved, was incomprehensible to him – and just plain crazy.

It was also becoming very cliquey on the boat. The crew naturally split into smokers (Carlo, Daniela and Imran) and non-smokers (me). And also into Italian speakers (Carlo, Daniela and Imran) and non-Italian speakers (me). And into night owls (Carlo, Daniela and Imran) and early birds (me). Daniela was always following the captain around like a puppy dog with her big brown eyes and stopped speaking to me beyond necessities. I think that she regarded me as a love rival for Carlo's affections, which was plain crazy. Imran spent a lot of time on the phone arguing with his wife and Carlo was always busy rearranging things just so. I was lonely and, stuck out at anchor, there was nothing I could do about it.

I'd never felt lonely on a boat before. I'd sailed with all kinds of people in a variety of circumstances up to this point, and I had always got on well with everyone. Even Steve and I had had fun, before it all turned weird. So I was very happy to find out that for our next charter we would be teaming up with another superyacht for the week and we would have three new almost-crewmates: Massimo, the owner/captain, and Lucia and Anton the deckhands.

The guests, from South America this time, were due to arrive on my thirty-third birthday. There were 11 of them – three families – split between *Panacea* and *Andante*. When they came, in a flamboyant Brazilian whirl, it was immediately clear that they were going to be more fun than the first set of guests. We had two families on our boat and *Andante* took the third family and the son of one of ours. That was the sleeping arrangements sorted; the rest was a lot more fluid. Sometimes we'd have eight on our boat for the morning; other times people would swim from one yacht to another so every time we moved anchorage we had different people on board. Like teachers on a school field trip, we had to be careful to make sure that between us we had all 11.

They had stated in their pre-charter preference form that they would eat most of their dinners ashore. That soon changed once they got a taste of Imran's cooking. It's that 200 calories of oil – ignorance is bliss and it does make everything very, very tasty. They chose to eat all meals on board, with often the adults taking lunch on our boat while the children ate on *Andante* and in the evening they swapped over. That made catering easier for both chefs and the ever-changing rota of guests more fun for me to serve. They were a happy and hyperactive bunch – every time one of the three teenage girls walked past me they would trill, 'Hi, Emma!' – and it was great to see them enjoying the boat: swimming, snorkelling, asking to go for rides in the tender to explore caves, rocks and bays. I was more than happy to do anything they asked: making flasks of camomile tea so the girls could try to lighten their hair in the sun, teaching their younger brother how to drive the dinghy.

Their mood permeated the crew, too, and Carlo allowed us to let our hair down a bit. After he had taken the guests to swim through sulphuric bubbles that wiggled their way up from cracks in the rocks around the Aeolian islands, he picked me up in the tender and let me swim, too. There were no fish around, just tiny mercurial spheres bubbling upwards in vertical lines. It was like floating in a glass of champagne.

Nose out of the water, it was a different matter, though: those pretty little bubbles stank to eggy high heaven.

'Em-ma,' Carlo said to me one morning, as I was clearing away the last of the Nutella-smeared breakfast plates, 'the guests have asked if you would like to join them to go to Stromboli.' This was unexpected. I had become used to only seeing the islands and towns we visited from the boat and had learned to suppress the urge to go exploring. *I am here to work*, I told myself, *not on holiday*. I'd never been up a live volcano before and I felt honoured to be invited.

Stromboli was one of the seven Aeolian islands, the area that *Panacea* mainly took charter guests to. Each island was very different from its neighbour and, with seven to visit, it was perfect for a week's charter itinerary. Most of Stromboli was an active volcano that put on a spectacular fireworks trip every night. One of *Panacea*'s tricks was to have a late dinner and then motor round to the far side of the island, where it was too deep to anchor, and just drift (keeping a careful lookout and a hand by the gear lever, obviously), to watch showers of sparks and big jets of flames spout from the volcano's mouth. On land, there was an organised trek to the top, starting just before sunset and reaching the pinnacle at about 10pm to enjoy the show before returning to the bottom about midnight.

Clad in hired heavy-duty boots and with bamboo poles in hand, we set off on the long trek up the volcano's side. All but one of the guests had come and Anton, the deckhand from *Andante*, had been invited, too. Anton was younger than me and about the same height. I had only seen him and *Andante*'s other deckhand, Lucia, briefly a couple of times. A Moldavian, Anton had a round, baby face but was strong from the boat work and a previous job in construction. The sun hat he wore tied under his chin reminded me of Tyrone.

The steep slope was hard going under the hot July sun and I was soon sweating, especially with the added extra water bottles I was carrying for the guests. Anton walked with me and, since he spoke no English and I not a word of Moldavian, his first language, we tried to muddle through by combining my tiny bit of Italian with liberal use of the international languages of pointing and of drawing pictures in the air.

'Guarda,' he said, plucking a blackberry from a bush we passed. 'Una mora. Come si dice, in inglese?'

'Blackberry,' I said.

'Bleck barry? Bleck barry!' he said, then giggled, miming using a telephone. 'Bleck barry.' He waved the fruit in the air as he tried out the word then popped it into my open mouth. *Uh-oh*.

As we climbed higher, the shrubs became fewer and fewer, until there was just the occasional fire-scorched blackened stump. A long, long way down, *Panacea* was a tiny black dot in a dark blue sea. The steep slope of the volcano continued below sea level and the water was deep, meaning we had our full 240 metres of chain out. I prayed the windlass would work, as it had been playing up the past couple of days, and I didn't fancy hauling all of that up by hand.

At the top we sat, where instructed by the guide, in black sand still warm from the afternoon's rays, and looked down on to popping and snapping flares of fire. I was glad of the warmth of the sand; now we had stopped climbing, and it was dark, cooling sweat was wicking the heat away from my body. I shivered in the thin long-sleeved top I had brought with me. The way back down, although far quicker, was tricky – we effectively had to ski down the sandy slope in our boots, using our bamboo poles as brakes.

'Vorrei offriti una pizza ed una birra,' Anton said at the bottom of the slope.

'OK. Grazie,' I replied, having understood enough to know birra was beer and pizza was… pizza.

We said goodbye to the guests and popped into a restaurant. After all the climbing, I was starving. In the loo I glanced in the mirror to see a face covered in grey ash. Looking good.

God knows how but I managed to understand enough of what Anton was telling me to glean that he was 26, had lived in Italy for six years and that this was his second summer on *Andante*. He could speak Moldavian, Romanian and Italian and, when he was a teenager, he had done a year's national service as an armed guard patrolling the Moldavian/Romanian border. His brother lived in Moldavia, his father was dead and he loved his mama and Moldavian techno music. The first parts, up to the national service, I was taking an educated guess at but I'm pretty sure I understood his last two points – mainly because he got out his phone to show me a picture of his mama (Eastern European. Headscarf. See?) and to play me some truly dreadful squawking electro racket.

He was a sweet boy, though, and I was glad to have a friend. *Andante* ran charters in a similar area to *Panacea*, so I knew I'd probably see him again from time to time through the summer.

And I did – the very next night. Both yachts were moored in a marina in Salina, so after dinner was finished, Carlo said we could go ashore if we wanted to.

'Vorrei offriti una birra ed una granita,' Anton said this time. He was nothing if not direct. I accepted, again. When I tried to pay he wouldn't let me.

The granita, not that far removed from the sugary confections that used to emerge from Mr Frosty's rotating belly, was tooth-achingly sweet and did not go with beer. So we switched to cocktails. When we ordered our second round, Anton asked for takeaway cups and we went for a stroll along the promenade. Italians like to stay up late but by this hour there were few people out on the streets. We walked towards the seafront and jumped across the breakwater rocks until we were by the water's edge. After a quick swim in our underwear and flip-flops to guard against the painful spines of the sea urchins we could see clinging to the rocks (the water was that clear even by moonlight), Anton kissed me and tried to take things further.

I moved away. 'No,' I said.

'Perchè no?'

'Perchè. No.'

'Perchè no?'

'Perchè. No.' Why no? Because. No.

'Pleeeease?' he begged. 'Pleeeease?' *So he does speak at least one word of English*, I thought, as I firmly shook my head and put my jeans and T-shirt back on in order to go back to the boat.

A week later, *Andante* moored next to us in Naples Mergellina marina and Anton asked me out for pizza and beer again. As we sat in a restaurant, over wine, ricotta and mozzarella, his phone rang, interrupting the flow of conversation – or, rather, the stilted, head-scratching game of charades crossed with Pictionary we were using to get by. It was his Mama. He leaned back in his chair and gabbled away at her in Moldavian. I sipped my wine, smiled politely and waited patiently, expecting him to make his excuses to his mother shortly and hang up. He talked. I sipped, smiled and waited. He talked some more. He looked at his plate and gesticulated over it. I started imagining their conversation, to pass the time. 'What have you had for your tea?' I guessed she was asking. 'Are you taking good care of yourself?' 'Ricotta, Mama. And yes, I am eating my vegetables. No, I'm not drinking too much. Yes, I am getting enough sleep.' Finally, after 20 minutes – 20 minutes! – he hung up.

I asked him what he did in the winter months, when he wasn't working on *Andante*. He told me he was going to go back to his brother's farm in Moldavia, where they kept pigs and had 1000 bottles of locally produced wine.

'You can come with me,' he said, in Italian. 'Spend the winter in Moldavia on the farm. Did I mention the 1000 bottles of wine? Maybe it is more – maybe 1500 by now.' So here I was again, being made an offer to don that headscarf and tuck myself away in a little former Soviet village in the middle of nowhere. I wasn't aware of having asked the universe to manifest me an Eastern European husband and a harsh winter existence to go with it, so why did these opportunities keep cropping up? It was weird. Again, like Sven's offer, it was so wide of the Caribbean mark that I didn't have to think twice about it turning it down. And, as I'd told Steve, not everything in my life was about getting a boyfriend. I had an image of me snuggling up in the barn with the pigs to keep off the Moldavian cold, mud smears on my face and straw sprigs in my hair, and clutching some gut-rotting potato wine. Thanks, Anton, but no thanks.

27

He made me an offer
I couldn't refuse

Em-ma! George Clooney! George Clooney!'
No, that wasn't a cry from an excitable Daniela, having just spotted a Hollywood A-lister driving along the Amalfitano coast in a roadster. It was an order for a coffee from the latest group of guests, a bunch of Italians who liked to have a laugh and a giggle – and to slap me on the bottom.

Even before they arrived, we sensed that they would be a difficult bunch. On their form, they stated that they wanted their privacy and Carlo instructed us all not to chat to them, just to serve them what they asked for and then move away to a discreet distance. Imran said they sounded like a solo female guest he had once had on another boat. The woman had stipulated that only one waiter must attend her at all her meals and that he must stand in a certain place on the deck. He was to remove her plates *immediately* she had finished eating but – and here's the rub – he must not, on any account, ever look at her. What his trick was for knowing she'd finished, I don't know. Maybe he held a little rear-view mirror out every two minutes to double-check she'd actually polished off her lobster. These rich people and their don't-look-at-me-or-feed-me-the-ends-of-tomatoes demands.

The ringleader of this group of six Italians asserted his dominance almost as soon as he had taken off his espadrilles and put them in the basket we kept at the top of the passerella, so that guests didn't bring grit from the street on to the decks.

'Where is the wine I ordered from the broker?' he barked. 'Is it here yet? We must have Champagne. Now.'

'Certainly, sir,' I replied, practically curtseying to him, and went off to find the 200-euros-a-bottle Veuve Clicquot he'd had sent on ahead. Of course, there was something wrong with it. 'It is too cold,' he said. 'Can't you get anything right? Where is the captain?'

At lunch, the bullying attitude continued as I cleared away the plates from the pasta vongole. They had eaten all of it, so I knew they must have liked it. But still there were complaints.

'There was sand in this one clam,' Mr Big Boss said. 'Fetch the chef.'

Imran was in the galley, putting the finishing touches to the calamari and polpo (octopus). 'Imran, they say there was sand in the vongole,' I told him. 'They are asking for you. Can you come?'

'What sand is?' he said, startled. 'I am washing it many times. Did they eat it?'

'Yes, they ate all of it. I'm sorry – please can you just come?'

Mr Big Boss gave Imran a public dressing down, treating him like an ignorant, inexperienced pot-washer, rather than the experienced chef who had cooked for the household of an Arabian prince that he was.

'Sand can ruin an entire dish,' Mr Big Boss went on with his lecture, while Imran hung his head and listened to the rant.

I walked back through to the galley with him to collect the main course.

'Now guest getting hungry, captain getting hungry,' he said.

'Hungry? They can't be that hungry – or bothered by the sand, Imran,' I pointed out. 'They ate the whole lot.'

'But if captain find out, he getting hungry with me.'

'Hungry? What are you on about?' I frowned as I balanced a heavy platter of seafood on my forearm. The penny dropped. 'Oh, angry. Yes, probably.'

We braced ourselves for Carlo to get really cross. He had recently bawled out Daniela so loudly that I could plainly hear every word he said while I was in the saloon and they were in the galley, with the door closed. I took to temporarily blocking up the fridge outlet vent with a towel if I thought he was going to blow a fuse so that the guests couldn't hear. Strangely, given the circumstances, he was calm for this charter.

And, now that Mr Big Boss had had a chance to show us who was, well, big boss, he relaxed and actually became quite pleasant, too. Possibly it had just taken him some time to relax from the stresses of big-city life and get into the holiday mood.

He and his friends were pleased when I told them we had a Nespresso machine on board. They nicknamed the coffees 'George Clooneys', because he advertises the machines, and ordered them after every meal. Each had a variation – a tall George Clooney, a decaf short George Clooney, a George Clooney so short and extra concentrated that it became a mere George Cloo.

After the thaw came jokes and japes and then macho stunts – diving into the water from the tender while I was driving it along, leading to a nasty gash on a foot and an order from the captain, who dressed it, not to go into the water again – and macho stunts descended to bum-slapping and inappropriate hugging. On their part, obviously. I wasn't going to slap some fifty-something hairy Italian ass, even if we had developed a working relationship that was almost akin to friendship.

One of the guests, an architect, was the first up every morning, and would read the paper over his George Clooney. He was my favourite of the group – he had been invited on the holiday by Mr Big Boss, who was footing the bill, and he wasn't obnoxious or rah rah but was a quiet, content and normal man. I glanced at a headline one morning – some kind of mass shooting.

'What happened?' I asked him, leaning over his shoulder to try to make sense of the pictures.

'In Norway,' he said. 'A man – how you say? – shoot... shot... many people with gun. Very sad.' He flicked through the pages of the newspaper so I could see the images and headlines. I couldn't understand much of what was written in the story but I gleaned enough from the layout, photos and numbers to understand that nearly 80 people had been killed in a car bomb and gun attack. I felt the old journalistic interest flicker to life – I always did love a hard news story like that one, sick as it may seem – but then I doused the little flame, cleared away the coffee things and went to fetch the breakfast food for the guests.

That little bit of journalistic interest would rear its head again a couple of weeks later, when reports started to come through about the London riots. Sitting on a luxury yacht at anchor in the tranquil waters of the Tyrrhenian Sea, surrounded by Champagne and Chanel, langoustine and

Loewe on a daily basis, it was surreal to imagine a bunch of disaffected youths smashing their way into Foot Locker and Curry's to nick a pair of Nikes and a microwave. Even stranger was to picture a gang of middle-class dads facing up to a council estate mob on Clapham's Northcote Road, where the rough shops meet the JoJo Maman Bébé branches, in order to protect their wives, children and shiny silver VW Golfs from harm. I know who my money'd be on in a scrap between the kids in my block in SW4 and a bunch of media-bespectacled, soft-in-the-middle Henrys and Barnabys. Far, far away in Italy, it was easy to see the satirical humour in the situation but from the postings I was seeing from London friends on Facebook, the reality was a lot more frightening. It was a big deal and an even bigger story in England but I found I didn't miss being in the newsroom one little bit. Far more exciting things were happening here, on *Panacea* – and I'm not talking about coffees, crew fallings-out or table presentation. No, these were exciting things to do with my epiphany: Guy had been in touch.

You remember him, right? Handsome devil, rides a motorbike, owns a yacht, lives a life as a free spirit in Asia? Big, beaming white smile? Long-lashed hazel eyes? I visited him a couple of times in Thailand? Was pleased for me when I told him about my epiphany but said that the 'Caribbean wouldn't work for him'? Yes, *that* Guy. Just as I was passing the half-way point of my time in Italy, starting to wonder what I'd do when it was finished, and was missing actually going sailing and feeling a bit lonely, here he was popping up again, being manifested by the universe. And he had an offer for me – an offer which, unlike Sven's and Anton's, I couldn't say no to.

28

I'm reviewing the situation

What seemed like a lifetime ago, I drew up a list of options, directions in which to steer my new life now it was freed of the old and rusting shackles of city life, social expectations, England and journalism. To recap, when I scrawled it down in a tattered notebook in the Andaman islands on board *Gillaroo*, it went something like this: Option 1: Get a job as crew in the Med in summer and in the Caribbean in winter. Option 2: Go home and settle down. Option 3. Carry on Cruisin'. Option 4: Go and find Guy. At the time the decision had been made for me: I'd been offered this job on *Panacea*, I'd accepted it and Guy had said that was a shame, as he'd been hoping I'd go sailing with him to Indonesia for the summer. I'd cheekily replied, 'Some other time?' and left it at that.

I had heard a bit from him from time to time over the past six months – he'd been on his boat in Malaysia, doing some jobs on it with a friend, then had left it anchored in some mangroves to go travelling in the Middle East. If we were both online on Facebook at the same time we'd have a quick catch-up chat, but I was forever having to drop my phone in my pocket to dash off to see to some guests' needs and we didn't really get beyond occasional snatched moments of small talk. I was always happy when his name cropped up in my messenger window but Thailand, travels and freedom were seeming very long ago now I was in the middle of a busy working life in Europe.

Time for a tangent. After Mr Big Boss and his friends departed in Naples, we had a couple of weeks without guests. It was the height of summer, what should have been our busiest and most profitable time, but instead we were languishing in Naples Mergellina marina for 300 euros a night. Mind you, it could have been worse – the megayachts moored just up from us were paying up to 3000 euros a night for their slots.

They were absolutely enormous things. Watching them come in to moor up was a spectacle not to be missed. If I was sleeping in my cabin and I heard the tell-tale fart of a bow thruster vibrate through the water I'd climb up out of my bunk on to the deck to catch the entertainment.

It being the height of the season, all the big boys were out – the 65-metre behemoths with shimmering white hulls and crews of 15 or 20. We looked like a grubby little sailing dinghy next to them, they were that big – as large as blocks of flats. The entrance to the marina was tight and they had to moor stern-to, Mediterranean style, and therefore turn through 90 degrees in the small gap between the anchor chains of the other megayachts and the little plastic day boats on the other side, and squeeze their way, in reverse, among the other billion-dollar gin palaces to stop just the perfect distance away from the quayside so that the owner's mistress could teeter off the back in her six-inch Manolos. Sometimes there'd be a queue of them waiting to come in. Imagine trying to get into a tight supermarket car park space that is only a foot wider than the car on either side, on a day when the tarmac is covered in black ice and while a whole host of other angry drivers, all desperate to claim the space for themselves, are all huffing and puffing and tooting their horns at you to get you to hurry up. They were very skilled drivers, these captains in their billion-dollar machines – and, of course, they always had a bevy of mini-skirt-clad stewardesses ready with metre-long inflatable fenders to cushion the blow and spare their blushes if they did get it just an inch or two off.

Their crew were always tanned and gorgeous – and often blonde. This is an industry that shamelessly hires staff on the basis of what they look like. Stories abound of chief stewardesses being sacked once they reach 35; or a captain – a man who had previously been like a best friend to the owner – being fired purely because he is balding and the missus can't abide it. When you send in your application for a job, you must always send in a photograph. It's not about glamour – women should wear their hair neatly tied back and there's none of the heavy make-up favoured by air stewardesses – but a natural prettiness in women, and a clean-shaven face for men, is a given. And if you don't like it – tough. There's a queue of other Mirandas and Petes lined up behind you, who are unencumbered by your modern sense of equality. Take it to your union rep. What's that? There isn't a union? Well, that's just hard luck, love.

Female deckhands were rare; I only saw a few others during my whole six months in Italy. Things might be different in America or Australia but in macho Italia, men do the men's work and women dress the flowers and plump the cushions. One afternoon in Naples I spotted a girl working on Roman Abramovich's former boat *Ecstasea* – he'd traded in the too-small 85-metre megayacht for the 165-metre *Eclipse*. Blonde and beautiful – naturally – she was suspended in a harness like an abseiler, dangling off the side of the boat, cleaning the topsides by dipping a long-handled brush into a bucket of suds that was tied round her waist and hanging by her ankles. A steel track, like a curtain rail, ran along the topsides above her, constructed solely for this reason – to suspend a human cleaner from on a weekly basis. Another deckhand, a guy, stood by the rail, sliding her forwards towards the bow as she finished scrubbing each section, and hosing off the soap suds behind her.

Cleaning was a proper industry on these boats – my paltry four-hour efforts were nothing compared to those of the megayacht crews. For two days we had the most beautiful yacht imaginable – the 36-metre 1930-built J Class sailing yacht *Shamrock V* – moored next but one to us. While I spent the morning switching between a variety of jobs, *Shamrock*'s bosun was 46 metres up her mast in his climbing harness, bottle of Glassex in one hand, polishing cloth in the other. He was up there at 8.30am, he was up there at 10.45am, he was still up there – although much closer to deck level by this point – at lunchtime. Five hours polishing a mast. Honestly, who can even see that far up?

I felt like a fraud next to these slick, competent, cool people. They weren't the friendliest bunch – no one said hello when we converged at the rubbish bins or hosepipe points. I don't know if it was a power *v.* sail thing – maybe they saw us as the pikeys of the marina. After all, these boats charter out at

450,000 euros a week – quite a lot more than we charged.

Carlo set me a task of polishing all of the bubbles out of the hull that had started to form between the black hull paint and the clear top coat. From a distance they looked like saltwater crystals but they didn't wash off and instead had to be sanded out. It was really a job that should have been done over the winter, in the boatyard, by a burly bloke with power tools, but here I was, bobbing about in the dingy, trying to scrub away at them with sandpaper in one hand while holding the dinghy flush to the yacht with the other. Whenever I pushed hard enough against the hull to start to see some effect, the dinghy moved until I was more than arm's reach away. I adapted a technique of stretching up and clinging on to the toe rail with the fingertips of my free arm, and that would work for a couple of minutes at a time until so much lactic acid built up in my extended arm that I had to let go and shake it until the burning subsided. Also, it was summer in Naples and it was incredibly hot and humid. Memories of Malaysia came back as sweat beaded on my back and rolled off the tip of my nose. I kept my head down, worried I was becoming a laughing stock among the other, better equipped exterior crews. *Ecstasea* Blondie looked way cooler, elegantly flying on her wire like a dancer in a show; I just looked like a scrubber. A frazzled, sweaty scrubber in men's clothes. And then, moving the dinghy from one hull to another, I got a rope tangled in the outboard engine's propeller. Proper schoolgirl error. I swore under my breath, hoping no one was watching me turning beetroot with shame.

'Em-ma! Carlo called down from *Panacea*'s deck. 'Take a break.' He didn't have to tell me twice. I climbed up the side of the hull and back down the ladder into the crew cabin.

The air-conditioning was bliss, working its way up from my ankles as I descended. Within a few minutes, under its cooling influence, I was more myself. I didn't feel like sleeping. *I'll work on my tan*, I decided. *Might as well try to even out these farmer's marks on my arms and legs while I have the chance.* Changing into a bikini and grabbing a towel and my iPod, I climbed back up into the sun. Towel rolled out on the guests' sunbathing deck – handily, the sunshades had been removed while we were in port – and prone position adopted, I closed my eyes and enjoyed the feeling of the sun on my back. *Ah, this is the life.*

'Em-ma!' I heard Carlo shouting through my reverie. 'What are you doing?'

I sat up. 'Taking a break, like you said.' A few weeks ago I would have felt weird to be in front of my boss dressed only in a bikini but I'd seen him in just his teeny-tiny black Speedos a fair few times by now, when he went into the water to check the underside of the boat, so I was less embarrassed about it.

'No, no, no. I am sorry but you cannot remain like this. I know a lot of the peoples here. What if they see you like this and tell the owner? You cannot remain.' I sighed quietly to myself and stood up. It's not like I was topless or anything. And, being in a bikini, who would even know I was crew rather than a guest, anyway? However, I should have remembered that this was *not* the life, *my* life. This was the guests' life. I wasn't cruising any more (and enjoying myself); I was working (and being told off). I sighed.

'OK, captain,' I said. 'I'm sorry. I didn't think.' I went back to my cabin and put my men's clothes back on again, resigning myself to having funny-looking patchy skin for ever.

The upside to being banished from sunbathing (and here we're off the tangent and back on track) was that I filled my time by going online. And, at the same time I was logged on to Facebook, so was Guy. I told him about my sunbathing boob and we chatted about the cruising life.

Wow, I miss it so much, I thought. *I'd be more than happy to forgo flushing toilets, aircon, hot water and silver plates for bucket showers, tins of beans and some freedom.*

I vented my frustrations at Guy on Messenger and he sympathised with me and somehow, without his directly asking me, the conversation turned to the winter and our going sailing together.

'It would be lovely to sail with you, if possible, nice to have someone who knows what they are doing for a change,' he wrote. 'I bet you could show me lots of stuff I don't know. It would be really interesting and fun as well. I have a boat, we should use it!'

'I am totally in,' I replied, wondering if this was for real or was just flirting. 'Where would we go? Still Indonesia and Papua New Guinea? I know if you go to Indo you need a special cruising licence.'

'Yeah I know all about that. It's called a cait and it's the reason I have never sailed in Indo, because you need to apply one month in advance with all the crew details,' Guy wrote. 'But if I knew it was you and me that would be a cinch.'

It sounds like he really does want me to go sailing with him, I thought. *But it's so hard to judge someone's tone over email or online chat. How to tell?*

'I really wanna set up somewhere I can dive casually and have a place in the sun!' he wrote.

I paused, fingers over my phone's keys, then decided to be

a bit cheeky and try my luck. 'Well, you should come to the Caribbean with me, then.' This was a bit naughty – I didn't actually have any plans to go to the Caribbean for the winter. *But hey*, I reasoned, *there's plenty of time to sort something out if he does call your bluff.*

The phone bleeped as his reply came through. 'I seriously am considering checking out the Caribbean with you,' he wrote. I blinked and re-read it. What was this? The guy who'd said the Caribbean 'wouldn't work for him' was now 'seriously considering' checking it out with me? This was bloody amazing. I read his message for a third time, in case I'd gotten the wrong end of the stick. Nope, there it was, in clear type, on the screen. He wanted to spend at least the winter with me. My heart did a little celebratory backflip and I did something unbelievably cheesy – I leapt up from my seat in the shade, jumped up and down on the deck and punched the air. Yes, that's right, I copied the high-energy moves of a bunch of mid-1980s, long-haired, stonewash-jeans-clad soft-rock singers. *That's* how thrilled I was.

Unable to wipe an enormous silly grin off my face, I wrote back, heart racing. 'OK in all seriousness, unless you meet the diving, poker-playing woman of your dreams and sail off into the sunset (sunrise I suppose if you're going east) with her, I'm inviting myself along on to the boat this winter.'

'It'd be funny if we sailed all the way to the Caribbean,' he replied. 'Seriously, I think winter would be lots of fun no matter where we go.'

'Good,' I said. 'Because I need some fun – there's a serious shortage of it at the moment. I think working can wait.'

Just like that, I had a plan of what to do once I left *Panacea* at the end of October. I was going to finish my old option

1, working as crew on a superyacht, and I was going to head off into the sunrise with Guy, which, in the same list I'd scribbled down six months ago, was option 4. And we were going to sail to Indonesia and Papua New Guinea, have amazing adventures and somehow end up in the Caribbean, thus fulfilling my epiphany. I did cheesy move number two and cast my eyes to the heavens. Could life get any better than this?

29

Hell hath no fury like
a fasting Muslim scorned

Imran was spilling over with excitement, humming loudly as he moved about the boat at our new anchorage, a wide smile on his bony face.

After five days in Naples marina, Carlo had decided we were going to stop haemorrhaging money and move to Salina in the Aeolian islands instead, where we could anchor for free. It was a beautiful anchorage, next to the main harbour, with views of low-rise white houses and green hills, punctuated with bright blooming bushes and the occasional moped put-putting its way up the steep roads. It was a far lovelier place to wait for our next charter than dirty, noisy Naples, with its polluted water, oil-stained tarmac and inbred feral cats with eyes that looked in different directions and that had parts of noses or ears missing.

'Imran,' I said, following him into the galley, where he started taking vegetables and herbs out of the fridge and plugging in his food processor. 'You seem different. What is it? Oh – no cigarette. And why are you so happy?'

'Hi, Golden Laydee,' he sang. 'Is Ramadan. First day today.'

I knew a little bit about Ramadan from my time in Borneo – we'd seen shopkeepers lolling about on the pavement, exhausted, sapped of all energy by the heat, humidity and lack of a good lunch, counting down the hours until sunset when they could eat – but not much more than that. Imran seemed a lot more upbeat than they had – but then he was a very faithful Muslim, having done Hajj the previous year.

'Does that mean no smoking as well as no eating?' I asked.

'No. Nothing in mouth. Even water.' He carried on humming as he worked.

I was horrified. 'No water? But it's 32 degrees outside.'

'Is OK,' he said, smashing cloves of garlic with the side of a knife. 'Is for God. And not too long. When moon finish, Ramadan finish.' He threw some ingredients in the blender and pulsed them together. 'You like pal-apple?'

I drew a blank. 'Pal-apple?'

'Yes, pal-apple. Food my country. Very good. You eat it.'

Pal-apple, pal-apple – what could he mean? I looked at the ingredients he had on the counter – some chickpeas, tomatoes, cumin, fresh coriander he'd picked up in the Asian area around the train station in Rome when he popped home to visit his family.

'You mean falafel?' I asked.

'Yes, pal-apple. I make for when Ramadan is finish tonight.'

Come sunset – he had a printed-out list of the official times so that he didn't eat a second too soon ('Sometimes mountain is coming in way of sun') – he prayed in his cabin, heated the oil and the smell of frying spices filled the boat. His jubilation was catching and everyone's spirits were lifted and we laughed and talked together over a relaxed meal, the first time we'd done that, it seemed, since before we had our first guests on board.

Next morning, though, it was a different story. I climbed out of my cabin and walked back towards the cockpit, to go below to make some tea. Imran was smoking a cigarette off the back of the boat, his shoulders hunched over.

'I break Ramadan,' he said, sadly, when I asked what had happened. The broad smile of the day before was gone. 'Captain say me no set alarm for 4am for to pray because he sleeping. Yesterday I wake up myself and go outside to pray. This morning, no wake up. So Ramadan broke.'

'Does that mean the whole thing is off?' I asked.

'No. I can do more day at end,' he said. 'Just for today Ramadan is not coming. Tomorrow I try.'

The third day, he did wake up in time 'for to pray' – while we had no guests on board he asked Carlo if he could temporarily move out of their shared cabin into another so that he didn't disturb him by rising in the middle of the night. By day five or six the humming, the big grins and the religious energy had faded. Instead, like those listless Malaysians I'd seen lounging outside their shop entrances, Imran took to lying around. And who could blame him? I imagine it's bad enough half starving yourself but having to quit the fags at the same time when you've a 50-a-day habit? He lay on the sofa, he lay on the table, he lay on the steps descending into the saloon. Anywhere that was big enough to accommodate him, he lay, staring into space, doing nothing. It was a good job we didn't have any charters – I don't know how he would have coped. Or how the guests would have coped, trying to pass the breakfast dishes over a prone, starving Muslim.

All that fasting must have been playing havoc with his

blood sugar levels, too, because he became an absolute Fury. That fight we'd had when we took the boat out for the first time was nothing on this. He screamed at me, inches from my face, when I asked him what I thought was something fairly innocuous about the breakfast dishes on about day ten of Ramadan. We had taken a last-minute five-day charter of 10 guests, which was more than we had space for, really – the woman who was paying for the whole trip was sleeping in the saloon. It was even more of a squeeze at the table at mealtimes and I just wanted to ask Imran to please put the breakfast food on small plates, so I could fit them all on.

His eyes grew wide and he sneered at me.

'Why you always like this?' he asked.

'Like what?'

'In morning, all...' In his anger he couldn't find the words and he broke off to wave his hands violently around, stabbing the air with a spoon he was holding. 'Women, always like this.' His voice rose to a loud shout and I worried the guests would hear. I tried to calm him down.

'It's not a big problem,' I said. 'It's just using small plat—'

He cut me off, shouting at me again. Steam was practically whistling out of both ears. I left. The next day he criticised the way I cleaned the boat apropos of nothing and that afternoon he got angry again when I set off to drive him ashore in the dinghy to do the food shopping. I decided to have a word with Carlo.

'He scream at me, too,' he said, 'when I buy two litre of milk. And at Daniela. This is no good. I going ask him to stop Ramadan.'

Oh God, I thought, feeling guilty. *That's not what I meant to happen.* I knew how important his religion was to him.

I had just wanted Carlo to have a quiet talk with Imran, to ask him to not be so rude.

The next morning, everything was back to normal, with Imran chain-smoking, downing espressos and eating – and acting like a normal human being.

'Captain tell me no do Ramadan,' he said, with a shrug. I was surprised he wasn't angry about it, but I suppose he'd never worked in the UK, with employee rights and religious equality. He was just used to having to do exactly what his boss told him.

'What will you do about Ramadan?' I asked him.

'Oh, I can do in winter. No problem. You want omelette, Golden Laydee?'

Carlo convinced me to use the free time we had again after the short charter to learn how to scuba dive. 'You need it, if you want to be a captain,' he said. 'You might have to check the anchor or the bottom of the boat or the propeller.' I hadn't the heart to tell him that I was changing my thinking and that I was going to head off for travelling and cruising fun again, rather than focusing on a superyacht career. Instead, I said I was a bit worried that it would hurt my ears. I didn't confess to being an absolute wuss in the water when it came to snorkelling, unless I had a couple of kind-hearted Aussies with me, in the shape of Greg and Debs.

'We will do a practice,' he said. 'I have diving gear and we will go down on the anchor chain, only five metre. Then you can try to clear your ear of the pressure.'

I found myself agreeing. Guy was a diver and he wanted us to go diving on our Indonesia trip. *And*, I reasoned with myself, *you grew to like snorkelling when you took your time and had a good teacher and, who knows, maybe the same thing will happen with diving and you'll forget about imagining scary, sharp-toothed sea monsters rising up from the deep to bite you. This whole leaving London thing and starting a new life was about being more open to trying new things. This is a chance to not automatically say no.* I agreed to the try dive.

It was awkward, using Carlo's spare regulator to breathe, which meant I had to stay inappropriately close to him while we descended, hand over hand, down the chain. I felt a bit nervous as I went, mainly because the regulator felt like it was going to pop out of my mouth, so I was holding on to that with one hand, the chain with the other and with both ankles, and was also having to let go of the regulator constantly to hold my nose while I blew out, to pop my ears. And I was trying not to get my naked legs tangled up with my boss's. Probably I was overdoing it a bit on the ear-popping but I was paranoid that I would hurt myself. Down and down we went, with not a sea monster in sight. In fact, there was nothing but blue water and Carlo's face, close up. He kept his eyes trained on mine, looking for signs of panic, and gave me a questioning OK sign every few seconds. I nodded my head in response, my hands being otherwise too occupied to make the same signal in reply.

At the surface he asked me how I felt.

'OK,' I said. 'But I felt like the regulator was being pulled out of my mouth the whole time.'

'That is because it is my spare one,' he said. 'Tomorrow we will borrow some equipment and you will find that easier. And, I tell you, we went to ten metre, not five metre, so you did very well.' I was astonished at that. I had made it down to ten metres, not panicked (too much) and not hurt my ears. I happily agreed to try again the next day.

He took Daniela down next but she freaked out and they didn't make it more than a metre below the surface. I moved away from the bow, not wanting to put her off by having an audience. But her panic made me feel even prouder of myself for staying calm.

Cumbersome dive gear donned the next day, Carlo again tried to coax Daniela into the water. We had taken the dinghy to a small pebble beach so that we could start in very shallow water. I left the pair of them to it and swam a little way off by myself, looking at a few small, light brown fish and grass peppering the sandy bottom. I had to concentrate hard on what I was doing and it was very distracting, which turned out to be a good thing, really. I hadn't quite got the hang of my buoyancy and my belly, in my wetsuit, scraped lightly along the floor as I swam along, my whole body tilted to the right so I resembled a fish with an infected swim bladder. I carried on and on, my dive mask inches from the sand. I was by myself and I felt absolutely fine – until I checked the depth gauge. I was 12 metres deep. I couldn't believe it. Because I had been following the bottom, I had no idea how much water was above me. I began to worry a little bit about the bends – I've seen *Baywatch*, so I know the dangers – as I didn't know if I should be diving to 12 metres. I turned 180 degrees and followed the seabed until my tank broke the surface of the water.

Sitting in the pebbly shallows, waiting for Carlo and Daniela to emerge, I felt jubilant. Not only had I done it, I had enjoyed it so much that I had lost track of where I was. Not once had

I freaked out or imagined nasty creatures of the deep. I had been utterly absorbed in the moment. In fact, I'd even go so far as to say that I had loved it.

'I bet you get the diving bug now,' Guy wrote when I went on to Facebook to babble excitedly about my day.

'Well, I decided to do it for you, because you said you want to dive in Indo,' I explained, 'but now I've discovered that I am actually doing it for me.'

I was as thrilled about it as I had been when I had had that first day of snorkelling in Mabul with Debs. But it wasn't the diving, specifically, that had given me such a boost; it was the fact that I had dared to try something that I had been pretty much convinced I was going to hate. A few years ago, back in the UK, I would have automatically demurred – in other words, wimped out. Now I was willing to give things a shot. Going off on a boat with people I didn't know; sailing into new countries with little more preparation or planning than 'point it that way and keep going 'til we get there'; being brave enough to try new, frightening things. Heading off on that original adventure and, now, having my dream life or epiphany to focus on, was opening up the world to me – and me to the world. *And it's not going to stop here*, I vowed. *This is just the beginning of seeing what I can achieve.*

30

Put your back into it
(or not, as it turns out)

Our little holiday over, it was back to work. And some work it was – I would start my cleaning marathon at 7am and climb, wearily, into my bunk at 4am, after the last of the customers had gone to bed. All day, every day, I was bending, lifting, twisting, pulling, carrying, stretching, reaching, loading, unloading. The good thing was that with all this physical exertion the extra pounds that I had put on when I first moved to Italy through over-enthusiastic consumption of carbs melted away. The downside was that something had to give – and that something, unfortunately, was my back.

I got up, as usual, early in the morning to start hosing down and polishing the cockpit area while the guests slept, preparing for breakfast. As I did every morning, I crouched down, cloth in hand, to reach into the awkward corners of the gunwales to remove any traces of salt residue or sand that showed clearly against the black paint. As I twisted and leant forwards, I felt my lower back ping. I stifled a yelp as I straightened up, hand to the back of my waist. Rubbing didn't ease the pain; sitting didn't help, nor did standing and pacing the deck. The only thing that seemed to make any difference to the waves of pain and the nauseous feeling it was creating was having a little cry. So I sat on the wooden rail and let the tears flow.

'Em-ma!' Daniela said, coming up from the saloon to smoke. 'What happened?'

'I've hurt my back,' I said. 'I don't know how but I can't really move.'

She went to wake the captain and, while he was dressing, came back with a heat pad and some painkillers and a glass of water. The captain had a look at my back – nothing to see, really: no jutting broken bones or giant swellings – and packed me off to my cabin to rest. For three whole days.

It was probably a good taster of what being sent to prison would be like. I was in a room maybe 6 foot by 6 foot, lying on a narrow slab that could only loosely be termed 'bed'. I was solitary, apart from when Daniela popped in to shower and change or sleep, and there was absolutely nothing to do. I slept, I woke, I ate, I stared at the ceiling until I was so bored that I fell asleep again, I ate, I slept some more. By listening to the timings of the engine starting and the anchor windlass grinding, I could work out roughly where we were in the routine of the day. After the first 24 hours I was able to lie in one position long enough to read but I'd soon worked through the couple of books I had stored on my Kindle and had nothing left, unless I started on the dictionary. I was completely and utterly bored. The boat's wifi couldn't penetrate the steel bulkhead between the crew cabin and the rest of the interior so I couldn't even kill time on the web.

By the second morning I was going so stir-crazy that I

gingerly climbed the ladder out of the cabin – extra tricky, given the twisting motion needed to get out of the bed and on to the rungs – and went up on deck. Jobs I could do upright, like hosing the floor, were fine, but as soon as I tried to lean forwards, pain seared through my back again. Carlo caught me wincing and sent me back to bed. I tried again on the third morning but it was still no-go. By the fourth, I was so fed up with being stuck in the cabin that I carried on through the pain, which was easing slightly and which I think was being helped by the movement. Carlo let me work – everyone else was feeling the burden of my absence, too, as they'd had to pick up the slack and do my work on top of their own (although not quite to my standards, I noticed, as I found pockets of dirt here and there).

'What you think cause it?' Daniela asked me.

I shrugged. 'I don't know. It has only happened to me once before in my life. Maybe all the heavy lifting?'

Carlo cut in. 'I think it is the mooring lines. This boat weighs 100 tonnes and you are pulling on these lines because we do not have the winches for them. Is no good. You see other boats, they have winches just for this job, for mooring. You cannot pull 100 tonnes by the hand.' He had a point.

A couple of days later, while I was still feeling a bit tender, we were moored in Vibo Valentia marina, next to a power megayacht, and I watched its deckhands at work. They were all men in their twenties or early thirties, all fit and strong, with broad backs and defined triceps. They wore tool belts and carried their power sanders around the boat with confidence, marking out areas to work on with blue tape and then starting their grinding, varnishing or fibreglassing tasks with practised ease like the skilled craftsmen they were.

I looked down into the cup of tea I was holding. *Who am I kidding? I'm not a deckhand, not really. I don't have any carpentry skills; I'm not an engineer; I can't look around the boat and identify what needs replacing, fixing or upgrading and know how to do it. There's a reason why I have barely seen any female deckhands working – and that's because it's not a woman's job. OK, so woodwork or fibreglassing skills can be learned, but what about everything else? Strength and power – they are the main attributes, for lifting and pulling things or climbing. I just don't have that. I'm a nine-stone weakling who gets a bad back from lifting a few suitcases and pulling on a few lines. Of course I can't be a deckhand; not really. Imran has to come out of the kitchen every time we enter or leave a marina to handle the big fenders because they're too heavy for me to lift over the guard rails. This is not an office; we can't have equality of the sexes here, smash through the glass ceiling to proportional representation in the boardroom. It comes down to natural differences between the genders. Carlo was right to make me the waitress – that's the job for a woman on a boat. Folding the towels, serving the coffees and smiling at the guests.*

I sighed. I had always worked in male-dominated environments, tried to find a way of being 'one of the lads' while still looking like a woman: by accepting being called by my surname, peppering my language with swear words or by bragging about how much I'd drunk the night before or how many minutes I'd managed to shave off my run or cycle home. That was different, though, it was just bravado. I couldn't fake this in the same way.

Over the following days I felt conflicted. I still loved everything about boats and the boating life: the familiar clinking noise of halyards hitting masts in the breeze in marinas, working outside, the instantly calming effect of the rippling water, the beautiful lines of the yachts, seeing the stars every night, the sunrises and sunsets. I didn't want to give all that up to go back to being a journalist in an office. But I didn't see how I could do this job again next summer.

It wasn't just the lack of strength and fear of injuring myself again; there were lots of other factors as well. Pretty high up was the lack of control I had over my own life: I couldn't decide when to get up, what to wear, what to eat, when to eat it or what time to go to bed. Even showering was dictated to me. I missed the freedom to do what I wanted, when I wanted to do it. I also really missed exercise – I had a theory that not being able to do my yoga or go running had weakened my core muscles and added to the back injury. And I hated not getting the opportunity to use my brain very much or to make decisions.

The upsides to this job were great, without a doubt – travelling around, meeting interesting people, earning good money. There was a problem with the Italian bank account I had opened when I arrived and I couldn't access any of my salary, which meant I was building up a tidy sum of savings. I had my tips in cash, as well, so I had access to money if I needed it, but, beyond the odd bottle of contact lens solution or a pretty scarf, there wasn't really the need to buy anything and we rarely had the opportunity to go to the shops, anyway, unless it was a trip to the supermarket to buy food for the guests. I worked out that, with holiday pay, I would be taking about £12,000 home with me. That's not a bad savings pot collected over just six months. It would certainly be enough to keep me going for a while out in Indonesia with Guy.

I found myself wishing that I'd known about the superyacht

industry when I was 22. Back then, the positives of travel and money would have far outweighed the negatives of lack of control. If I'd started 10 years ago I could have been a chief stewardess by now, amassed an absolute fortune and possibly been well on my way to retirement. It was a great industry, for sure – just not one to be breaking into when you're a slightly cynical, washed-up 33-year-old weedy ex-journalist, perhaps.

I wasn't ready to quit the yachting life, though. *What I need to do*, I decided, *is find a different way of working around boats, one where I am in control so I get the benefits without the drawbacks. And one where I don't have to physically damage myself in the process.*

Obviously one way of getting to hang around boats for a while longer was my upcoming trip to Indonesia with Guy. OK, so I wasn't going to be earning big bucks, but I'd still have the travel, meeting new people and being around boats parts sorted. Plus, there'd be all that fantastic Asian food to eat – and I was presuming I'd be able to choose my own bedtime. Pure luxury. Just that, you know, what with no hot water, aircon, washing machine, etc, it'd be pure luxury without the luxuries.

'I'm looking forward to it as well,' Guy wrote, 'but we do need to decide where to go. I am busy programming during the day. So I haven't had much time to get into it. Are we talking about being in Langkawi in early, mid or late November?'

My sister's first baby was due at the end of November and I wanted to be in the UK for that so we settled on early December for meeting up in Malaysia. That would give me a few weeks after leaving Italy to visit friends and family in England and get everything sorted out. I felt the familiar thrill as we sketched out a rough plan to sail to Sumatra. One little doubt was niggling away at me – that I'd never lived with a boyfriend before, let alone spent 24/7 with one on a 36-foot yacht in a place so remote we were likely to go weeks without seeing anyone else. Steve had promised me lots of other boats around; *Gillaroo* had had a big crew; *Panacea* was work. *Incognito* was just Guy and me. Boyfriend part aside, I was a bit of an old hand at going to live on boats with virtual strangers by now, so it wasn't hard to suppress the little niggle. Also, planning the trip – looking at weather and current patterns, charts and immigration information, would give me something to do in the five weeks between having our last charter and flying home.

'An adventure. Woo hoo!' I wrote to Guy, before slipping my phone in my pocket to go and take another order for coffee and gelato. *I can't wait.*

31

Down time

Ironically, once the charters were finished, I missed the guests. Their demands, their annoying habits and their rudeness had at least given the four of us as a crew something to bond over. Now that we were on our own, as a team we grew apart again, although Carlo and Daniela were getting increasingly closer. Stuck in Naples marina for five weeks, with no anchors to drop, no tender to have to drive, no elaborate meals to prepare and serve and no cleaning to do, it was deathly dull.

Carlo headed off to Genoa, to the boat show, and then on to Rome, to attend to 'business'. He was trying to work out where would be the best – and cheapest – place to keep the boat over the winter and so far Sicily, Turkey and Tunisia had been mentioned. Daniela, coincidentally, went with him to Rome, apparently to collect her passport in case we left for a country that wouldn't, unlike Croatia, allow her to use her Italian ID card to gain entry. I caught her Veeting her bikini line the day before the pair of them set off for the train station. *Presumably you are hoping that that'll be for the benefit of the captain,* I thought, *rather than for the Italian passport office civil servants.*

Imran and I stayed behind, to take care of the boat in the windy October weather. As soon as September finished, the sun vanished and heavy rain and wind storms rolled violently in over the Mediterranean to strike the Bay of Naples. *Panacea*, held in place by two mooring lines and six thick stern lines, strained at her ties in the wind and swell like a huge dog after the scent of a rabbit at its leash. I was worried that, if there was a problem, I would have to motor the boat out of the marina and re-park it. I had done it before – but with a 38-foot plastic sailing yacht in spacious marinas in calm weather, not a 1-million-euro, 100-tonne steel behemoth in a howling gale.

'Imran,' I asked, 'can you drive this boat if we need to move?' He claimed he could but I had my doubts. I crossed my fingers that we wouldn't need to.

In my boredom, I watched a lot of TV. There was a flat screen in the saloon and we could get a decent enough signal at certain times of the day if it wasn't too windy and if we stuck the portable antenna outside, on the coachroof. I discovered that they didn't dub over *CSI* in Italian, and after a couple of weeks I became quite knowledgeable about the work of early-millennium crime investigation labs in Miami, LA and Vegas.

Imran ignored the American-language TV but was hooked on Italian-dubbed romantic Swiss soap operas, quiz shows and movies. We watched the start of the remake of *Planet of the Apes* together one evening.

'When they make it, this movie,' he asked me, through a thick fug of cigarette smoke in the saloon that I was trying my best to ignore, 'do they go film it in space?' *Ah, bless,*

I thought, and tried to explain CGI to him but he was the kind of man who struggled to work a non-smart mobile phone, so I think the concept was lost on him.

When I wasn't catching up with 10-year-old formulaic US dramas, and when it wasn't so windy that the gusts blew me sideways into the Naples promenade traffic, I ran. After my back injury, I was conscious of trying to do whatever I could to strengthen my back and core muscles. I had running shoes – covered in paint and a bit frayed in some parts where I'd accidentally sanded part of them away with my power tools back in the boatyard – a sports bra and my iPod shuffle, so I was good to go. Whenever I'd been to the supermarket to get bread or tomatoes for the boat I'd noticed that there seemed to be a constant stream of people jogging along the waterfront. So I laced up my shoes, did a loose attempt at stretching, and limped out to join them.

It turned out to be more like an army obstacle course than a running track. There were slow-moving, talking and gesticulating Italians to weave through and piles of dog poop to leap over. When dusk came, and with it the cover of darkness and protection from prying police eyes, African immigrants spread bedsheets over the pavement and carefully arranged their precious cargo of fake Gucci and Dolce & Gabbana handbags, belts and purses. These were the only black men I saw in Naples, crouching against the sea wall in their djellabas, mirrored hats jammed on to their heads. I think the police mainly turned a blind eye, as long as the transactions only proceeded after dark. Occasionally, probably as an exercise in meeting arrest quotas, a cop car pulled up and the knock-off goods instantly vanished into the bedsheets and the streets of Naples became dotted with men toting these giant bundles, trying to look for all the world like black Dick Whittingtons seeking the fabled streets of gold.

Naples waterfront is a busy place, full of tourists and locals, strolling, chatting and kissing. My god, were there a lot of lovers there. Teenagers, twenty-somethings, even fifty-year-olds were constantly engaged in public displays of affection, snogging and wrapping their arms so tightly around each other that it was difficult to tell which denim-jacket-clad arm belonged to whom. Boys sat on the low wall, or on the breakwater rocks, and their girlfriends clambered on to their laps to straddle them, face-to-face, all the better for full-on, passionate Frenching. Evening, mid-afternoon, morning – the time of day didn't seem to make a lot of difference. It was enough to make a prudish jogging Englishwoman blush.

On my third or fourth run, when I reached my halfway point, I stopped momentarily to catch my breath before turning back. I felt my pulse throbbing in my face and could tell, from the colour my lower arms had turned, that my entire head was now a fetching shade of puce. As I paced, fiddling with my iPod to find a motivating tune that would encourage me to carry on, a man in running gear stopped me.

'Scusi,' he said and I removed my earphones to hear a fast stream of Italian.

'Mi dispiace. Non parlo italiano,' I said, shrugging and holding the earphone between my fingers, ready to put it back in my ear.

'Ah, you Eengleesh?' he asked, jogging on the spot. 'What you do here in Napoli?'

I told him I worked on a boat.

'I live in Venice, not here, but I am here working,' he said. 'I stay here two weeks. I am not knowing anybody.'

Madonna! I thought, to borrow an Italian term of exasperation. (Mamma mia! was another one I had adopted – yes, Italians really do use it.) *Madonna! Don't tell me I am being chatted up, on the street, by a stranger, while I'm in the middle of a run. I look a mess. I am fluorescent pink. I am sweating so much that salt crystals are starting to cling to the underside of my chin. And droplets are dangling from the tip of my nose while I am talking to him. These Italians – they certainly are an amorous bunch. And none too fussy, it appears.*

'Maybe you would like to meet me for a drink?' the man asked me. I made a lightning assessment in my head. He was good-looking, yes, liked keeping fit, obviously, had plenty of confidence, apparently. But I doubted I'd be able to overcome the horror of his having seen me in this kind of stinking, perspiring mess. So I politely declined, making up a lie about having to attend to some guests on the boat, and took off, running faster than my natural pace to get away from him, self-conscious that he would be checking out my bouncing bum, putting enough distance between us until I felt it was safe to stop and catch my breath and prevent myself from having the heart attack I felt was coming on, I'd pushed myself that hard.

Amorous advances aside, once I was through the pain barrier of the first four or five jogs, I started to really enjoy it. Each day I went out I strayed a little further along the path, increasing the distance of my route. At first I could barely make it past the bag sellers to the stone Castel dell'Ovo and back before my lungs ordered me to stop. But over the course of a couple of weeks I added more sights to my route: a second, small marina, outdoor tennis courts, a third marina, a park, a lido, the cruise ship dock. Eventually I was up to nearly an hour and enjoying feeling fit. My back was no longer giving me any trouble. I added in some Pilates-style moves in the (un)comfort but privacy of my cabin. I had moved into the twin guest cabin opposite Carlo and Imran's – Daniela had taken an aft double – but it was still so small (my bed was 28 inches wide) that it was tricky finding ways to fit outstretched legs and arms into the space. But at least I could sit up in bed and I no longer had to perch sideways on the loo.

The rhythm of running became a sort of therapy and I let my thoughts wander as I ran, straying here, there and everywhere. Most of the time, they landed on Guy and our upcoming trip. We still had not much more of a plan other than to meet in Langkawi in early December. As I jogged, I looked around at the strangers I passed, but none of them seemed as interesting, as different, or as good-looking as him. Little of shivers of excitement about my new adventure with Guy shuddered their way up from my belly whenever I thought about it.

A message came through one empty, endless afternoon from a friend, Grace, who I had done a sailing course with. She was working as a cook and hostess on a French yacht for the season and they were coming in to Naples for one night, on their way to France. Did I want to meet her for a beer? Did I ever.

I took a taxi up the darkening streets of Naples, past beautiful old houses with enviable views over the bay. The Irish pub was empty this Monday evening but I didn't care. It had – oh joy of joys – pints of Heineken and deep-fried cheesy bar snacks. It was heaven.

'I thought you'd enjoy a taste of home,' Grace said, sucking on a gin and tonic. She introduced me to her boyfriend Mark and the captain of her boat, an Aussie. They were without owners at the moment, on passage from Croatia to the south of France.

We swapped tales of our torture. Grace and the boys were on a private 40-metre motor boat that mainly catered to the owners – one of whom was a teenage boy worth 40 million euros.

'He just spends all his time inside on his iPad,' Grace said. 'He never wants to go ashore. He says he can do all that when he's old.'

I felt my eyebrows rise. Because there were few guests, other than friends of the owners, the crew had more time to themselves. But when the owners came on board they worked even harder than I did. 'I did a week of 22-hour days,' Grace told me.

My eyebrows shot even higher. 'How do you cope?' I asked.

She shrugged. 'It's hard but it's only for a week at a time. And the money's good. I mean, I'm not a trained chef, only a cook-stew, but I'm on 3500 euros a month.'

I almost spat out the mouthful of beer I'd just taken. 'Three thousand five hundred? And do you get tips on top?'

'Oh, probably about, um, five thousand over the four months.'

'Christ!' I told her. 'I'm in the wrong job.'

The more we chatted, the more it seemed that I really was in the wrong job. I'd been happy to take the position on *Panacea* because it was my entry to that sphere. Sail boats paid less than motor yachts, I knew, but I'd thought that that would be fine if I was being paid to do something I loved, sailing. In reality, we hadn't sailed once. And I was a glorified cleaner-cum-waitress stuck with a crew I didn't really get on with.

Grace was in her second season working on her boat, and she got to live and work with her boyfriend and had a really nice, friendly captain. With the pots of cash they were managing to save, they planned to buy an old wreck of a house in France and renovate it. I was, to pinch an Essex girl phrase, well jel.

'She got a bad boat,' Grace had told Mark when he'd come back from the bar with a fresh round of drinks. She said it matter-of-factly, like there were good boats and bad boats out there, and I'd just had shitty luck. It set me thinking.

As I took a taxi back to Naples Mergellina – paid for by Grace's captain, who had shoved a 50-euro note in the hand of the driver to cover a 15-euro journey, after paying for all of the drinks and food (their boat even had a crew fun fund) – half-formed ideas tumbled around my drunken mind. Maybe I could do this. If I could swallow my pride about being a 'servant', I could earn serious cash and have to work only for a few months each year. If things worked out with Guy, he could come with me, too, as crew. It was a bit odd to think that I was now reconsidering a career that only a few weeks ago I had summarily written off. *But that's the beauty of this new life*, I told myself. *You're just finding your feet. And you decided to be less of a planner, more impulsive. So maybe you don't write it off. You leave the door open and see what blows through it.*

Two days later, while I was idly wondering why my knees and elbows hurt – a hangover, it turned out; it'd been a while – Carlo and Daniela came back from Rome, on the same train (coincidence?) – Daniela with a chic new wardrobe, hairstyle and push-up bra (coincidence? – I still couldn't work out if they were officially a couple or not) and Carlo with an important announcement.

'I have called the boatyard in Tunisia but there is no spaces,' he said. 'It is the financial creases – everybody looking for somewhere cheap to go.' *That's a shame*, I thought. *I was looking forward to visiting a new country – and eating some spicy food for a change.*

'I do not want to go to Turkey,' the captain went on. 'The wind there is too strong and the trip is terrible. So instead we go to Licata. There is a very good deal for us – just 3000 euro for the winter. And it is not so far. We leave on Friday.'

'Where is Licata?' I asked.

'Sicilia.' *OK, so not a new country but I've never been to Sicily before. Cool. Mafiosi, here we come.*

The life cycle of *Panacea* came full circle – in June there had been a mad rush to get her ready and out of the boatyard for the charters; now the boredom and sitting around was over and it was all hands on deck to get her packed up and into the boatyard for the winter. Rugs, linens, snorkelling gear and silver platters were packed into the bilges. Leftover cases of wine, expensive olive oil, the prosciutto-slicing machine that we had used only once and my George-Clooney-maker vanished into the back of a van and off to a warehouse. We hoisted the tender, lifted the anchor, dropped the mooring lines, cast off the stern lines and set off on our final journey to Sicily.

The crossing was rough and cold and the wind didn't stop even when we were in the supposed shelter of Licata marina, meaning I only managed one of my two days of deep cleaning. All of a sudden, it seemed, time had caught up with me and, before I knew it, it was the last day of October, All Hallow's Eve, the time for naughty spirits to rise up from their secret hiding places – and for deckhands to fly home because they've reached the end of their contract.

Carlo rose with me at 4.30am to see me off. He woke Daniela, who gave me a hug and a nice smile – the first I'd had from her since we left Castellamare – but Imran stayed in bed, sleeping.

Carlo thanked me for everything as he handed my bag to the taxi driver. The fact that we would never see each other again, that I wouldn't be returning to *Panacea*, lay unspoken between us. It didn't need to be verbalised and for once I was grateful for his Italian manner – had he been English, he'd have been compelled to politely say maybe he'd see me again next year, and I'd have had to mutter some half excuse in response and we'd both have been left with the annoying feeling that we shouldn't have said that.

He stuck out a hand for me to shake – no Italian two or even three kisses, just formal business – and I felt the rough calluses of both our palms (yes, I had grown them, too) scratch against each other. With a small wave I got into the taxi to take me to the bus stop, to get to the airport, then the other airport, then the tube and train ride it would involve to get me back to Derbyshire.

There was no overwhelming sense of relief that my time on a 'bad boat' was over, that I wouldn't have to serve another coffee or scrub a deck as I watched the dry hills of Sicily shrink beneath us when my plane took off. Nor was there any of the nostalgic sadness that normally sets in when you leave a job, a home or even a lover. I didn't feel anything really, apart from when I checked in my travel wallet for my passport and happily saw the three crisp 500-euro notes nestling in there, tucked in with some other 200s, 100s and 50s. That Monopoly money symbolised freedom. *It's going to buy me a fair bit of time to go cruising, especially in Asia, maybe six months*, I thought, resting my forehead against the cool glass of the plane window. *Work, and especially worrying about what kind of work I'll end up doing, can wait. Now there's just fun, travel, sun, sailing – and Guy.*

32

Casting Off

It was the day before I was due to fly to Langkawi, when I was in the middle of shopping for plain popcorn kernels – Guy had asked me to bring some: 'It makes a good snack for cockpit parties' – that I handed in my notice to myself after deciding to quit English life.

'I'm off,' I told my former British self. 'To Malaysia. To live on a boat. With a man. But not with a cat.' And I felt ridiculously pleased with myself for it.

The canned foods aisle of Sainsbury's in the Derbyshire former mining town of Ripley was the last place I'd have expected to experience another one of my epiphanies, to be hit by a little bubble of bliss. On a tropical beach, almost definitely. While admiring a spectacular view, probably. But in a fluorescent-lit identikit supermarket while crowded on all sides by the blue-rinse brigade shuffling past with their half-laden trolleys, hems of their trousers damp from the November rain flooding the pot-holey car park? Not the most obvious of locations.

However, descend a little bubble did, enveloping me

with its carefree attitude and lightness of spirit. The bubble accompanied me back from the supermarket to my parents' house, it helped me pack my (one, reasonably light) bag, it came with me to visit my friends, it drove with me to my sister's house to hold my tiny, two-day-old nephew for the first time and watch in awe as his impossibly small fingers grasped my thumb. *I've got to stop having these little epiphanic daydreams*, I thought, *or eventually they're going to lead me to the loony bin*. But I only half meant it: I was enjoying these blissful moments too much to care.

And so, once again I found myself at Gatwick, clutching a one-way budget ticket to Asia, with no more of a plan than to fly to Malaysia, take a taxi to an agreed location and then wait for a man to turn up in his dinghy to whisk me off to his yacht.

I have got enough brain cells to recognise that I was following a path that I had taken before, and which hadn't worked out too well. But things were different this time: different place, different boat, different man. The main change was in how I felt about that man. I liked this one, really liked him – which was something of an unusual situation for me. And I was a different person, too, much more laidback and more confident, less worried about planning, about a career path, about what the future held. I was much better at going with the flow, at trusting fate and knowing that, somehow, everything would work out fine. Apart from when I'd been offered two positions as a 'wife' in eastern Europe, I hadn't thought about marriage, children or detached homes with gardens for months. And this time I didn't have a bill for £100-worth of excess baggage in my pocket – that at least showed that I'd learned something.

On the plane, I ate the meals I'd paid for, I slept when I could, knowing that jetlag was inevitable and that I'd get through it in a few days, and stepped off the plane in a pair of light linen trousers, a thin T-shirt and flip-flops to collect that one bag, which came through the clear plastic flaps on to the carousel with no delay.

No worrying about brushes with drugs enforcement officers this time, I thought, poking fun at my former self as I swung it lightly on to one shoulder.

The airport was empty and I walked straight up to the desk to pay in advance for my taxi. A battered yellow and red car pulled up outside, its number matching the one printed on my voucher, and I smiled as I recalled that all Malaysian cabs looked like that.

Bright green palms and giant ferns lined the roads, looking obscenely verdant and full of life in the bright sunlight. The sky seemed bigger than I remembered, full of towering grey cumulus keeping everyone guessing about whether they were about to dump their heavy load over the island or not. The taxi wasn't air-conditioned and I started to sweat lightly under my T-shirt. I'd chosen a white and pale pink striped one because it wouldn't show the damp patches and it had a high neck to avoid causing offence to the locals. I pulled at it gently, to stop it from sticking to my back, but I didn't mind the humidity too much. After the freezing air-conditioning on *Panacea* and the bitter cold of an English early winter, it felt good to feel a bit uncomfortably hot. Besides, there was no aircon on *Incognito*. Temperatures inside *Gillaroo* had reached 36°C when we were in this part of the world. I'd have to get used to it.

As we drove along the dusty road, passing the odd

motorcyclist wearing a coat backwards, it felt like a homecoming. Part of it was a sense of familiarity with Langkawi, with the sights, sounds and smells of South-East Asia. In Italy I'd missed the food – and its associated fragrant scents – badly. One time, when I caught a whiff of soy and garlic in the air, I'd followed my nose to an Asian fusion restaurant, the only one I'd seen in six months, and been so pleased that I'd bitten into my spring rolls too soon in my enthusiasm and burnt the roof of my mouth. Now, the smells of chicken satay being barbecued, of hot roads and exhaust fumes from the motorbikes blew into the taxi through the open window. I took a deep (albeit poisonous) lungful. I looked, greedily, at every tropical plant we passed and I remembered how much I'd loved the jungle and its beautiful vulgarity.

We passed a moped rider going the wrong way along the side of the carriageway, against the flow of traffic, and then we were at a crossroads I recognised, on the outskirts of Kuah town. I rooted in my bag for my phone.

'Just coming into Kuah now,' I texted Guy. 'Where shall I meet you?'

'Tell your taxi driver the blue jetty, where the ferries come in,' came the reply, almost immediately.

I leaned forward, to make myself heard to the driver over the radio. 'Can we go to the blue jetty, please?'

He looked at me blankly in the rear view mirror of the car, uncomprehending.

I tried pigeon English. 'Blue jetty. Ferry. You know?' His eyes crinkled as he understood me.

'Ah, yes, perry. Perry chetty.'

I sat back, but then remembered there was another jetty

across the bay from where the boats anchored, where the large ferries from the mainland docked.

I tried to explain to the driver where I wanted to go.

'Not big one, not with eagle. Blue one,' I said, using my hands to mark out big and small, as if that would help.

'Yes, perry chetty,' he said.

Crap. We were going to the wrong place. *So much for my being confident in knowing what I am doing now.*

'I think he might be taking me to the big jetty, with the Eagle statue,' I texted Guy, hoping he hadn't set off in the dinghy already to the wrong place.

'OK. I'll head there,' came the reply.

But then we were pulling off the road and round the side of a restaurant I recognised and I realised the driver had understood me after all.

'I'm at the blue jetty,' I texted. My cool, calm confidence had eroded a bit but I thanked the driver, 'Terima kasih,' and set off along the path I remembered down to the waterfront.

A gaggle of pale-faced Chinese holidaymakers were making their way excitedly off a boat, chatting about the day's fun, still wearing their bright orange life preservers. I stood aside to let them pass and followed the snaking concrete path out to the bobbing blue plastic pontoons where the dinghies were moored.

The sun was beginning to set and the water was sparkling in the low light as the onshore breeze that had built up through the heat of the day rippled across the reflective surface, breaking it into a million diamonds of yellow-white light. I lifted my hand to my eyes to shield them from the glare and looked out into the bay, where a flotilla of yachts bobbed gently on their anchors, turned to silhouettes by the descending sun. Already the sky had started to turn lilac. As I watched, a black dot separated itself from one of the boats and began to zigzag its way towards me like a bee skimming low across the sea. It got closer and closer until I recognised the outline of *Incognito*'s dinghy, and Guy driving it. There was an age, in which I'm not sure I breathed, before he pulled up in front of me.

'Hi,' he said, knocking the engine into neutral, and I saw that big, white welcoming smile.

'Hi,' I said, and stepped into the dinghy, reached back, took hold of the line tying me to the shore and cast off.

(NOT) THE END.

RATHER A BEGINNING.